# Other Books and Series by Jeff Bowen

*Applications for Enrollment of Chickasaw Newborn Act of 1905*
*Volumes I thru VII*

*Cherokee Intermarried White 1906 Volume I thru X*

*Applications for Enrollment of Creek Newborn Act of 1905*
*Volumes I thru XIV*

*Applications for Enrollment of Choctaw Newborn Act of 1905*
*Volume I, II, III, IV, V, VI & VII*

Visit our website at **www.nativestudy.com** to learn more about these and other books and series by Jeff Bowen

# APPLICATIONS FOR ENROLLMENT OF CHOCTAW NEWBORN ACT OF 1905

# VOLUME VIII

TRANSCRIBED BY
JEFF BOWEN
NATIVE STUDY
Gallipolis, Ohio
USA

# Other Books and Series by Jeff Bowen

*1901-1907 Native American Census Seneca, Eastern Shawnee, Miami, Modoc, Ottawa, Peoria, Quapaw, and Wyandotte Indians (Under Seneca School, Indian Territory)*

*1932 Census of The Standing Rock Sioux Reservation with Births And Deaths 1924-1932*

*Census of The Blackfeet, Montana, 1897- 1901 Expanded Edition*

*Eastern Cherokee by Blood, 1906-1910, Volumes I thru XIII*

*Choctaw of Mississippi Indian Census 1929-1932 with Births and Deaths 1924-1931 Volume I*
*Choctaw of Mississippi Indian Census 1933, 1934 & 1937, Supplemental Rolls to 1934 & 1935 with Births and Deaths 1932-1938, and Marriages 1936-1938 Volume II*

*Eastern Cherokee Census Cherokee, North Carolina 1930-1939 Census 1930-1931 with Births And Deaths 1924-1931 Taken By Agent L. W. Page Volume I*
*Eastern Cherokee Census Cherokee, North Carolina 1930-1939 Census 1932-1933 with Births And Deaths 1930-1932 Taken By Agent R. L. Spalsbury Volume II*
*Eastern Cherokee Census Cherokee, North Carolina 1930-1939 Census 1934-1937 with Births and Deaths 1925-1938 and Marriages 1936 & 1938 Taken by Agents R. L. Spalsbury And Harold W. Foght Volume III*

*Seminole of Florida Indian Census, 1930-1940 with Birth and Death Records, 1930-1938*

*Texas Cherokees 1820-1839 A Document For Litigation 1921*

*Choctaw By Blood Enrollment Cards 1898-1914 Volumes I thru XVII*

*Starr Roll 1894 (Cherokee Payment Rolls) Districts: Canadian, Cooweescoowee, and Delaware Volume One*
*Starr Roll 1894 (Cherokee Payment Rolls) Districts: Flint, Going Snake, and Illinois Volume Two*
*Starr Roll 1894 (Cherokee Payment Rolls) Districts: Saline, Sequoyah, and Tahlequah; Including Orphan Roll Volume Three*

*Cherokee Intruder Cases Dockets of Hearings 1901-1909 Volumes I & II*

*Indian Wills, 1911-1921 Records of the Bureau of Indian Affairs Books One thru Seven;*
*Native American Wills & Probate Records 1911-1921*

# Other Books and Series by Jeff Bowen

*Turtle Mountain Reservation Chippewa Indians 1932 Census with Births & Deaths, 1924-1932*

*Chickasaw By Blood Enrollment Cards 1898-1914 Volume I thru V*

*Cherokee Descendants East An Index to the Guion Miller Applications Volume I*
*Cherokee Descendants West An Index to the Guion Miller Applications Volume II (A-M)*
*Cherokee Descendants West An Index to the Guion Miller Applications Volume III (N-Z)*

*Applications for Enrollment of Seminole Newborn Freedmen, Act of 1905*

*Eastern Cherokee Census, Cherokee, North Carolina, 1915-1922, Taken by Agent James E. Henderson*  *Volume I (1915-1916)*
*Volume II (1917-1918)*
*Volume III (1919-1920)*
*Volume IV (1921-1922)*

*Complete Delaware Roll of 1898*

*Eastern Cherokee Census, Cherokee, North Carolina, 1923-1929, Taken by Agent James E. Henderson*  *Volume I (1923-1924)*
*Volume II (1925-1926)*
*Volume III (1927-1929)*

*Applications for Enrollment of Seminole Newborn Act of 1905 Volumes I & II*

*North Carolina Eastern Cherokee Indian Census 1898-1899, 1904, 1906, 1909-1912, 1914 Revised and Expanded Edition*

*1932 Hopi and Navajo Native American Census with Birth & Death Rolls (1925-1931) Volume 1 - Hopi*
*1932 Hopi and Navajo Native American Census with Birth & Death Rolls (1930-1932) Volume 2 - Navajo*

*Western Navajo Reservation Navajo, Hopi and Paiute 1933 Census with Birth & Death Rolls 1925-1933*

*Cherokee Citizenship Commission Dockets 1880-1884 and 1887-1889 Volumes I thru V*

Copyright © 2013
by Jeff Bowen

ALL RIGHTS RESERVED
No part of this publication may be reproduced
or used in any form or manner whatsoever
without previous written permission from the
copyright holder or publisher.

Originally published:
Baltimore, Maryland
2013

Reprinted by:

Native Study LLC
Gallipolis, OH
www.nativestudy.com
2020

Library of Congress Control Number: 2020918113

ISBN: 978-1-64968-101-0

*Made in the United States of America.*

This series is dedicated to the descendants of the Choctaw newborn listed in these applications.

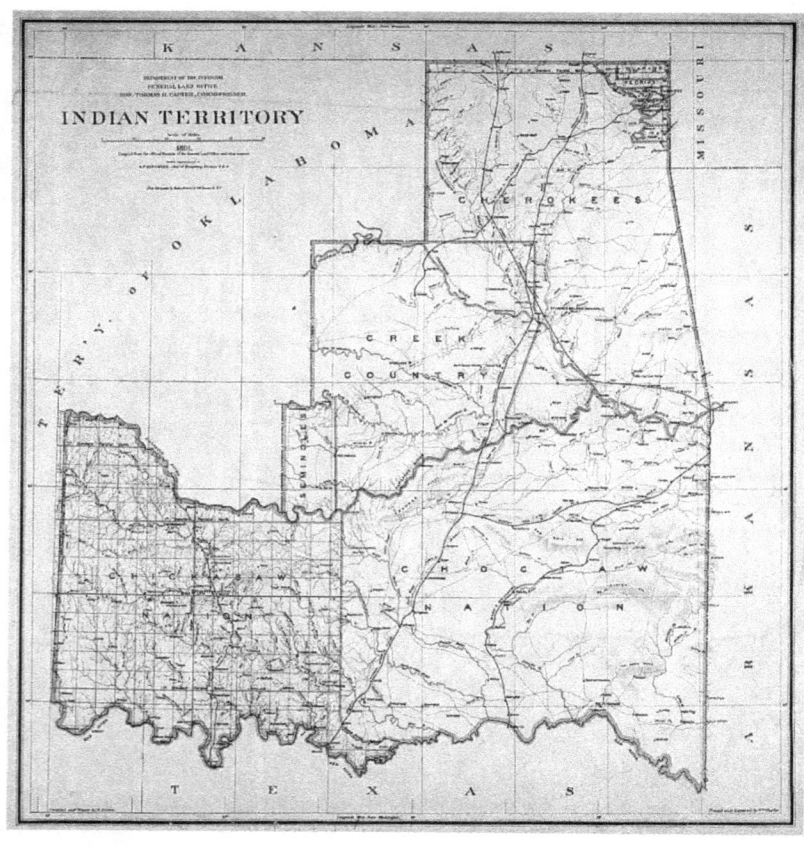

This map of Indian Territory shows how large the Choctaw and Chickasaw Nations' land base was that contained huge deposits of asphalt and coal. Just the size and territory involved was flooded with the "Grafters".

DEPARTMENT OF THE INTERIOR.
Commissioner to the Five Civilized Tribes.

# NOTICE.

## Opening of Land Office at Wewoka,
### IN THE SEMINOLE NATION, INDIAN TERRITORY.

Notice is hereby given that on Monday, September 4, 1905, the Commissioner to the Five Civilized Tribes will establish a land office at Wewoka, in the Seminole Nation, Indian Territory, for the purpose of allowing citizens and freedmen of the Seminole Nation to select allotments of land for their minor children enrolled under the Act of Congress approved March 3, 1905 (33 Stat. L 1060), and for the further purpose of allowing citizens and freedmen of the Seminole Nation, whose allotments are incomplete, to select additional land in order to bring the value of their allotments up to the standard of $309.09, as nearly as may be practicable.

Each child whose enrollment in accordance with the Act of March 3, 1905, has been duly approved by the Secretary of the Interior, is entitled to receive an allotment of forty acres without regard to the character or value of the land selected.

Selection of allotments for minor children must be made by their citizen or freedmen parents or by a duly appointed guardian, or curator, or by a duly appointed administrator.

TAMS BIXBY,
Commissioner.

Muskogee, Indian Territory,
July 29, 1905.

*This particular notice for the Seminole and Creek Newborn makes mention of the Act of 1905. It is likely that a similar notice was posted in the Choctaw and Chickasaw Nations for the registration of newborn children.*

# DEPARTMENT OF THE INTERIOR,
## Commission to the Five Civilized Tribes.

Rules and Regulations Governing the Selection of Allotments and the Designation of Homesteads in the Choctaw and Chickasaw Nations.

1. Selections of allotments and designations of homesteads for adult citizens and selections of allotments for adult freedmen must be made in person except as herein otherwise provided.

2. Applications to have land set apart and homesteads designated for duly identified Mississippi Choctaws must be made personally before the Commission to the Five Civilized Tribes. Fathers may apply for their minor children and if the father be dead the mother may apply. Husbands may apply for wives. Applications for orphans, insane persons and persons of unsound mind may be made by duly appointed guardian or curator, and for aged and infirm persons and prisoners by agents duly authorized thereunto by power of attorney, in the discretion of said Commission.

3. At the time of the selection of allotment each citizen and duly identified Mississippi Choctaw shall designate as a homestead out of said selection land equal in value to one hundred and sixty acres of the average allottable land of the Choctaw and Chickasaw Nations, as nearly as may be.

4. Each Choctaw and Chickasaw freedman, at the time of selection shall designate as his or her allotment of the lands of the Choctaw and Chickasaw Nations, land equal in value to forty acres of the average allottable land of the Choctaw and Chickasaw Nations.

5. Citizens, freedmen and identified Mississippi Choctaws who are married, whether they have attained their majority or not, will be regarded as of age for the purpose of making selections.

6. Selections may be made by citizen and freedman parents for unmarried male children under twenty-one years of age and for unmarried female children under eighteen years of age, and a male citizen or freedman may make selection for his wife, if she is entitled to make selection, unless she shall, at the time or previously thereto, protest in writing.

7. Where the father of an unmarried minor citizen, freedman or identified Mississippi Choctaw is a non-citizen, the citizen, freedman or identified Mississippi Choctaw mother of such children must make selection in person in behalf of said children.

8. Selections of allotments and designations of homesteads for minor freedmen may be made by the citizen father or mother or freedman father or mother, as the case may be, or by a guardian, curator, or an administrator having charge of their estate, in the order named.

9. Selections of allotments and designations of homesteads for citizen, and selections of allotment for freedmen, prisoners, convicts, aged and infirm persons and soldiers and sailors of the United States on duty outside of Indian Territory, may be made by duly appointed agents under power of attorney, and for incompetents by guardians, curators, or other suitable person akin to them.

10. Selections may be made and homesteads designated by duly identified Mississippi Choctaws, who have, within one year after the date of their identification as such, made satisfactory proof of bona fide settlement within the Choctaw-Chickasaw country, at any time within six months after the date of their said identification.

11. Persons authorized to make selections by power of attorney, as provided in rules 2 and 9 hereof, must be the husband or wife, or a relative not further removed than a cousin of the first degree of the person for whom such selection is made.

12. It shall be the duty of the Commission to the Five Civilized Tribes to see that selections of allotments and designations of homesteads for the classes of persons mentioned in rules 2, 6, 7, 8 and 9 hereof, are made for the best interests of such persons.

13. Selections of allotments for citizens, freedmen and identified Mississippi Choctaws who have died subsequent to September 25, 1902, and before making a selection of allotment, shall be made by a duly appointed administrator or executor. If, however, such administrator or executor be not duly and expeditiously appointed, or fails to act promptly when appointed, or for any other cause such selections be not so made within a reasonable and practicable time, the Commission to the Five Civilized Tribes shall designate the lands thus to be allotted.

14. In determining the value of a selection the appraised value of the land selected shall be increased by the appraised value of such pine timber on such land as has heretofore been estimated by the Commission to the Five Civilized Tribes.

15. Selections of allotments may be made only by citizens and freedmen whose enrollment has been approved by the Secretary of the Interior, and by persons duly identified by the Commission to the Five Civilized Tribes as Mississippi Choctaws, and by none others.

16. When a selection of land has been made by a citizen, freedman or identified Mississippi Choctaw, and the land so selected is claimed by a person whose rights as a citizen or freedman have not been finally determined, contest for the land so selected may be instituted by the person claiming the land, formal application for the land being first made as is required by the Rules of Practice in Choctaw and Chickasaw allotment contest cases.

THE COMMISSION TO THE FIVE CIVILIZED TRIBES.
TAMS BIXBY, Chairman.

Muskogee, Indian Territory, March 24, 1903.

The above statement published prior to 1905, was established for what was supposed to be a set of guidelines when it came to allotments. But with supplemental agreements and Congressional legislation, time frames as well as rules and regulations often changed and were not the same for every tribe.

# INTRODUCTION

The *Applications for Enrollment of Choctaw Newborn Act of 1905*, National Archive film M-1301, Rolls 50-57, are found under the heading of Applications for Enrollment of the Commission to the Five Civilized Tribes. For this series, I have transcribed the application forms filled out by individuals applying for enrollment in the Five Civilized Tribes under the Dawes Commission. These applications contain considerably more information than stated on the census cards found in series M-1186. M-1301 possesses its own numerical sequence, separate from M-1186. To find each party's roll number you would have to reference M-1186.

The Choctaw as well as the Chickasaw allotments were likely some of the most sought after properties in Indian Territory. There was supposed to be a 25-year restriction on the sale or lease of any Indian lands so as to insure that the owners wouldn't be swindled, but that isn't what happened. This fact is borne out in the Dawes Commission General Allotment Act, of February 8, 1887, Section 5, which "Provides that after an Indian person is allotted land, the United States will hold the land 'in trust [1] for the sole use and benefit of the Indian' (or his heirs if the Indian landowner dies) for a period of 25 years. (Land held in trust by the United States government cannot be sold or in anyway alienated by the Indian landowner, since the United States government considers the underlying ownership of the land held by itself and not the tribe. After the period of trust ends, the Indian landowner is free to sell the land and is free from any encumbrance from the United States.)"[1] Instead, Native Americans were exploited by the devious. The Choctaw and Chickasaw Districts both had huge asphalt and coal deposits, so there was pressure from outsiders to acquire them from the minute they were discovered. After repeated attacks throughout the years and many legislative changes, President "Roosevelt finally signed the Five Tribes Bill at noon on April 26, 1906, the forces seeking to end all restrictions were disappointed. Section 19 removed restrictions from the sale of all inherited land but directed that no full-bloods could sell their land for twenty-five years. The Act also prohibited leases for more than one year without the approval of the Secretary of the Interior."[2]

Angie Debo described the opportunists that wanted these Native American allotments as, "Grafters". The parents of the newborns enumerated within this series would no sooner receive the approval for their child's allotment than there would be someone there with cash in hand holding a new deed or lease for the parents to sign their child's birthright away. Angie Debo said it best, "As the business incapacity of the allottees became apparent, a horde of despoilers fastened themselves upon their property." According to Debo, "The term 'grafter' was applied as a matter of course to dealers in Indian land, and was frankly accepted by them. The speculative fever also affected Government employees so that it was almost impossible to prevent them from making personal investments."[3]

---

[1] General Allotment Act, Act of Feb. 8, 1887 (24 Stat. 388, ch. 119, 25 USCA 331)
[2] The Dawes Commission and the Allotment of the Five Civilized Tribes, 1893-1914 by Kent Carter, pg. 173
[3] And Still the Waters Run, Angie Debo, p. 92.

# INTRODUCTION

According to the Department of Interior in 1905, "It is estimated that there will be added to the final rolls of the citizens and freedmen of the Choctaw and Chickasaw nations the names of 2,000 persons, including 1,500 new-born children to be enrolled under the provisions of the act of Congress approved March 3, 1905."[4]

The quote below explains, in detail, the requirements for qualifying as a newborn Choctaw, "By the act of Congress approved March 3, 1905 (H.R. 17474), entitled 'An act making appropriations for the current and contingent expenses of the Indian Department and for fulfilling treaty stipulations with various Indian tribes for the fiscal year ending June 30, 1906, and for other purposes,' it was provided as follows:

'That the Commission to the Five Civilized Tribes is hereby authorized for sixty days after the date of the approval of this act to receive and consider applications for enrollment of infant children born prior to September twenty-fifth, nineteen hundred and two, and who were living on said date, to citizens by blood of the Choctaw and Chickasaw tribes of Indians whose enrollment has been approved by the Secretary of the Interior prior to the date of the approval of this act; and to enroll and make allotments to such children.'

'That the Commission to the Five Civilized Tribes is authorized for sixty days after the date of the approval of this act to receive and consider applications for enrollment of children born subsequent to September twenty-fifth, nineteen hundred and two, and prior to March fourth, nineteen hundred and five, and who were living on said latter date, to citizens by blood of the Choctaw and Chickasaw tribes of Indians whose enrollment has been approved by the Secretary of the Interior prior to the date of the approval of this act; and to enroll and make allotments to such children.'

"Notice is hereby given that the Commission to the Five Civilized Tribes will, up to and inclusive of midnight, May 2, 1905, receive applications for the enrollment of infant children born prior to September 25, 1902, and who were living on said date, to citizens by blood of the Choctaw and Chickasaw tribes of Indians whose enrollment has been approved by the Secretary of the Interior prior to March 3, 1905."[5]

Following is the scope of these transcriptions: Besides the applications themselves, researchers will find the identities of other individuals within these applications -- doctors, lawyers, mid-wives, and other relatives -- that may help with you genealogical research.

Jeff Bowen
Gallipolis, Ohio
*NativeStudy.com*

---

[4] Annual Reports of the Department of the Interior For the Fiscal Year Ended June 30, 1905, p. 609.
[5] Annual Reports of the Department of the Interior For the Fiscal Year Ended June 30, 1905, p. 593.

# Applications for Enrollment of Choctaw Newborn
## Act of 1905   Volume VIII

<u>Choc New Born 435</u>
    Randall Henry Swink   b. 11-3-02

---

**COPY.**

N.B. 435.

Muskogee, Indian Territory, April 7, 1905.

William Swink,
    Valliant, Indian Territory.

Dear Sir:

    There is enclosed you herewith for execution application for the enrollment of your infant child, Henry Swink, born November 3, 1902.

    Your affidavit heretofore filed with the Commission show that the applicant was living on December 3, 1902. It is necessary that the child be enrolled, that he was living on March 4, 1905.

    Neither the affidavit of the mother nor that of the attending physician or mid-wife have been filed in this office. These two affidavits are necessary; but in the event that the mother is dead or that there was no physician or mid-wife in attendance it will be necessary that you secure the affidavits of two persons who have actual knowledge of the fact that the child was born, the date of his birth, that he was living on March 4, 1905 and that Nannie Swink is his mother. You will please insert the age of the mother in the place left blank for that purpose.

    In having these affidavits executed care should be exercised to see that all names are written in full, as they appear in the body of the affidavit, and in the event that either of the persons signing the affidavit are unable to write, signatures by mark must be attested by two witnesses. Each affidavit must be executed before a Notary Public and the notarial seal and signature of the officer must be attached to each separate affidavit.

                          Respectfully,

        SIGNED

LM 7-14
                              *T. B. Needles.*
                              Commissioner in Charge.

## Applications for Enrollment of Choctaw Newborn
## Act of 1905   Volume VIII

Choctaw N.B. 435.

Muskogee, Indian Territory, May 2, 1905.

William Swink,
    Valliant, Indian Territory.

Dear Sir:

    Receipt is hereby acknowledged of the affidavits of Nannie Swink and D. G. Spencer to the birth of Randell[sic] Henry Swink, son of William and Nannie Swink, November 3, 1902, and the same have been filed with our records in the matter of the enrollment of said child.

Respectfully,

Chairman.

**BIRTH AFFIDAVIT.**

DEPARTMENT OF THE INTERIOR.
**COMMISSION TO THE FIVE CIVILIZED TRIBES.**

    IN RE APPLICATION FOR ENROLLMENT, as a citizen of the    Choctaw    Nation, of Randell[sic] Henry Swink    , born on the  3rd  day of  November  , 1902

Name of Father: William Swink      a citizen of the ........................Nation.
Name of Mother: Nannie Swink      a citizen of the  Choctaw    Nation.

Postoffice    Valiant[sic] I.T.

AFFIDAVIT OF MOTHER.

UNITED STATES OF AMERICA, Indian Territory, }
..........................................DISTRICT. }

    I, Nannie Swink    , on oath state that I am  36   years of age and a citizen by blood   , of the   Choctaw    Nation; that I am the lawful wife of    William Swink  , who is a citizen, by Intermarriage    of the    Choctaw    Nation; that a    male child was born to me on 3rd    day of    November   , 1902; that said child has been named  Randell[sic] Henry Swink    , and was living March 4, 1905.

Nannie Swink

Witnesses To Mark:
{
{

## Applications for Enrollment of Choctaw Newborn
## Act of 1905 Volume VIII

Subscribed and sworn to before me this   27   day of    April    , 1905

H L Fowler<br>Notary Public.

---

### AFFIDAVIT OF ATTENDING PHYSICIAN OR MID-WIFE.

UNITED STATES OF AMERICA, Indian Territory,  }
Central                    DISTRICT.

I,   D.O. Spencer M.D.   , a   Physician   , on oath state that I attended on Mrs.  Nannie Swink   , wife of   William Swink   on the   3$^{rd}$   day of November   , 1902; that there was born to her on said date a   male   child; that said child was living March 4, 1905, and is said to have been named Randell[sic] Henry Swink

D.O. Spencer M.D.

Witnesses To Mark:
{

Subscribed and sworn to before me this   27   day of    April    , 1905

H L Fowler<br>Notary Public.

---

BIRTH AFFIDAVIT.

## Department of the Interior,
### COMMISSION TO THE FIVE CIVILIZED TRIBES.

IN RE APPLICATION FOR ENROLLMENT, as a citizen of the   Choctaw   Nation, of   Henry Swink   , born on the   3   day of   November   , 190 2

Name of Father: William Swink              a citizen of the   Choctaw   Nation.
Name of Mother: Nanny[sic] Swink           a citizen of the   Choctaw   Nation.

Post-Office:   Valiant[sic] I.T.

---

AFFIDAVIT OF ~~MOTHER~~. father

UNITED STATES OF AMERICA,  }
  INDIAN TERRITORY,
Central            District.

I,   William Swink   , on oath state that I am   34   years of age and a citizen by   adoption  , of the   Choctaw   Nation; that I am the lawful ~~wife~~

3

# Applications for Enrollment of Choctaw Newborn
## Act of 1905   Volume VIII

husband of   Nanny Swink   , who is a citizen, by blood   of the   Choctaw Nation; that a   male   child was born to ~~me~~ her on 3 day of November , 190 2, that said child has been named   Henry Swink   , and is now living.

William Swink

WITNESSES TO MARK:
{

*Subscribed and sworn to before me this  3   day of   December   , 190 2*

H.C. Risteen<br>
*Notary Public.*

---

Choc New Born 436
        Edward C. Marcum   b. 4-7-04

Choctaw 5841

Muskogee, Indian Territory, March 30, 1905.

Henry W. Marcum,
        Cairo, Indian Territory.

Dear Sir:

   Receipt is hereby acknowledged of the affidavits of Cordelia Marcum and W. A. Spindle to the birth of Edward C. Marcum, son of Henry W. and Cordelia Marcum, April 27, 1904, and the same have been filed with our records as an application for the enrollment of said child.

Respectfully,

Chairman.

## Applications for Enrollment of Choctaw Newborn
## Act of 1905  Volume VIII

7-NB-436.

**COPY**

Muskogee, Indian Territory, April 25, 1905.

Henry W. Marcum,
    Cairo, Indian Territory.

Dear Sir:

    Receipt is hereby acknowledged of the affidavits of Cordelia Marcum and W. A. Spindle, to the birth of Edward C. Marcum, child of Henry W. and Cordelia Marcum, April 27, 1904, and the same have been filed with our records in the matter of the enrollment of said child.

Respectfully,
SIGNED

*Tams Bixby*
Chairman.

---

**COPY.**

N.B. 436

Muskogee, Indian Territory, April 10, 1905.

Henry W. Marcum,
    Cairo, Indian Territory.

Dear Sir:

    There is inclosed you herewith for execution application for the enrollment of your infant child, Edward C. Marcum, born April 27, 1904.

    In having these affidavits executed care should be exercised to see that all names are written in full, as they appear in the body of the affidavit, and in the event that either of the persons signing the affidavit are unable to write, signatures by mark must be attested by two witnesses. Each affidavit must be executed before a Notary Public and the notarial seal and <u>signature</u> of the officer must be attached to each separate affidavit.

Respectfully,
SIGNED

*T. B. Needles.*
Commissioner in Charge.

SEV 8-10.

# Applications for Enrollment of Choctaw Newborn
## Act of 1905   Volume VIII

**BIRTH AFFIDAVIT.**

## DEPARTMENT OF THE INTERIOR.
## COMMISSION TO THE FIVE CIVILIZED TRIBES.

**IN RE APPLICATION FOR ENROLLMENT,** as a citizen of the   Choctaw   Nation, of Edward C. Marcum   , born on the   27   day of   April   , 1904

Name of Father: Henry W. Marcum   a citizen of the   Choctaw   Nation.
Name of Mother: Cordelia Marcum   a citizen of the   Choctaw   Nation.

Postoffice   Cairo, Ind. Ter.

**AFFIDAVIT OF MOTHER.**

**UNITED STATES OF AMERICA, Indian Territory,**
   Central   **DISTRICT.**

I, Cordelia Marcum   , on oath state that I am   29   years of age and a citizen by   Blood   , of the   Choctaw   Nation; that I am the lawful wife of Henry W. Marcum   , who is a citizen, by Intermarriage   of the   Choctaw   Nation; that a   male   child was born to me on   27"   day of   April   , 1904; that said child has been named   Edward C. Marcum   , and was living March 4, 1905.

Cordelia Marcum

Witnesses To Mark:
{

Subscribed and sworn to before me this   21   day of   April   , 1905

W.B. *(Illegible)*
Notary Public.

**AFFIDAVIT OF ATTENDING PHYSICIAN OR MID-WIFE.**

**UNITED STATES OF AMERICA, Indian Territory,**
   Central   **DISTRICT.**

I,   W.A. Spindle   , a   Physician   , on oath state that I attended on Mrs.   Cordelia Marcum   , wife of   Henry W. Marcum   on the   27"   day of April   , 1904; that there was born to her on said date a   male   child; that said child was living March 4, 1905, and is said to have been named   Edward C. Marcum

W.A. Spindle

Witnesses To Mark:
{

# Applications for Enrollment of Choctaw Newborn
## Act of 1905   Volume VIII

Subscribed and sworn to before me this  17  day of   April     , 1905

                             W.B. *(Illegible)*
                             Notary Public.

**BIRTH AFFIDAVIT.**

### DEPARTMENT OF THE INTERIOR.
### COMMISSION TO THE FIVE CIVILIZED TRIBES.

**IN RE APPLICATION FOR ENROLLMENT,** as a citizen of the   Choctaw   Nation, of  Edward C. Marcum   , born on the  27  day of April  , 1904

Name of Father:  Henry W. Marcum        a citizen of the   Choctaw   Nation.
Name of Mother:  Cordelia Marcum        a citizen of the   Choctaw   Nation.

                   Postoffice    Cairo, I.T.

**AFFIDAVIT OF MOTHER.**

UNITED STATES OF AMERICA, Indian Territory, }
   Central                      DISTRICT. }

    I,  Cordelia Marcum   , on oath state that I am   29   years of age and a citizen by   Blood  , of the   Choctaw   Nation; that I am the lawful wife of Henry W. Marcum   , who is a citizen, by  Marriage   of the   Choctaw Nation; that a   male   child was born to me on  27  day of   April  , 1904; that said child has been named   Edward C. Marcum   , and was living March 4, 1905.

                             Cordelia Marcum

Witnesses To Mark:
  { Henry Brock
    G W Allen

    Subscribed and sworn to before me this  25  day of  March    , 1905

                             Notary Public.

# Applications for Enrollment of Choctaw Newborn
## Act of 1905   Volume VIII

### AFFIDAVIT OF ATTENDING PHYSICIAN OR MID-WIFE.

UNITED STATES OF AMERICA, Indian Territory,
Central      DISTRICT.

I,   W.A. Spindle   , a   Physician   , on oath state that I attended on Mrs.   Cordelia Marcum   , wife of   Henry W. Marcum   on the 27 day of April   , 1904; that there was born to her on said date a   male   child; that said child was living March 4, 1905, and is said to have been named   Edward C. Marcum

W.A. Spindle

Witnesses To Mark:
{ W.N. Stringfield
{ W<sup>m</sup> Gayner

Subscribed and sworn to before me this   20 day of   March   , 1905

W.B. *(Illegible)*
Notary Public.

---

Choc New Born 437
Vey V. Agent   b. 2-15-03

7-5613

Muskogee, Indian Territory, March 24, 1905.

Annie G. Agent,
Sallisaw, Indian Territory.

Dear Madam:

Receipt is hereby acknowledged of your affidavit and the affidavit of V. W. Hudson to the birth of Vey V. Agent daughter of Henry Clay and Annie G. Agent, February 15. 1903, and the same have been filed with our records as an application for the enrollment of said child.

Respectfully,

Chairman.

# Applications for Enrollment of Choctaw Newborn
## Act of 1905   Volume VIII

BIRTH AFFIDAVIT.

### DEPARTMENT OF THE INTERIOR.
### COMMISSION TO THE FIVE CIVILIZED TRIBES.

IN RE APPLICATION FOR ENROLLMENT, as a citizen of the   Choctaw   Nation, of Vey V Agent   , born on the 15   day of   Feby   , 1903

Name of Father: Henry Clay Agent   a citizen of the   Choctaw   Nation.
Name of Mother: Annie G. Agent   a citizen of the   Choctaw   Nation.

Postoffice   Sallisaw, Ind. Ter.

### AFFIDAVIT OF MOTHER.

UNITED STATES OF AMERICA, Indian Territory, }
Northern   DISTRICT. }

I,   Annie G. Agent   , on oath state that I am   37   years of age and a citizen by   Blood   , of the   Choctaw   Nation; that I am the lawful wife of   Henry Clay Agent   , who is a citizen, by   Adoption   of the   Choctaw   Nation; that a   Female   child was born to me on   15   day of   Feby   , 1903; that said child has been named   Vey V. Agent   , and was living March 4, 1905.

Annie G. Agent

Witnesses To Mark:
{

Subscribed and sworn to before me this   20"   day of   March   , 1905

W.L. Curtis *(Illegible)*
Notary Public.
Commissioner, Sallisaw I.T.

### AFFIDAVIT OF ATTENDING PHYSICIAN OR MID-WIFE.

UNITED STATES OF AMERICA, Indian Territory, }
Northern   DISTRICT. }

I,   Dr. V.W. Hudson   , a   Physician   , on oath state that I attended on Mrs. Annie G. Agent   , wife of   Henry Clay Agent   on the 15   day of   Feby   , 1903; that there was born to her on said date a   Female   child; that said child was living March 4, 1905, and is said to have been named Vey V. Agent

V.W. Hudson M.D.

# Applications for Enrollment of Choctaw Newborn
# Act of 1905   Volume VIII

Witnesses To Mark:
{
      Subscribed and sworn to before me this  20"  day of   March   , 1905

                               W.L. Curtis *(Illegible)*
                                    Notary Public.
                            *(Illegible)* Commissioner
                                      Sallisaw I.T.

---

Choc New Born 438
    Wilson Caldwell   b. 7-3-03

**NEW-BORN AFFIDAVIT.**

        Number............

## ...Choctaw Enrolling Commission...

    IN THE MATTER OF THE APPLICATION FOR ENROLLMENT, as a citizen of the Choctaw          Nation, of          Wilson Caldwell

born on the   3rd   day of   July        190 3

Name of father    Willie Caldwell         a citizen of    Choctaw
Nation final enrollment No.  2719
Name of mother   Mary Ann Caldwell      a citizen of    Choctaw
Nation final enrollment No............................

                                Postoffice     Rufe I.T.

**AFFIDAVIT OF MOTHER.**

UNITED STATES OF AMERICA
INDIAN TERRITORY
    Central        DISTRICT

        I         Mary Ann Caldwell               , on oath state that I am   26       years of age and a citizen by   blood    of the   Choctaw          Nation, and as such have been placed upon the final roll of the     Choctaw   Nation, by the Honorable Secretary of the Interior my final enrollment number being ..................... ; that I am the lawful wife of   Willie Caldwell          , who is a citizen of the   Choctaw          Nation, and as such

## Applications for Enrollment of Choctaw Newborn
## Act of 1905   Volume VIII

has been placed upon the final roll of said Nation by the Honorable Secretary of the Interior, his final enrollment number being   2719   and that a   Male   child was born to me on the 3$^{rd}$   day of July   190 3; that said child has been named   Wilson Caldwell , and is now living.

Mary Ann Caldwell

Witnesseth.

Must be two Witnesses who are Citizens. } Jesse Christy
H B Jacob

Subscribed and sworn to before me this   22   day of   Feb   190 5

W A Shoney<br>Notary Public.

My commission expires:   Jan 10 1909

---

## AFFIDAVIT OF ATTENDING PHYSICIAN OR MIDWIFE

UNITED STATES OF AMERICA
INDIAN TERRITORY
    Central   DISTRICT

I,   Lettie Hekabe   a   midwife on oath state that I attended on Mrs.   Mary Ann Caldwell   wife of   Willie Caldwell on the 3$^{rd}$   day of July , 190 3, that there was born to her on said date a   male   child, that said child is now living, and is said to have been named   Wilson Caldwell

her<br>Lettie x Hekabe   M.D.<br>mark

WITNESSETH:

Must be two witnesses who are citizens and know the child. { Jesse Christy
H B Jacob

Subscribed and sworn to before me this, the   22   day of   Feb   190 5

W A Shoney   Notary Public.

We hereby certify that we are well acquainted with   Lettie Hekabe   a   midwife   and know   her   to be reputable and of good standing in the community.

{ Jesse Christy<br>H.B. Jacob

## Applications for Enrollment of Choctaw Newborn
## Act of 1905 Volume VIII

**BIRTH AFFIDAVIT.**

### DEPARTMENT OF THE INTERIOR.
### COMMISSION TO THE FIVE CIVILIZED TRIBES.

IN RE APPLICATION FOR ENROLLMENT, as a citizen of the Choctaw Nation, of Wilson Caldwell , born on the 3 day of July , 1903

Name of Father: Willey Caldwell     a citizen of the Choctaw Nation.
Name of Mother: Mary Ann Caldwell     a citizen of the Choctaw Nation.

Postoffice     Rufe I.T.

**AFFIDAVIT OF MOTHER.**

UNITED STATES OF AMERICA, Indian Territory, }
    Central     DISTRICT.

I, Mary Ann Caldwell , on oath state that I am 26 years of age and a citizen by Blood , of the Choctaw Nation; that I am the lawful wife of Willie Caldwell , who is a citizen, by Blood of the Choctaw Nation; that a male child was born to me on 3 day of July , 1903; that said child has been named Wilson Caldwell , and was living March 4, 1905.

                          Mary Ann Caldwell
Witnesses To Mark:              by mark
    { John W Fowler
      Jesse L Christie

Subscribed and sworn to before me this 25 day of March , 1905

                          H L Fowler
                               Notary Public.

**AFFIDAVIT OF ATTENDING PHYSICIAN OR MID-WIFE.**

UNITED STATES OF AMERICA, Indian Territory, }
    Central     DISTRICT.

I, Lidia Hickby , a ................., on oath state that I attended on Mrs. May Ann Caldwell , wife of Willie Caldwell on the 3 day of July , 1903; that there was born to her on said date a mail[sic] child; that said child was living March 4, 1905, and is said to have been named Wilson Caldwell

                         her
                      L dia x Hickby
                         mark

## Applications for Enrollment of Choctaw Newborn
## Act of 1905  Volume VIII

Witnesses To Mark:
{ John W Fowler
{ Jesse L Christie

    Subscribed and sworn to before me this  25  day of  March  , 1905

                        H L Fowler
                            Notary Public.

---

Choc New Born 439
    Roberth R. Wilson  b. 8-3-03

**BIRTH AFFIDAVIT.**

### DEPARTMENT OF THE INTERIOR.
### COMMISSION TO THE FIVE CIVILIZED TRIBES.

    **IN RE APPLICATION FOR ENROLLMENT,** as a citizen of the  Choctaw  Nation, of  Roberth R. Wilson  , born on the  3  day of August  , 1903

Name of Father: Edward H Wilson      a citizen of the  Choctaw  Nation.
Name of Mother: Emma Wilson      a citizen of the  Choctaw  Nation.

                Postoffice     Fort Towson Ind Ter

**AFFIDAVIT OF MOTHER.**

UNITED STATES OF AMERICA, Indian Territory, }
    Central         DISTRICT. }

    I,  Emma Wilson  , on oath state that I am  29  years of age and a citizen by  Blood  , of the  Choctaw  Nation; that I am the lawful wife of  Edward H. Wilson  , who is a citizen, by  Blood  of the  Choctaw  Nation; that a  male  child was born to me on  3  day of  August  , 1903; that said child has been named  Roberth R Wilson  , and was living March 4, 1905.

                        Emma Wilson

Witnesses To Mark:
{
{

# Applications for Enrollment of Choctaw Newborn
## Act of 1905   Volume VIII

Subscribed and sworn to before me this 22 day of March , 1905

                        Thomas Fennell
                        Notary Public.

**AFFIDAVIT OF ATTENDING PHYSICIAN OR MID-WIFE.**

UNITED STATES OF AMERICA, Indian Territory,
Central      DISTRICT.

I, Mary Gross , a Midwife , on oath state that I attended on Mrs. Emma Wilson , wife of Edward H Wilson on the 3 day of August , 1903; that there was born to her on said date a male child; that said child was living March 4, 1905, and is said to have been named Roberth R Wilson

                        her
                    Mary x Gross
Witnesses To Mark:        mark
  { Alford Gross
    Minerva M Christan[sic]

Subscribed and sworn to before me this 24th day of March , 1905

                        Thomas Fennell
                        Notary Public.

---

Choc New Born 440
    Dora May McClure  b. 4-6-04

                                  7-2282

                Muskogee, Indian Territory, March 31, 1905.

Poker J. McClure,
    Calvin, Indian Territory.

Dear Sir:

    Receipt is hereby acknowledged of the affidavits of Ida McClure and J. C. Bentley to the birth of Dora May McClure, daughter of Poker J. and Ida McClure, April 6, 1904, and the same have been filed with our records as an application for the enrollment of said child.

## Applications for Enrollment of Choctaw Newborn
## Act of 1905 Volume VIII

Respectfully,

Chairman.

7 NB 440

Muskogee, Indian Territory, May 19, 1905.

P. J. McClure,
    Calvin, Indian Territory.

Dear Sir:

    Receipt is hereby acknowledged of your letter of May 11, 1905, asking if the roll numbers of yourself and wife Ida McClure given in the affidavits to the birth of your child Dora May McClure are correct and stating that if not you will forward other affidavits if necessary.

    In reply to your letter you are advised that it appears from our records that the roll numbers given in the affidavits to the birth of your child Dora May McClure which were filed with the Choctaw Enrolling Commission are correct and the affidavits heretofore forwarded to the birth of your child Dora May McClure have been filed with our records as an application for her enrollment.

Respectfully,

Chairman.

**NEW-BORN AFFIDAVIT.**

Number............

## ...Choctaw Enrolling Commission...

    IN THE MATTER OF THE APPLICATION FOR ENROLLMENT, as a citizen of the Choctaw Nation, of Dora May McClure

born on the 6$^{th}$ day of April 1904

Name of father    Poker J McClure    a citizen of    Choctaw Nation final enrollment No. 716
Name of mother    Ida McClure    a citizen of    Choctaw Nation final enrollment No. 6613

## Applications for Enrollment of Choctaw Newborn
## Act of 1905   Volume VIII

Postoffice   Calvin, Ind Ter

### AFFIDAVIT OF MOTHER.

UNITED STATES OF AMERICA
INDIAN TERRITORY
Central   DISTRICT

I   Ida McClure   , on oath state that I am 27 years of age and a citizen by Blood of the Choctaw Nation, and as such have been placed upon the final roll of the Choctaw Nation, by the Honorable Secretary of the Interior my final enrollment number being 6613 ; that I am the lawful wife of Poker J McClure , who is a citizen of the Choctaw Nation, and as such has been placed upon the final roll of said Nation by the Honorable Secretary of the Interior, his final enrollment number being 716 and that a Female child was born to me on the 6th day of April 190 4; that said child has been named Dora May McClure , and is now living.

Ida McClure

Witnesseth.
Must be two Witnesses who are Citizens.   Eva B Loving
Johnson Frazier

Subscribed and sworn to before me this 24 day of Feb 190 5

H B Harrell
Notary Public.

My commission expires:   Jan 10/1906

## AFFIDAVIT OF ATTENDING PHYSICIAN OR MIDWIFE

UNITED STATES OF AMERICA
INDIAN TERRITORY
Central   DISTRICT

I,   John C Bentley   a   Physician on oath state that I attended on Mrs. Ida McClure wife of Poker J McClure on the 6th day of April , 190 4, that there was born to her on said date a Female child, that said child is now living, and is said to have been named Dora May McClure

J C Bentley   M.D.

WITNESSETH:
Must be two witnesses who are citizens and know the child.   Eva B Loving
Johnson Frazier

# Applications for Enrollment of Choctaw Newborn
## Act of 1905 Volume VIII

    Feb      Subscribed and sworn to before me this, the    24    day of 190 5

                                                  H B Harrell      Notary Public.

We hereby certify that we are well acquainted with    Dr J C Bentley    a   Physician   and know   him   to be reputable and of good standing in the community.

                                   { Eva B Loving  
                                     Johnson Frazier

**BIRTH AFFIDAVIT.**

## DEPARTMENT OF THE INTERIOR.
## COMMISSION TO THE FIVE CIVILIZED TRIBES.

**IN RE APPLICATION FOR ENROLLMENT,** as a citizen of the    Choctaw    Nation, of Dora May McClure      , born on the 6th   day of April   , 1904

Name of Father: Poker J McClure      a citizen of the   Choctaw   Nation.  
Name of Mother: Ida McClure        a citizen of the   Choctaw   Nation.

                         Postoffice    Calvin, I.T.

**AFFIDAVIT OF MOTHER.**

**UNITED STATES OF AMERICA, Indian Territory,**  
     Central               **DISTRICT.**

I,   Ida McClure      , on oath state that I am   27    years of age and a citizen by Blood    , of the    Choctaw     Nation; that I am the lawful wife of    Poker J McClure , who is a citizen, by Marriage    of the      Choctaw      Nation; that a     Female child was born to me on   $6^{th}$    day of    April     , 1904; that said child has been named Dora May McClure     , and was living March 4, 1905.

                                           Ida McClure

Witnesses To Mark:  
    { Calvin Paxson  
      Eva B Loving

       Subscribed and sworn to before me this   25   day of    March     , 1905

         My commission                H B Harrell  
         Expires 10/1906              Notary Public.

## Applications for Enrollment of Choctaw Newborn
## Act of 1905 Volume VIII

### AFFIDAVIT OF ATTENDING PHYSICIAN OR MID-WIFE.

UNITED STATES OF AMERICA, Indian Territory, }
   Central            DISTRICT. }

    I, ................................., a     Physician   , on oath state that I attended on Mrs. Ida McClure   , wife of Poker J McClure   on the 6th day of April , 1904; that there was born to her on said date a   Female   child; that said child was living March 4, 1905, and is said to have been named Dora May McClure

                              J C Bentley M.D.

Witnesses To Mark:
  { Calvin Paxson
    Eva B Loving

    Subscribed and sworn to before me this 25 day of   March   , 1905.

    My commission          H B Harrell
    Expires 10/1906            Notary Public.

---

Choc New Born 441
    Edna May Hooe b. 10-2-02
    Robert Isreal Hooe b. 3-12-04

                                  7-3092

                Muskogee, Indian Territory, March 31, 1905.

Archie F. Hooe,
    Kiowa, Indian Territory.

Dear Sir:

    Receipt is hereby acknowledged of the affidavits of Mattie Hooe and Nettie Fulsom[sic] to the birth of Edna May Hooe, daughter of Archie F. and Mattie Hooe, October 2, 1902; also affidavits of Mattie Hooe and Edith Watts to the birth of Robert Isreal Hooe, son of Archie F. and Mattie Hooe, March 12, 1904, and the same have been filed with our records as an application for the enrollment of said children.

                            Respectfully,

                                      Chairman.

## Applications for Enrollment of Choctaw Newborn
## Act of 1905   Volume VIII

**NEW-BORN AFFIDAVIT.**

Number..............

### ...Choctaw Enrolling Commission...

IN THE MATTER OF THE APPLICATION FOR ENROLLMENT, as a citizen of the Choctaw Nation, of Edna May Hooe born on the 2nd [9th crossed] day of ___October___ 190 2

| | | |
|---|---|---|
| Name of father Archie F Hooe | a citizen of | Choctaw |
| Nation final enrollment No. 737 | | |
| Name of mother Mattie Hooe | a citizen of | Choctaw |
| Nation final enrollment No. 9013 | | |

Postoffice    Kiowa IT

**AFFIDAVIT OF MOTHER.**

UNITED STATES OF AMERICA
INDIAN TERRITORY
  Central    DISTRICT

I Mattie Hooe , on oath state that I am 28 years of age and a citizen by Blood of the Choctaw Nation, and as such have been placed upon the final roll of the Choctaw Nation, by the Honorable Secretary of the Interior my final enrollment number being 9013 ; that I am the lawful wife of Archie F Hooe , who is a citizen of the Choctaw Nation, and as such has been placed upon the final roll of said Nation by the Honorable Secretary of the Interior, his final enrollment number being 737 and that a Female child was born to me on the 2nd day of October 190 2; that said child has been named Edna May Hooe , and is now living.

Mattie Hooe

Witnesseth.

Must be two Witnesses who are Citizens.   J J Bohneer
                                          A Bohrue

Subscribed and sworn to before me this 18 day of Jan 190 5

H B Rowley<br>Notary Public.

My commission expires: ....................

## Applications for Enrollment of Choctaw Newborn
## Act of 1905   Volume VIII

## AFFIDAVIT OF ATTENDING PHYSICIAN OR MIDWIFE

UNITED STATES OF AMERICA
INDIAN TERRITORY
Central    DISTRICT

I, Nettie Thompson a Midwife on oath state that I attended on Mrs. Mattie Hooe wife of Archie F Hooe on the 2nd day of October, 1902, that there was born to her on said date a Female child, that said child is now living, and is said to have been named Edna May Hooe

Mrs Nettie Thompson    *midwife*  *M.D.*

Subscribed and sworn to before me this, the 18 day of January 1905

H B Rowley    Notary Public.

WITNESSETH:
Must be two witnesses { J J Bohneer
who are citizens         { A Bohrue

We hereby certify that we are well acquainted with Mrs Nettie Thompson a midwife and know her to be reputable and of good standing in the community.

J J Bohneer              R E McDaniel

A. Bohrue                C. W. West

**NEW-BORN AFFIDAVIT.**

Number..........

...Choctaw Enrolling Commission...

IN THE MATTER OF THE APPLICATION FOR ENROLLMENT, as a citizen of the Choctaw Nation, of Robert Israel Hooe

born on the 12th day of  March  1904

Name of father   Archie F Hooe          a citizen of   Choctaw
Nation final enrollment No. 737
Name of mother   Mattie Hooe            a citizen of   Choctaw
Nation final enrollment No. 9013

Postoffice   Kiowa IT

## Applications for Enrollment of Choctaw Newborn
## Act of 1905    Volume VIII

### AFFIDAVIT OF MOTHER.

UNITED STATES OF AMERICA
INDIAN TERRITORY
Central    DISTRICT

I    Mattie Hooe    , on oath state that I am 28 years of age and a citizen by Blood of the Choctaw Nation, and as such have been placed upon the final roll of the Choctaw Nation, by the Honorable Secretary of the Interior my final enrollment number being 9013 ; that I am the lawful wife of Archie F Hooe , who is a citizen of the Choctaw Nation, and as such has been placed upon the final roll of said Nation by the Honorable Secretary of the Interior, his final enrollment number being 737 and that a male child was born to me on the 12 day of March 190 4; that said child has been named Robert Isreal Hooe , and is now living.

    Mattie Hooe

Witnesseth.
  Must be two Witnesses who are Citizens.    Nettie Thompson
  A Bohrue

Subscribed and sworn to before me this 18 day of Jan 190 5

    H B Rowley
    Notary Public.

My commission expires: _____

---

## AFFIDAVIT OF ATTENDING PHYSICIAN OR MIDWIFE

UNITED STATES OF AMERICA
INDIAN TERRITORY
Central    DISTRICT

I, Edith Watts a Midwife on oath state that I attended on Mrs. Mattie Hooe wife of Archie F Hooe on the 12 day of March , 190 4 , that there was born to her on said date a male child, that said child is now living, and is said to have been named Robert Israel Hooe

    Edith Watts   midwife M.D.

Subscribed and sworn to before me this, the 18 day of January 190 5

WITNESSETH:    H B Rowley    Notary Public.
  Must be two witnesses who are citizens    Nettie Thompson
  A Bohrue

# Applications for Enrollment of Choctaw Newborn
## Act of 1905  Volume VIII

We hereby certify that we are well acquainted with     Mrs Edith Watts a    midwife    and know    her    to be reputable and of good standing in the community.

Nettie Thompson                                R E McDaniel

A. Bohrue                                      Birdie Rhine

---

**BIRTH AFFIDAVIT.**

## DEPARTMENT OF THE INTERIOR.
## COMMISSION TO THE FIVE CIVILIZED TRIBES.

---

IN RE APPLICATION FOR ENROLLMENT, as a citizen of the     Choctaw     Nation, of Robert Isreal Hooe    , born on the 12   day of March   , 1904

Name of Father: Archie F Hooe        a citizen of the   Choctaw    Nation.
Name of Mother: Mattie Hooe          a citizen of the   Choctaw    Nation.

Postoffice    Kiowa IT

---

**AFFIDAVIT OF MOTHER.**

UNITED STATES OF AMERICA, Indian Territory, ⎫
Central                 DISTRICT. ⎭

I, Mattie Hooe   , on oath state that I am   29   years of age and a citizen by Blood   , of the   Choctaw    Nation; that I am the lawful wife of   Archie F Hooe , who is a citizen, by  inter marriage    of the    Choctaw     Nation; that a    male child was born to me on   12$^{th}$   day of    March    , 1904; that said child has been named   Robert Isreal Hooe    , and was living March 4, 1905.

Mattie Hooe

Witnesses To Mark:

Subscribed and sworn to before me this 25$^{th}$   day of    March    , 1905.

WN Vernon
Notary Public.

# Applications for Enrollment of Choctaw Newborn
## Act of 1905   Volume VIII

### AFFIDAVIT OF ATTENDING PHYSICIAN OR MID-WIFE.

UNITED STATES OF AMERICA, Indian Territory, }
Central                                    DISTRICT. }

I, Edith Watts, a midwife, on oath state that I attended on Mrs. Mattie Hooe, wife of Archie F Hooe on the 12 day of March, 1904; that there was born to her on said date a male child; that said child was living March 4, 1905, and is said to have been named Robert Isreal Hooe

Edith Watts

Witnesses To Mark:
{

Subscribed and sworn to before me this 25 day of March, 1905

WN Vernon
Notary Public.

BIRTH AFFIDAVIT.

### DEPARTMENT OF THE INTERIOR.
### COMMISSION TO THE FIVE CIVILIZED TRIBES.

IN RE APPLICATION FOR ENROLLMENT, as a citizen of the Choctaw Nation, of Edna May Hooe, born on the $2^{nd}$ day of Oct, 1902

Name of Father: Archie F Hooe          a citizen of the Choctaw Nation.
Name of Mother: Mattie Hooe            a citizen of the Choctaw Nation.

Postoffice   Kiowa IT

### AFFIDAVIT OF MOTHER.

UNITED STATES OF AMERICA, Indian Territory, }
Central                                    DISTRICT. }

I, Mattie Hooe, on oath state that I am 29 years of age and a citizen by Blood, of the Choctaw Nation; that I am the lawful wife of Archie F Hooe, who is a citizen, by inter marriage of the Choctaw Nation; that a Female child was born to me on $2^{nd}$ day of October, 1902; that said child has been named Edna May Hooe, and was living March 4, 1905.

Mattie Hooe

Witnesses To Mark:
{

## Applications for Enrollment of Choctaw Newborn
## Act of 1905   Volume VIII

Subscribed and sworn to before me this 25$^{th}$ day of   March   , 1905

                                                    WN Vernon
                                                    Notary Public.

### AFFIDAVIT OF ATTENDING PHYSICIAN OR MID-WIFE.

**UNITED STATES OF AMERICA, Indian Territory,**
     Central                   **DISTRICT.**

     I,   Mrs Nettie Thompson  , a   midwife   , on oath state that I attended on Mrs.  Mattie Hooe  , wife of   Archie F Hooe   on the 2$^{nd}$  day of  October  , 1902; that there was born to her on said date a   Female   child; that said child was living March 4, 1905, and is said to have been named Edna May Hooe

                                        Mrs Nettie Thompson

Witnesses To Mark:

Subscribed and sworn to before me this 25$^{th}$ day of   March   , 1905

                                                WH Vernon
                                                Notary Public.

---

Choc New Born 442
         Estella Owens  b. 10-28-02

**BIRTH AFFIDAVIT.**
                             **DEPARTMENT OF THE INTERIOR.**
### COMMISSION TO THE FIVE CIVILIZED TRIBES.

     **IN RE APPLICATION FOR ENROLLMENT,** as a citizen of the   Choctaw   Nation, of   Estella Owens   , born on the  28th  day of  Oct.  , 1902

Name of Father:  John Ownes[sic]          a citizen of the   Choctaw   Nation.
Name of Mother:  Katie Owens             a citizen of the   Choctaw   Nation.

                                Postoffice   Caddo Indian Territory

# Applications for Enrollment of Choctaw Newborn
## Act of 1905   Volume VIII

**AFFIDAVIT OF MOTHER.**

UNITED STATES OF AMERICA, Indian Territory,　}
　　Central　　　　　DISTRICT.

I,　Katie Owens　, on oath state that I am　27　years of age and a citizen by marriage　, of the　Choctaw　Nation; that I am the lawful wife of　John Owens , who is a citizen, by blood　of the　Choctaw　Nation; that a　female　child was born to me on　28th　day of　Oct　, 1902; that said child has been named Estella Owens　, and was living March 4, 1905.

　　　　　　　　　　　　　　　　Katie Owens

Witnesses To Mark:
{

　Subscribed and sworn to before me this 25th　day of　March　, 1905

　　　　　　　　　　　　　　JL Rappolee
　　　　　　　　　　　　　　　　Notary Public.

---

**AFFIDAVIT OF ATTENDING PHYSICIAN OR MID-WIFE.**

UNITED STATES OF AMERICA, Indian Territory,　}
　　Central　　　　　DISTRICT.

I,　W. J. Melton　, a　Physician　, on oath state that I attended on Mrs.　Katie Owens　, wife of　John Owens　on the 28th day of　Oct　, 1902; that there was born to her on said date a　female　child; that said child was living March 4, 1905, and is said to have been named　Estella Owens

　　　　　　　　　　　　　　　　W.J. Melton

Witnesses To Mark:
{

　Subscribed and sworn to before me this 25th　day of　March　, 1905

　　　　　　　　　　　　　　JL Rappolee
　　　　　　　　　　　　　　　　Notary Public.

## Applications for Enrollment of Choctaw Newborn
## Act of 1905   Volume VIII

7-3525.

Muskogee, Indian Territory, December 18, 1902.

John Owens,
    Caddo, Indian Territory.

Dear Sir:

    Receipt is hereby acknowledged of the application for enrollment as a citizen of the Choctaw Nation of Stella Owens, infant daughter of John and Katie Owens, born October 28, 1902.

    You are advised that the Commission is without authority to enroll this child as a citizen of the Choctaw Nation, it appearing that said child was born October 28, 1902, subsequent to the ratification by the citizens of the Choctaw and Chickasaw Nations on September 25, 1902, of an act of Congress approved July 1, 1902 (32 Stats., 641).

    Section twenty-eight thereof provides as follows:

    "The names of all persons living on the date of the final ratification of this agreement entitled to be enrolled as provided in section 27 hereof shall be placed upon the rolls made by said Commission; and no child born thereafter to a citizen or freedman and no person intermarried thereafter to a citizen shall be entitled to enrollment or to participate in the distribution of the tribal property of the Choctaws and Chickasaws."

    Respectfully,

    Acting Chairman.

---

BIRTH AFFIDAVIT.

## Department of the Interior,
### COMMISSION TO THE FIVE CIVILIZED TRIBES.

---

    IN RE APPLICATION FOR ENROLLMENT, as a citizen of the Choctaw Nation, of Stella Owen[sic], born on the 28 day of Oct., 1902

Name of Father: John Owens    a citizen of the Choctaw Nation.
Name of Mother: Katie Owens    a citizen of the Choctaw Nation.

    Post-Office:    Caddo I.T.

# Applications for Enrollment of Choctaw Newborn
## Act of 1905  Volume VIII

### AFFIDAVIT OF MOTHER.

UNITED STATES OF AMERICA,  
    INDIAN TERRITORY,  
Cent District.

I, Katie Owens , on oath state that I am ............ years of age and a citizen by marriage , of the Choctaw Nation; that I am the lawful wife of John Owens , who is a citizen, by blood of the Choctaw Nation; that a female child was born to me on 28 day of Oct , 190 2, that said child has been named Stella Owens , and is now living.

                                her  
                            Katie x Owens

*WITNESSES TO MARK:*                         mark  
  Lee Payne  
  John Clark

*Subscribed and sworn to before me this* 12 *day of* Dec , *1902*

                            JL Rappolee  
                            *Notary Public.*

---

### AFFIDAVIT OF ATTENDING PHYSICIAN OR MID-WIFE.

UNITED STATES OF AMERICA,  
    INDIAN TERRITORY,  
Cent District.

I, W J Melton , a Physician , on oath state that I attended on Mrs. Katie Owens , wife of John Owens on the 28 day of Oct , 190 2; that there was born to her on said date a female child; that said child is now living and is said to have been named Stella Owen[sic]

                            W.J. Melton  
*WITNESSES TO MARK:*

*Subscribed and sworn to before me this* 6th *day of* Dec , *190* 2

                            J L Rappolee  
                            *Notary Public.*

Applications for Enrollment of Choctaw Newborn
Act of 1905   Volume VIII

**NEW-BORN AFFIDAVIT.**

Number..............

## Choctaw Enrolling Commission.

IN THE MATTER OF THE APPLICATION FOR ENROLLMENT, as a citizen of the Choctaw   Nation, of   Stella Owens

born on the 28$^{th}$   day of   October   190 2

Name of father   John Owens                   a citizen of   Choctaw Nation
Nation final enrollment No   14357
Name of mother   Katie Owens                  a citizen of   Choctaw Nation
Nation final enrollment No 664

Postoffice   Caddo IT

**AFFIDAVIT OF MOTHER.**

UNITED STATES OF AMERICA, ⎫
   INDIAN TERRITORY,        ⎬
Cent        DISTRICT        ⎭

I   Katie Owens                   on oath state that I am   28   years of age and a citizen by   marriage   of the   Choctaw   Nation, and as such have been placed upon the final roll of the   Choctaw   Nation, by the Honorable Secretary of the Interior my final enrollment number being   664   ; that I am the lawful wife of   John Owens        , who is a citizen of the   Choctaw   Nation, and as such has been placed upon the final roll of said Nation by the Honorable Secretary of the Interior, his final enrollment number being   14357   and that a   female   child was born to me on the   28   day of   Oct       190 2; that said child has been named   Stella Owens       , and is now living.

Katie Owens

WITNESSETH:
Must be two ⎫   S.J. Homer
Witnesses who ⎬
are Citizens. ⎭   F Manning

Subscribed and sworn to before me this   17$^{th}$   day of   Jan       190 5

J L Rappolee
Notary Public.

My commission expires   Nov 19$^{th}$ 1907

## Applications for Enrollment of Choctaw Newborn
## Act of 1905   Volume VIII

*Affidavit of Attending Physician or Midwife*

UNITED STATES OF AMERICA,  
   INDIAN TERRITORY,  
Cent      DISTRICT

I, W J Melton a Regular Practicing Physician on oath state that I attended on Mrs. Katie Owens wife of John Owens on the 28th day of Oct, 190 2, that there was born to her on said date a female child, that said child is now living, and is said to have been named Stella Owens

                        W.J. Melton        M. D.

Subscribed and sworn to before me this the 17th day of Jan 1905

                        J L Rappolee
                                  Notary Public.

**WITNESSETH:**

Must be two witnesses who are citizens and know the child.
{ S J Homer
{ F Manning

We hereby certify that we are well acquainted with W J Melton a Physician and know him to be reputable and of good standing in the community.

                  Must be two citizen witnesses.
                  { F Manning
                  { S J Homer

---

<u>Choc New Born 443</u>
    Mattie Fay Worley   b. 9-28-03

## Applications for Enrollment of Choctaw Newborn
### Act of 1905   Volume VIII

**BIRTH AFFIDAVIT.**

## DEPARTMENT OF THE INTERIOR,
### COMMISSION TO THE FIVE CIVILIZED TRIBES.

*IN RE Application for Enrollment,* as a citizen of the   Choctaw   Nation, of   Mattie Fay Worley  , born on the  28    day of  September   , 1903

Name of Father: Jesse A Worley        a citizen of the   Choctaw   Nation.
Name of Mother: Annie Worley         a citizen of the   Choctaw   Nation.

Post-Office:   Antioch I.T.

### AFFIDAVIT OF MOTHER.

UNITED STATES OF AMERICA,
   INDIAN TERRITORY.
   Southern       District.

I,   Annie Worley     , on oath state that I am  23    years of age and a citizen by   Blood   , of the   Choctaw   Nation; that I am the lawful wife of   Jesse Worley   , who is a citizen, by   intermarriage   of the Choctaw   Nation; that a   female   child was born to me on  28th    day of   September  , 1903 , that said child has been named   Mattie Fay Worley   , and is now living.

                                                      Annie Worley

**WITNESSES TO MARK:**
   G L Grisham

*Subscribed and sworn to before me this*  25   day of   March   , 1905.

                                                      G L Grisham
                                                      NOTARY PUBLIC.

### AFFIDAVIT OF ATTENDING PHYSICIAN OR MID-WIFE.

UNITED STATES OF AMERICA,
   INDIAN TERRITORY.
   Southern       District.

I,   Mrs E.A. Cobler     , a   Midwife    , on oath state that I attended on Mrs.   Annie Worley   , wife of   Jesse Worley   on the  28th   day of   September   ,

## Applications for Enrollment of Choctaw Newborn
## Act of 1905   Volume VIII

1903 ; that there was born to her on said date a   Female   child; that said child is now living and is said to have been named   Mattie Fay Worley

                                                    my
                               Mrs E.A. Cobler   x
                                                  mark

**WITNESSES TO MARK:**
{ J D Cobble
{ GL Grisham

      *Subscribed and sworn to before me this*   25   *day of*   March   , 1905.

                                  G L Grisham
                                  *NOTARY PUBLIC.*
My com exp Dec the 11 1909

---

Choc New Born 444
     William Downard Trueblood   b. 8-22-04

**BIRTH AFFIDAVIT.**

### DEPARTMENT OF THE INTERIOR.
### COMMISSION TO THE FIVE CIVILIZED TRIBES.

**IN RE APPLICATION FOR ENROLLMENT,** as a citizen of the   Choctaw   Nation, of William Downard Trueblood   , born on the   22nd day of   August   , 1904

Name of Father: A.H. Trueblood       a citizen of the   Choctaw   Nation.
Name of Mother: Mary J. Trueblood      a citizen of the   Choctaw   Nation.

                        Postoffice   Purcell, Indian Territory.

**AFFIDAVIT OF MOTHER.**

**UNITED STATES OF AMERICA, Indian Territory,** }
   Southern               **DISTRICT.** }

     I,   Mary J. Trueblood   , on oath state that I am   31   years of age and a citizen by   Blood   , of the   Choctaw   Nation; that I am the lawful wife of   A. H. Trueblood   , who is a citizen, by   inter-marriage   of the   Choctaw Nation; that a   Male   child was born to me on   22nd   day of   August   , 1904; that said child has been named   William Downard Trueblood   , and was living March 4, 1905.

# Applications for Enrollment of Choctaw Newborn
## Act of 1905   Volume VIII

Mary J Trueblood

Witnesses To Mark:
{ My Commission
Expires Feby 29" 1908

Subscribed and sworn to before me this 27th day of March , 1905

W H Downard
Notary Public.

---

**AFFIDAVIT OF ATTENDING PHYSICIAN OR MID-WIFE.**

UNITED STATES OF AMERICA, Indian Territory, }
Southern                DISTRICT.

I, J. S. Childs , a Physician , on oath state that I attended on Mrs. Mary J. Trueblood , wife of A. H. Trueblood on the 22nd day of August , 1904; that there was born to her on said date a Male child; that said child was living March 4, 1905, and is said to have been named William Downard Trueblood

J.S. Childs, M.D.

Witnesses To Mark:
{

Subscribed and sworn to before me this 27th day of March , 1905

WH Downard
Notary Public.

My Commission
Expires Feby 29" 1908

Applications for Enrollment of Choctaw Newborn
Act of 1905   Volume VIII

Choc New Born 445
　　　Gertie B. Guthrie  b. 9-9-04

**BIRTH AFFIDAVIT.**

# DEPARTMENT OF THE INTERIOR,
### COMMISSION TO THE FIVE CIVILIZED TRIBES.

*IN RE Application for Enrollment,* as a citizen of the　　Choctaw　　Nation, of　Gertie B Guthrie　, born on the　9$^{th}$　day of September　, 1904

Name of Father: William W Guthrie　　　a citizen of the　Choctaw　Nation.
Name of Mother: Rebecca Guthrie　　　　a citizen of the　　　"　　Nation.

　　　　　　　　　　　Post-Office:　　　Antioch, Ind Ter

### AFFIDAVIT OF MOTHER.

UNITED STATES OF AMERICA,　⎫
　　**INDIAN TERRITORY.**　　　　　⎬
Southern Judicial　　District.　⎭

　　　I,　　Rebecca Guthrie　　, on oath state that I am　39　years of age and a citizen by　blood　, of the Choctaw　Nation; that I am the lawful wife of　William W Guthrie　, who is a citizen, by　Intermarriage　of the Choctaw　Nation; that a female　child was born to me on　9$^{th}$　day of September　, 1904, that said child has been named　Gertie B Guthrie　, and is now living.

　　　　　　　　　　　　　　　　　　　　　　　my
　　　　　　　　　　　　　　　　Rebecca Guthrie　x
**WITNESSES TO MARK:**　　　　　　　　　　　　mark
　　⎰ M.C. Grisham
　　⎱ G.L. Grisham

　　　*Subscribed and sworn to before me this*　14$^{th}$　*day of*　March　, 1905.

　　　　　　　　　　　　　　　　G.L. Grisham
　　　　　　　　　　　　　　　　*NOTARY PUBLIC.*

## Applications for Enrollment of Choctaw Newborn
## Act of 1905 Volume VIII

**AFFIDAVIT OF ATTENDING PHYSICIAN OR MID-WIFE.**

UNITED STATES OF AMERICA,   State of Missouri
INDIAN TERRITORY.            City St Louis
................................ District.

I, E. Sullivan , a physician , on oath state that I attended on Mrs. Rebecca Guthrie , wife of William W Guthrie on the 9th day of September , 1904 ; that there was born to her on said date a female child; that said child is now living and is said to have been named Gertie B Guthrie

E Sullivan

**WITNESSES TO MARK:**
{ *(Name Illegible)*
  *(Name Illegible)*

Subscribed and sworn to before me this 20th day of March , 1905.

*(Name Illegible)*
**NOTARY PUBLIC.**

---

Choc New Born 446
   Lonie Harral Jones b. 4-19-04

**BIRTH AFFIDAVIT.**

# DEPARTMENT OF THE INTERIOR,
**COMMISSION TO THE FIVE CIVILIZED TRIBES.**

*IN RE Application for Enrollment,* as a citizen of the Choctaw Nation, of Lewie[sic] Haral[sic] Jones , born on the 19th day of April , 1904

Name of Father: Charles P Jones     a citizen of the Choctaw Nation.
Name of Mother: Vera E Jones         a citizen of the Choctaw Nation.

Post-Office:   Hewett I.T.

# Applications for Enrollment of Choctaw Newborn
## Act of 1905   Volume VIII

**AFFIDAVIT OF MOTHER.**

UNITED STATES OF AMERICA,  
    INDIAN TERRITORY.  
  So[sic]      District.

    I, Vera E Jones, on oath state that I am 22 years of age and a citizen by Birth, of the Choctaw Nation; that I am the lawful wife of Charles P Jones, who is a citizen, by inter marriage of the Choctaw Nation; that a male child was born to me on 19$^{th}$ day of April, 1904, that said child has been named Lewie Haral Jones, and is now living.

                                      Vara[sic] E Jones

**WITNESSES TO MARK:**

    *Subscribed and sworn to before me this* 1$^{st}$ *day of* May, *1905.*

                                        WA Darling  
                                        *NOTARY PUBLIC.*

**AFFIDAVIT OF ATTENDING PHYSICIAN OR MID-WIFE.**

UNITED STATES OF AMERICA,  
    INDIAN TERRITORY.  
  So      District.

    I, John Tidmore, a Physician, on oath state that I attended on Mrs. Vera E Jones, wife of Charles P Jones on the 19$^{th}$ day of April, 1904; that there was born to her on said date a male child; that said child is now living and is said to have been named Lewie Haral Jones

                                      Dr John Tidmore

**WITNESSES TO MARK:**

    *Subscribed and sworn to before me this* First *day of* May, *1905.*

                                       WAS Darling  
                                      *NOTARY PUBLIC.*

## Applications for Enrollment of Choctaw Newborn
## Act of 1905  Volume VIII

**BIRTH AFFIDAVIT.**

## DEPARTMENT OF THE INTERIOR.
## COMMISSION TO THE FIVE CIVILIZED TRIBES.

**IN RE APPLICATION FOR ENROLLMENT,** as a citizen of the Choctaw Nation, of Lonie Harral Jones, born on the 19 day of April, 1904

Name of Father: Charles P Jones  a citizen of the Chocktaw[sic]Nation.
Name of Mother: Vara[sic] E Jones  a citizen of the Chocktaw Nation.

Postoffice Hewitt Ind T.

**AFFIDAVIT OF MOTHER.**

UNITED STATES OF AMERICA, Indian Territory,
Southern DISTRICT.

I, Vara E Jones, on oath state that I am 21 years of age and a citizen by Blood, of the Chocktaw Nation; that I am the lawful wife of Charles P Jones, who is a citizen, by Inter marriage of the Chocktaw Nation; that a male child was born to me on 19 day of April, 1904; that said child has been named Lonie Harral Jones, and was living March 4, 1905.

Vara E Jones

Witnesses To Mark:
{

Subscribed and sworn to before me this 24 day of March, 1905

J O Grimsley
Notary Public.

**AFFIDAVIT OF ATTENDING PHYSICIAN OR MID-WIFE.**

UNITED STATES OF AMERICA, Indian Territory,
Southern DISTRICT.

I, John Tidmore, a Physician, on oath state that I attended on Mrs. Vara E Jones, wife of Charles P Jones on the 19 day of April, 1904; that there was born to her on said date a male child; that said child was living March 4, 1905, and is said to have been named Lonie Harral Jones

Dr John Tidmore

Witnesses To Mark:
{

## Applications for Enrollment of Choctaw Newborn
## Act of 1905   Volume VIII

Subscribed and sworn to before me this 24 day of March , 1905

J O Grimsley
Notary Public.

---

Choc New Born 447
    James Anderson Bully   b. 7-15-03
    John Bully   b. 7-15-03

Choctaw 542[sic]
Choctaw 3839

Muskogee, Indian Territory, March 31, 1905.

Anderson Bully,
    Bennington, Indian Territory.

Dear Sir:

    Receipt is hereby acknowledged of your letter of March 27, inclosing affidavits of Amanda A. Bully and Tennessee Wilson to the birth of James Anderson Bully and John Bully, children of Anderson and Amanda A. Bully, July 15, 1903, and the same have been filed with our records as an application for the enrollment of said child[sic].

Respectfully,

Chairman.

---

**BIRTH AFFIDAVIT.**

**DEPARTMENT OF THE INTERIOR.**
**COMMISSION TO THE FIVE CIVILIZED TRIBES.**

**IN RE APPLICATION FOR ENROLLMENT,** as a citizen of the   Choctaw   Nation, of John Bully   , born on the 15$^{th}$   day of July   , 1903

Name of Father: Anderson Bully   a citizen of the   Choctaw   Nation.
Name of Mother: Amanda Bully (nee Christie)   a citizen of the   Choctaw   Nation.

Postoffice   Bennington, I.T.

## Applications for Enrollment of Choctaw Newborn
## Act of 1905 Volume VIII

### AFFIDAVIT OF MOTHER.

UNITED STATES OF AMERICA, Indian Territory, }
    Central             DISTRICT.

    I, Amanda Bully, on oath state that I am 25 years of age and a citizen by blood, of the Choctaw Nation; that I am the lawful wife of Anderson Bully, who is a citizen, by blood of the Choctaw Nation; that a male child was born to me on 15th day of July, 1903; that said child has been named John Bully, and was living March 4, 1905.

                                            her
                                 Amanda A x Bully
Witnesses To Mark:                  mark
  { George William
    David Byington

    Subscribed and sworn to before me this 27th day of Mch, 1905

                                 BW Williams
                                 Notary Public.

---

### AFFIDAVIT OF ATTENDING PHYSICIAN OR MID-WIFE.

UNITED STATES OF AMERICA, Indian Territory, }
    Cent                 DISTRICT.

    I, Tennessee Wilson, a midwife, on oath state that I attended on Mrs. Amanda Bully, wife of Anderson Bully on the 15th day of July, 1903; that there was born to her on said date a male child; that said child was living March 4, 1905, and is said to have been named John Bully

                                 Tennessee Wilson

Witnesses To Mark:
  {

    Subscribed and sworn to before me this 27th day of Mch, 1905

                                 B.W. Williams
                                 Notary Public.

# Applications for Enrollment of Choctaw Newborn
## Act of 1905  Volume VIII

BIRTH AFFIDAVIT.

## DEPARTMENT OF THE INTERIOR.
## COMMISSION TO THE FIVE CIVILIZED TRIBES.

IN RE APPLICATION FOR ENROLLMENT, as a citizen of the Choctaw Nation, of James Anderson Bully, born on the 15$^{th}$ day of July, 1903

Name of Father: Anderson Bully  a citizen of the Choctaw Nation.
Name of Mother: Amanda Christie now Bully  a citizen of the Choctaw Nation.

Postoffice  Bennington, I.T.

### AFFIDAVIT OF MOTHER.

UNITED STATES OF AMERICA, Indian Territory, }
    Central             DISTRICT. }

I, Amanda Bully, on oath state that I am 25 years of age and a citizen by blood, of the Choctaw Nation; that I am the lawful wife of Anderson Bully, who is a citizen, by blood of the Choctaw Nation; that a male child was born to me on 15th day of July, 1903; that said child has been named James Anderson Bully, and was living March 4, 1905.

                        her
            Amanda A x Bully
Witnesses To Mark:      mark
  { George William
    David Byington

Subscribed and sworn to before me this 27th day of Mch, 1905

            B.W. Williams
                Notary Public.

### AFFIDAVIT OF ATTENDING PHYSICIAN OR MID-WIFE.

UNITED STATES OF AMERICA, Indian Territory, }
    Cent               DISTRICT. }

I, Tennessee Wilson, a midwife, on oath state that I attended on Mrs. Amanda Bully, wife of Anderson Bully on the 15th day of July, 1903; that there was born to her on said date a male child; that said child was living March 4, 1905, and is said to have been named James Anderson Bully

            Tennessee Wilson

## Applications for Enrollment of Choctaw Newborn
## Act of 1905  Volume VIII

Witnesses To Mark:
{

    Subscribed and sworn to before me this 27th  day of  Mch  , 1905

                                      B.W. Williams
                                      Notary Public.

---

Choc New Born 448
    Simon Nelson  b. 1-17-05

**BIRTH AFFIDAVIT.**
                    **DEPARTMENT OF THE INTERIOR.**
              **COMMISSION TO THE FIVE CIVILIZED TRIBES.**

    **IN RE APPLICATION FOR ENROLLMENT,** as a citizen of the  Choctaw  Nation, of
Simon Nelson  , born on the  17  day of  January  , 1905

Name of Father:  Richard Nelson          a citizen of the  Choctaw  Nation.
Name of Mother:  Alice Nelson           a citizen of the  Choctaw  Nation.

                    Postoffice  Boswell, I.T.

                  **AFFIDAVIT OF MOTHER.**

**UNITED STATES OF AMERICA, Indian Territory,** }
    Central Judicial         **DISTRICT.**

    I,  Alice Nelson  , on oath state that I am  18  years of age and a citizen by blood  , of the  Choctaw  Nation; that I am the lawful wife of  Richard Nelson  , who is a citizen, by blood  of the  Choctaw  Nation; that a  male  child was born to me on  17  day of  January  , 1905; that said child has been named  Simon  , and was living March 4, 1905.

                                    Alice Nelson

Witnesses To Mark:
{

## Applications for Enrollment of Choctaw Newborn
## Act of 1905   Volume VIII

Subscribed and sworn to before me this  25   day of   Mch   , 1905

L.D. Horton
Notary Public.

---

**AFFIDAVIT OF ATTENDING PHYSICIAN OR MID-WIFE.**

UNITED STATES OF AMERICA, Indian Territory,
Central Judicial            DISTRICT.

I, Nancy Chatman , a midwife , on oath state that I attended on Mrs. Alice Nelson , wife of Richard Nelson on the 17 day of January , 1905; that there was born to her on said date a   male   child; that said child was living March 4, 1905, and is said to have been named Simon

her
Nancy x Chatman
mark

Witnesses To Mark:
{ J.E. M<sup>c</sup>Cleary
{ LD Horton

Subscribed and sworn to before me this  25   day of   Mch   , 1905

L.D. Horton
Notary Public.

---

**NEW-BORN AFFIDAVIT.**

Number............

## ...Choctaw Enrolling Commission...

---

IN THE MATTER OF THE APPLICATION FOR ENROLLMENT, as a citizen of the Choctaw         Nation, of         Simon Nelson

born on the   17   day of   January       190 5

Name of father     J R Nelson                          a citizen of     Choctaw
Nation final enrollment No. 9387
Name of mother     Alice Nelson nee Crowder     a citizen of     Choctaw
Nation final enrollment No. 4070

Postoffice       Boswell I.T.

## Applications for Enrollment of Choctaw Newborn
## Act of 1905 Volume VIII

### AFFIDAVIT OF MOTHER.

UNITED STATES OF AMERICA
INDIAN TERRITORY
   Central    DISTRICT

        I    Alice Nelson nee Crowder    , on oath state that I am 18 years of age and a citizen by blood of the Choctaw Nation, and as such have been placed upon the final roll of the Choctaw Nation, by the Honorable Secretary of the Interior my final enrollment number being 4070 ; that I am the lawful wife of Richard Nelson , who is a citizen of the Choctaw Nation, and as such has been placed upon the final roll of said Nation by the Honorable Secretary of the Interior, his final enrollment number being 9387 and that a Male child was born to me on the 17 day of January 190 5; that said child has been named Simon Nelson , and is now living.

                                Alice Nelson

Witnesseth.
Must be two Witnesses who are Citizens.
    Jas C. Goode
    Sam Bench

    Subscribed and sworn to before me this 24 day of Feb 190 5

                              SH Downing
                                    Notary Public.

My commission expires: March 14th 1908

---

## AFFIDAVIT OF ATTENDING PHYSICIAN OR MIDWIFE

UNITED STATES OF AMERICA
INDIAN TERRITORY
   Central    DISTRICT

    I, Nancie[sic] Chatman a Midwife on oath state that I attended on Mrs. Allice[sic] Nelson wife of Richard Nelson on the 17 day of January , 190 5, that there was born to her on said date a male child, that said child is now living, and is said to have been named Simon Nelson

                        Nancie x Chatman    Midwife

WITNESSETH:
Must be two witnesses who are citizens and know the child.
    Jas C Goode
    Sam Bench

## Applications for Enrollment of Choctaw Newborn
## Act of 1905   Volume VIII

Subscribed and sworn to before me this, the  24  day of Feb  190 5

SH Downing   Notary Public.

We hereby certify that we are well acquainted with  Nancie Chatman  a  Midwife  and know  her  to be reputable and of good standing in the community.

$\left\{\begin{array}{l}\text{Jas C Goode} \\ \text{Sam Bench}\end{array}\right.$

*(The affidavit below typed as given.)*

United States of America,
    Indian Territory,
Central Judicial District.

    I, Richard Nelson, after having been first duly sworn state: I am 20 years of age and reside near Boswell, I.T. I am a citizen by blood of the Choctaw Nation: On the 6th day of March 1903 I was married to Alice Crowder, a Choctaw citizen by blood near Boswell, I.T.-M.T.Dwight, then County Judge of Jackson County performed the marriage ceremony-He gave me a marriage certificate and when I was at the Land Office at Atoka. About August 1903 to make our filings the officers of the land office took up my certificate and kept it- Upon presenting said certificate, they allowed me to file for myself and also for my wife.

Richard Nelson

Subscribed and sworn to before me this the 25th day of March 1905.

L.D. Horton
Notary Public.

---

Choc New Born 449
    Lilly B. Henderson   b. 12-8-02

## Applications for Enrollment of Choctaw Newborn
## Act of 1905   Volume VIII

Choctaw 1988.

Muskogee, Indian Territory, March 31, 1905.

Samuel N. Henderson,
    Stringtown, Indian Territory.

Dear Sir:

    Receipt is hereby acknowledged of the affidavits of Ida Henderson and J. A. Dabney to the birth of Lilly B. Henderson, daughter of Samuel N. and Ida Henderson, December 8, 1902, and the same have been filed with our records as an application for the enrollment of said child.

                     Respectfully,

                                  Chairman.

### *Affidavit of Attending Physician or Midwife*

UNITED STATES OF AMERICA,  
    INDIAN TERRITORY,  
Central Judicial DISTRICT

    I,    J.A. Dabney     a    Practicing Physician on oath state that I attended on Mrs. Ida Henderson    wife of Samuel M Henderson on the 8$^{th}$ day of Dec , 190 2, that there was born to her on said date a    female   child, that said child is now living, and is said to have been named   Lillie B. Henderson

                                J.A. Dabney      M. D.

Subscribed and sworn to before me this the    22$^{nd}$   day of   Feby     1905

                                D.S. Kennedy
                                    Notary Public.

WITNESSETH:

Must be two witnesses who are citizens and know the child. { Christopher D Moore  
Henry J Bond

    We hereby certify that we are well acquainted with    J.A. Dabney a    Practicing Physician    and know    him    to be reputable and of good standing in the community.

                          Must be two citizen witnesses. { Christopher D Moore  
Henry J Bond

Applications for Enrollment of Choctaw Newborn
Act of 1905   Volume VIII

# NEW BORN AFFIDAVIT

No ............

## CHOCTAW ENROLLING COMMISSION

IN THE MATTER OF THE APPLICATION FOR ENROLLMENT as a citizen of the Choctaw Nation, of   Lillie B Henderson   born on the 8th day of   Dec.   190 2

Name of father   Samuel M Henderson   a citizen of   Choctaw   Nation, final enrollment No......................
Name of mother   Ida Henderson   a citizen of   Choctaw   Nation, final enrollment No.   5694

Stringtown, I.T.   Postoffice.

### AFFIDAVIT OF MOTHER

UNITED STATES OF AMERICA  
INDIAN TERRITORY  
DISTRICT   23

I   Ida Henderson   , on oath state that I am   29   years of age and a citizen by   blood   of the   Choctaw   Nation, and as such have been placed upon the final roll of the   Choctaw   Nation, by the Honorable Secretary of the Interior my final enrollment number being   5694   ; that I am the lawful wife of   Samuel M Henderson   , who is a citizen of the   Choctaw   Nation, and as such has been placed upon the final roll of said Nation by the Honorable Secretary of the Interior, his final enrollment number being ............ and that a   female   child was born to me on the   8th   day of   Dec   190 5[sic]; that said child has been named   Lillie B Henderson   , and is now living.

WITNESSETH:                                   Ida Henderson
Must be two witnesses   { Christopher Moore
who are citizens          Henry J Bond

Subscribed and sworn to before me this, the   22nd   day of   Feby   , 190 5

D.S. Kennedy
Notary Public.

My Commission Expires:   Nov. 1st 1905

## Applications for Enrollment of Choctaw Newborn
## Act of 1905  Volume VIII

BIRTH AFFIDAVIT.

## DEPARTMENT OF THE INTERIOR.
## COMMISSION TO THE FIVE CIVILIZED TRIBES.

IN RE APPLICATION FOR ENROLLMENT, as a citizen of the Choctaw Nation, of Lilly B. Henderson , born on the 8$^{th}$ day of Dec , 1902

Name of Father: Samuel M Henderson     a citizen of the Choctaw Nation.
Name of Mother: Ida Henderson     a citizen of the Choctaw Nation.

Postoffice Stringtown, I.T.

### AFFIDAVIT OF MOTHER.

UNITED STATES OF AMERICA, Indian Territory,
Central Judicial     DISTRICT.

I, Ida Henderson , on oath state that I am 29 years of age and a citizen by blood , of the Choctaw Nation; that I am the lawful wife of Samuel M Henderson , who is a citizen, by marriage of the Choctaw Nation; that a female child was born to me on 8$^{th}$ day of Dec , 1902; that said child has been named Lilly B. Henderson , and was living March 4, 1905.

                          Ida Henderson

Witnesses To Mark:
{

Subscribed and sworn to before me this 27$^{th}$ day of Mch , 1905

                       D.S. Kennedy
                          Notary Public.

### AFFIDAVIT OF ATTENDING PHYSICIAN OR MID-WIFE.

UNITED STATES OF AMERICA, Indian Territory,
Central Judicial     DISTRICT.

I, J.A. Dabney , a Physician , on oath state that I attended on Mrs. Ida Henderson , wife of Samuel M Henderson on the 8$^{th}$ day of Dec , 1902; that there was born to her on said date a female child; that said child was living March 4, 1905, and is said to have been named Lilly B Henderson

                       J.A. Dabney MD

Witnesses To Mark:
{

## Applications for Enrollment of Choctaw Newborn
## Act of 1905  Volume VIII

Subscribed and sworn to before me this 27<sup>th</sup> day of    Mch   , 1905

D.S. Kennedy
Notary Public.

---

Choc New Born 450
    Benjamin Hibbert Norman   b. 3-27-03

7-2220

Muskogee, Indian Territory, March 29, 1905.

Reuben Norman,
    Coaldale, Arkansas.

Dear Sir:

    Receipt is hereby acknowledged of the affidavits of Sarah J. Norman and M. A. Stewart to the birth of Benjamin Hibbert Norman, Indian Territory son of Reuben and Sarah J. Norman, Indian Territory March 27, 1903, and the same have been filed with our records as an application for the enrollment of said child.

Respectfully,

Chairman.

# NEW BORN AFFIDAVIT

No _____

## CHOCTAW ENROLLING COMMISSION

IN THE MATTER OF THE APPLICATION FOR ENROLLMENT as a citizen of the Choctaw Nation, of   Benjamin H. Norman   born on the 27 day of   march   190 3

Name of father   Ruben Norman    a citizen of   Choctaw   Nation, final enrollment No. ———

Name of mother   Sarah J Norman   a citizen of   Choctaw   Nation, final enrollment No.  6425

## Applications for Enrollment of Choctaw Newborn
## Act of 1905   Volume VIII

Coaldale, Ark.                    Postoffice.

### AFFIDAVIT OF MOTHER

UNITED STATES OF AMERICA  
   INDIAN TERRITORY  
DISTRICT    Central

I    Sarah J Norman    , on oath state that I am   40   years of age and a citizen by   blood   of the   Choctaw   Nation, and as such have been placed upon the final roll of the   Choctaw   Nation, by the Honorable Secretary of the Interior my final enrollment number being   6425   ; that I am the lawful wife of   Ruben Norman   , who is a citizen of the   non   Nation, and as such has been placed upon the final roll of said Nation by the Honorable Secretary of the Interior, his final enrollment number being — and that a   male   child was born to me on the   27   day of   March   190 3; that said child has been named   Benjamin H Norman   , and is now living.

WITNESSETH:                                Sarah J Norman  
Must be two witnesses { Ada Williams  
who are citizens         { Bettie M Justice

Subscribed and sworn to before me this, the   16   day of   February   , 190 5

                         James Bower  
                             Notary Public.

My Commission Expires:  
   Sept 23-1907

### *Affidavit of Attending Physician or Midwife*

UNITED STATES OF AMERICA,  
   INDIAN TERRITORY,  
Central    DISTRICT

I,   M.A. Stewart   a   Practicing Physician on oath state that I attended on Mrs.   Sarah J Norman   wife of   Ruben Norman   on the   27   day of   March   , 190 3, that there was born to her on said date a   male   child, that said child is now living, and is said to have been named   Benjamin H Norman

                      M.A. Stewart          M. D.

Subscribed and sworn to before me this the   16   day of   February   1905

                        James Bower  
                            Notary Public.

## Applications for Enrollment of Choctaw Newborn
## Act of 1905   Volume VIII

WITNESSETH:
Must be two witnesses who are citizens and know the child.
{ Ada Williams
  Bettie M Justice

We hereby certify that we are well acquainted with M.A. Stewart a Practicing Physician and know him to be reputable and of good standing in the community.

Must be two citizen witnesses.
{ Ada Williams
  Bettie M. Justice

BIRTH AFFIDAVIT.

### DEPARTMENT OF THE INTERIOR.
### COMMISSION TO THE FIVE CIVILIZED TRIBES.

**IN RE APPLICATION FOR ENROLLMENT,** as a citizen of the Choctaw Nation, of Benjamin Hibbert Norman, born on the 27th day of March, 1903

Name of Father: Reubin Norman   a citizen of the United States Nation.
Name of Mother: Sarah J Norman   a citizen of the Choctaw Nation.

Postoffice   Coaldale, Arkansas

**AFFIDAVIT OF MOTHER.**

UNITED STATES OF AMERICA, Indian Territory,
Central DISTRICT.

I, Sarah J Norman, on oath state that I am 40 years of age and a citizen by blood, of the Choctaw Nation; that I am the lawful wife of Reuben Norman, who is a citizen, by .................. of the United States ~~Nation~~; that a male child was born to me on 27th day of March, 1903; that said child has been named Benjamin Hibbert Norman, and was living March 4, 1905.

Sarah J Norman

Witnesses To Mark:
{

Subscribed and sworn to before me this 21st day of March, 1905

Wirt Franklin
Notary Public.

## Applications for Enrollment of Choctaw Newborn
## Act of 1905 Volume VIII

**AFFIDAVIT OF ATTENDING PHYSICIAN OR MID-WIFE.**

UNITED STATES OF AMERICA, Indian Territory, }
Central       DISTRICT.

    I, M A Stewart , a Practicing Physician , on oath state that I attended on Mrs. Sarah J Norman , wife of Reuben Norman on the 27 day of March, 1903; that there was born to her on said date a male child; that said child was living March 4, 1905, and is said to have been named Benjamin Hibbert Norman

                                    M.A. Stewart M.D.

Witnesses To Mark:
{

    Subscribed and sworn to before me this 22 day of March , 1905

                                    NS Contelow
                                    Notary Public.
My Com Expr Mch 20-1907        Havener I.T.

---

Choc New Born 451
    Esther Julia Hill b. 4-21-03

**NEW-BORN AFFIDAVIT.**

            Number................

## ...Choctaw Enrolling Commission...

    IN THE MATTER OF THE APPLICATION FOR ENROLLMENT, as a citizen of the Choctaw Nation, of Esther J Hill

born on the 21$^{st}$ day of ___April___ 190 3

| | | |
|---|---|---|
| Name of father Cornelius D. Hill | a citizen of | Choctaw |
| Nation final enrollment No. 101 | | |
| Name of mother Izora Hill | a citizen of | Choctaw |
| Nation final enrollment No. 6479 | | |

                                    Postoffice Poteau Indian Territory

## Applications for Enrollment of Choctaw Newborn
## Act of 1905   Volume VIII

### AFFIDAVIT OF MOTHER.

UNITED STATES OF AMERICA
INDIAN TERRITORY
Central   DISTRICT

I   Izora Hill   , on oath state that I am 37   years of age and a citizen by   blood   of the   Choctaw   Nation, and as such have been placed upon the final roll of the   Choctaw   Nation, by the Honorable Secretary of the Interior my final enrollment number being   6479   ; that I am the lawful wife of   Cornelius D. Hill   , who is a citizen of the   Choctaw   Nation, and as such has been placed upon the final roll of said Nation by the Honorable Secretary of the Interior, his final enrollment number being   101   and that a   female   child was born to me on the 21$^{st}$   day of   April   190 3; that said child has been named   Esther J. Hill   , and is now living.

Izora Hill

Witnesseth.
Must be two Witnesses who are Citizens.   TB Wall
WH Harrison

Subscribed and sworn to before me this   14$^{th}$   day of   Jan   190 5

Malcolm E Rosser
Notary Public.

My commission expires:..................

---

## AFFIDAVIT OF ATTENDING PHYSICIAN OR MIDWIFE

UNITED STATES OF AMERICA
INDIAN TERRITORY
Central   DISTRICT

I,   W. E. Jones   a   Physician   on oath state that I attended on Mrs.   Izora Hill   wife of   Cornelius D. Hill   on the   21$^{st}$   day of   April   , 190 3, that there was born to her on said date a   female   child, that said child is now living, and is said to have been named   Esther J Hill

W.E. Jones   𝓂.𝒟.

Subscribed and sworn to before me this, the   14$^{th}$   day of   January   190 5

WITNESSETH:
Must be two witnesses who are citizens   TB Wall
W.H. Harrison

Malcolm E Rosser   Notary Public.

# Applications for Enrollment of Choctaw Newborn
## Act of 1905 Volume VIII

We hereby certify that we are well acquainted with W.E. Jones a Physician and know him to be reputable and of good standing in the community.

_____  T B Wall

_____  WH Harrison

**BIRTH AFFIDAVIT.**

### DEPARTMENT OF THE INTERIOR.
### COMMISSION TO THE FIVE CIVILIZED TRIBES.

IN RE APPLICATION FOR ENROLLMENT, as a citizen of the Choctaw Nation, of Esther Julia Hill , born on the 21$^{st}$ day of April , 1903

Name of Father: Cornelius D. Hill     a citizen of the Choctaw Nation.
Name of Mother: Izora Hill     a citizen of the Choctaw Nation.

Postoffice Poteau Indian Territory

**AFFIDAVIT OF MOTHER.**

UNITED STATES OF AMERICA, Indian Territory, }
    Central      DISTRICT. }

I, Izora Hill , on oath state that I am 37 years of age and a citizen by blood , of the Choctaw Nation; that I am the lawful wife of Cornelius D Hill , who is a citizen, by intermarriage of the Choctaw Nation; that a female child was born to me on the 21$^{st}$ day of April , 1903; that said child has been named Esther Julia Hill , and was living March 4, 1905.

                                            Izora Hill

Witnesses To Mark:
{

Subscribed and sworn to before me this 25$^{th}$ day of March , 1905

My Comm. expires                    Malcolm E Rosser
    Dec 11 1906                           Notary Public.

## Applications for Enrollment of Choctaw Newborn
## Act of 1905   Volume VIII

### AFFIDAVIT OF ATTENDING PHYSICIAN OR MID-WIFE.

UNITED STATES OF AMERICA, Indian Territory, }
Central        DISTRICT.

    I,   William E. Jones   , a   Physician   , on oath state that I attended on Mrs.   Izora Hill   , wife of   Cornelius D Hill   on the   21$^{st}$ day of April   , 1903; that there was born to her on said date a   female   child; that said child was living March 4, 1905, and is said to have been named   Esther Julia Hill

                                           William E Jones

Witnesses To Mark:
{

    Subscribed and sworn to before me this  25$^{th}$  day of   March   , 1905

My Comm. expires             Malcolm E Rosser
Dec 11 1906                   Notary Public.

---

BIRTH AFFIDAVIT.

## DEPARTMENT OF THE INTERIOR,
### COMMISSION TO THE FIVE CIVILIZED TRIBES.

    *IN RE Application for Enrollment,* as a citizen of the   Choctaw   Nation, of   Esther J Hill   , born on the   21   day of   April   , 1903

Name of Father:  Cornelius D Hill        a citizen of the   Choctaw   Nation.
Name of Mother:  Izora Hill             a citizen of the   Choctaw   Nation.

                   Post-Office:   Poteau I.T.

### AFFIDAVIT OF MOTHER.

UNITED STATES OF AMERICA, }
   INDIAN TERRITORY.
Central        District.

    I,   Izora Hill   , on oath state that I am   35   years of age and a citizen by Blood   , of the   Choctaw   Nation; that I am the lawful wife of   Cornelius D Hill   , who is a citizen, by   marriage   of the Choctaw Nation; that a   Female   child was born to me on   21   day of   April   , 1903 , that said child has been named   Esther J Hill   , and is now living.

                                  Izora Hill

# Applications for Enrollment of Choctaw Newborn
## Act of 1905  Volume VIII

**WITNESSES TO MARK:**

{

    *Subscribed and sworn to before me this* 25   *day of*  Aug   , 1903

                                        LL Smith
                                        *NOTARY PUBLIC.*

### AFFIDAVIT OF ATTENDING PHYSICIAN OR MID-WIFE.

UNITED STATES OF AMERICA,
    INDIAN TERRITORY.
Central        District.

I,  W E Jones  , a  Physician  , on oath state that I attended on Mrs.  Izora Hill  , wife of  Cornelius D Hill  on the  21  day of  April  , 1903; that there was born to her on said date a  Female  child; that said child is now living and is said to have been named  Esther J Hill

                                    W E Jones M.D.

**WITNESSES TO MARK:**

{

    *Subscribed and sworn to before me this* 25   *day of*  Aug   , 1903

                                        LL Smith
                                        *NOTARY PUBLIC.*

7-2236

Muskogee, Indian Territory, August 28, 1903.

Cornelius D. Hill,
    Poteau, Indian Territory.

Dear Sir:

    Receipt is hereby acknowledged of the affidavits of Izora Hill and W. E. Jones relative to the birth of Esther J. Hill, infant daughter of Cornelius D. and Izora Hill, April 21, 1903, which it is presumed has been forwarded to this office as an application for enrollment of the above named child as a citizen of the Choctaw Nation.

    You are advised that under the provisions of the Act of Congress approved July 1, 1902, (32 Stats., 641), the Commission is now without authority to receive or consider

## Applications for Enrollment of Choctaw Newborn
## Act of 1905   Volume VIII

the original application for enrollment of any person whomsoever as a citizen of either the Choctaw or Chickasaw Nation.

Respectfully,

Chairman.

---

7-NB-451

Muskogee, Indian Territory, July 24, 1905.

Cornelius D. Hill,
Poteau, Indian Territory.

Dear Sir:

Receipt is hereby acknowledged of your letter of July 15, 1905, by reference from J. D. Ward in which you ask if you will be notified when the enrollment of your child Esther J. Hill has been approved.

In reply to your letter you are advised that when the enrollment of a child for whom application was made under the act of March 3, 1905, has been approved by the Secretary of the Interior the proper adult persons will be notified.

Respectfully,

Commissioner.

---

7-NB-451.

Muskogee, Indian Territory, November 3, 1905.

Cornelius D. Hill,
Poteau, Indian Territory.

Dear Sir:

Receipt is hereby acknowledged of your letter of October 30, 1905, asking if your new born child Esther Julia Hill is entitled to a pro ratio share of the townsite money.

In reply to your letter you are advised that the payment of moneys to citizens of the Choctaw and Chickasaw Nations is a matter which is within the jurisdiction of the United States Indian Agent and this office can give you no information upon the subject.

Respectfully,

Commissioner.

## Applications for Enrollment of Choctaw Newborn
## Act of 1905   Volume VIII

Choc New Born 452
    Dessie Williams   b. 1-19-03

7-NB-452

Muskogee, Indian Territory, July 31, 1905.

Ada Williams,
    Coalgate, Indian Territory.

Dear Madam:

Receipt is hereby acknowledged of your letter of July 24, 1905, asking if the name of your child Dessie Williams has been approved so that you can now select allotment for her.

In reply to your letter you are advised that on July 22, 1905, the Secretary of the Interior approved the enrollment of your child Dessie Williams as a citizen by blood of the Choctaw Nation and selection of allotment may now be made in her behalf.

Respectfully,

Commissioner.

# NEW BORN AFFIDAVIT

No

## CHOCTAW ENROLLING COMMISSION

IN THE MATTER OF THE APPLICATION FOR ENROLLMENT as a citizen of the Choctaw Nation, of   Dessie Williams   born on the 19 day of   January   190 3

Name of father   Lum Williams   a citizen of   Choctaw   Nation, final enrollment No.   ———
Name of mother   Ada Williams   a citizen of   Choctaw   Nation, final enrollment No.   6499

Coaldale - Ark.   Postoffice.

## Applications for Enrollment of Choctaw Newborn
## Act of 1905   Volume VIII

### AFFIDAVIT OF MOTHER

UNITED STATES OF AMERICA  
   INDIAN TERRITORY  
DISTRICT   Central

   I   Ada Williams   , on oath state that I am   26   years of age and a citizen by   blood   of the   Choctaw   Nation, and as such have been placed upon the final roll of the   Choctaw   Nation, by the Honorable Secretary of the Interior my final enrollment number being   6499   ; that I am the lawful wife of   Lum Williams   , who is a citizen of the   non   Nation, and as such has been placed upon the final roll of said Nation by the Honorable Secretary of the Interior, his final enrollment number being.................. and that a   female   child was born to me on the 19   day of   January   190 3; that said child has been named   Dessie Williams   , and is now living.

WITNESSETH:                                 Ada Williams  
  Must be two witnesses { Samuel R Wilson  
  who are citizens      John Folsom

   Subscribed and sworn to before me this, the   16   day of   February   , 190 5

                                            James Bower  
                                                      Notary Public.

My Commission Expires:  
    Sept 23-1907

### *Affidavit of Attending Physician or Midwife*

UNITED STATES OF AMERICA,  
   INDIAN TERRITORY,  
  Central   DISTRICT

   I,   Bettie Kirksey   a   midwife on oath state that I attended on Mrs.   Ada Williams   wife of   Lum Williams   on the   19   day of   January   , 190 3, that there was born to her on said date a   female   child, that said child is now living, and is said to have been named   Dessie Williams

                                        Bettie M. Kirksey   ~~M. D.~~

   Subscribed and sworn to before me this the   16   day of   February   1905

                                        James Bower  
                                              Notary Public.

WITNESSETH:  
  Must be two witnesses   { Samuel R Wilson  
  who are citizens and  
  know the child.          John Folsom

# Applications for Enrollment of Choctaw Newborn
## Act of 1905   Volume VIII

We hereby certify that we are well acquainted with   Bettie Kirksey   a   midwife   and know   her   to be reputable and of good standing in the community.

Must be two citizen witnesses. { Samuel R Wilson
John Folsom

BIRTH AFFIDAVIT.

## DEPARTMENT OF THE INTERIOR.
## COMMISSION TO THE FIVE CIVILIZED TRIBES.

IN RE APPLICATION FOR ENROLLMENT, as a citizen of the   Choctaw   Nation, of Dessie Williams   , born on the 19th   day of   January   , 1903

Name of Father: Lum Williams         a citizen of the   Choctaw   Nation.
Name of Mother: Ada Williams         a citizen of the   Choctaw   Nation.

Postoffice   Coaldale, Arkansas

### AFFIDAVIT OF MOTHER.

UNITED STATES OF AMERICA, Indian Territory,
Central                DISTRICT.

I,   Ada Williams   , on oath state that I am   27   years of age and a citizen by blood   , of the   Choctaw   Nation; that I am the lawful wife of   Lum Williams   , who is a citizen, by ................ of the   United States   ~~Nation~~; that a   female   child was born to me on   19th   day of   January   , 1903; that said child has been named   Dessie Williams   , and was living March 4, 1905.

Ada Williams

Witnesses To Mark:
{

Subscribed and sworn to before me this   27th   day of   March   , 1905.

Wirt Franklin
Notary Public.

## Applications for Enrollment of Choctaw Newborn
## Act of 1905   Volume VIII

**AFFIDAVIT OF ATTENDING PHYSICIAN OR MID-WIFE.**

UNITED STATES OF AMERICA, Indian Territory, }
   Central             DISTRICT.

I, Amanda Loving, a mid-wife, on oath state that I attended on Mrs. Ada Williams, wife of Lum Williams on the 19th day of January, 1903; that there was born to her on said date a female child; that said child was living March 4, 1905, and is said to have been named Dessie Williams

                                her
                          Amanda x Loving
Witnesses To Mark:            mark
  { LB Kinslow
    W$^m$ C Page

Subscribed and sworn to before me this 27th day of March, 1905

                              Wirt Franklin
                              Notary Public.

---

Choc New Born 453
    James Russell Scantlen  b. 7-8-03

                                                Choctaw 2457

                  Muskogee, Indian Territory, March 31, 1905.

James M. Scantlen,
    Garland, Indian Territory.

Dear Sir:

    Receipt is hereby acknowledged of the affidavits of Laurena Scantlen, Joshua Christy and William Kinch to the birth of James Russell Scantlen, son of James M. and Laurena Scantlen, July 8, 1903, and the same have been filed with our records as an application for the enrollment of said child.

                              Respectfully,

                                                Chairman.

## Applications for Enrollment of Choctaw Newborn
## Act of 1905   Volume VIII

7-N.B. 453.

Muskogee, Indian Territory, April 25, 1905.

James M. Scantlin[sic],
    Garland, Indian Territory.

Dear Sir:

    Receipt is hereby acknowledged of your letter of May 18, asking if your baby has been approved so that you can file for him.

    In reply to your letter you are advised that the enrollment of your child, James Russell Scantlin, has not yet been approved by the Secretary of the Interior, and pending his approval no selecting of allotment can be made in his behalf. You will be notified of such further action as is taken in this case.

                        Respectfully,

                                      Chairman.

**BIRTH AFFIDAVIT.**

## DEPARTMENT OF THE INTERIOR,
### COMMISSION TO THE FIVE CIVILIZED TRIBES.

**In Re Application for Enrollment,** as a citizen of the  Choctaw  Nation, of James Russell Scantlen  , born on the  8$^{th}$  day of  July  , 1903

Name of Father: James M. Scantlen    a citizen of the  Choctaw  Nation.
Name of Mother: Laurena Scantlen    a citizen of the  Choctaw  Nation.

                      Post-office    Garland

**AFFIDAVIT OF MOTHER.**

UNITED STATES OF AMERICA, }
    INDIAN TERRITORY,
    Central        District.

    I, Laurena Scantlen  , on oath state that I am  27  years of age and a citizen by  Blood  , of the  Choctaw  Nation; that I am the lawful wife of  James M. Scantlen  , who is a citizen, by Intermarriage of the  Choctaw  Nation; that a male  child was born to me on  8$^{th}$  day of  July  , 190 3, that said child has been named  James Russell  , and is now living.

## Applications for Enrollment of Choctaw Newborn
## Act of 1905   Volume VIII

Laurena Scantlen

**WITNESSES TO MARK:**

Subscribed and sworn to before me this 18$^{th}$ day of August , 1904

C C Jones
**NOTARY PUBLIC.**

---

**AFFIDAVIT OF ATTENDING PHYSICIAN OR MID-WIFE.**

UNITED STATES OF AMERICA,
**INDIAN TERRITORY,**
.................................... District.

    I, James M Scantlen , a ................................, on oath state that I attended on Mrs. Laurena Scantlen , wife of James M Scantlen on the 8$^{th}$ day of July , 190 3; that there was born to her on said date a male child; that said child is now living and is said to have been named James Russel[sic]

James M Scantlen

**WITNESSES TO MARK:**

Subscribed and sworn to before me this 18$^{th}$ day of August , 1904

C C Jones
**NOTARY PUBLIC.**

---

**NEW-BORN AFFIDAVIT.**

Number................

## ...Choctaw Enrolling Commission...

    IN THE MATTER OF THE APPLICATION FOR ENROLLMENT, as a citizen of the Choctaw Nation, of Russell J[sic] Scantlen

born on the 8 day of ___July___ 190 3

Name of father  James M Scantlen      a citizen of    the Choctaw
Nation final enrollment No. 517
Name of mother  Laurena Scantlen      a citizen of    Choctaw
Nation final enrollment No. 14752

# Applications for Enrollment of Choctaw Newborn
## Act of 1905 Volume VIII

Postoffice     Garland I.T.

### AFFIDAVIT OF MOTHER.

UNITED STATES OF AMERICA
INDIAN TERRITORY
Central     DISTRICT

I     Laurena Scantlen     , on oath state that I am 24 years of age and a citizen by Blood of the Choctaw Nation, and as such have been placed upon the final roll of the Choctaw Nation, by the Honorable Secretary of the Interior my final enrollment number being     14752 ; that I am the lawful wife of     James M Scantlen     , who is a citizen of the Choctaw Nation, and as such has been placed upon the final roll of said Nation by the Honorable Secretary of the Interior, his final enrollment number being     517     and that a     Male     child was born to me on the 8 day of July     190 3; that said child has been named Russell J Scantlen , and is now living.

Laurena Scantlen

Witnesseth.

Must be two Witnesses who are Citizens.     Josiah Garland
     Ward Garland Jr

Subscribed and sworn to before me this     3rd     day of Mar     190 5

C C Jones
Notary Public.

My commission expires: 3/3/1907

---

## AFFIDAVIT OF ATTENDING PHYSICIAN OR MIDWIFE

UNITED STATES OF AMERICA
INDIAN TERRITORY
.................................... DISTRICT

I,     J. M. Scantlen     a     Husband     on oath state that I attended on Mrs.     J. M. Scantlen     wife of     J M Scantlen     on the 8 day of July     , 190 3, that there was born to her on said date a     male     child, that said child is now living, and is said to have been named     Russell Scantlen

J M Scantlen

Subscribed and sworn to before me this, the     3rd     day of March     190 5

C C Jones     Notary Public.

WITNESSETH:
Must be two witnesses who are citizens     Josiah Garland
     Ward Garland Jr

62

## Applications for Enrollment of Choctaw Newborn
## Act of 1905   Volume VIII

We hereby certify that we are well acquainted with    J.M. Scantlen a    Husband    and know    him    to be reputable and of good standing in the community.

    Josiah Garland    _____

    Ward Garland Jr.    _____

    _____

United States of America  )
Indian Territory           ) SS
Central District           )

    I,    Joshua Christy   , on oath state that I am personally acquainted with Mrs. Laurena Scantlen and know that she is the wife of James M. Scantlen and that on the 8th day of July, 1903 there was born to her a male child; that said child was living on March 4, 1905 and is said to have been named James Russell Scantlen.

                                                        Joshua Christy

Witnesses to mark

_____

_____

Subscribed and sworn to before me this   25$^{st}$[sic]   day of   March   1905.

                                                        C C Jones
                                                        Notary Public.

    _____

United States of America  )
Indian Territory           ) SS
Central District           )

    I,   Wm Kinch   , on oath state that I am personally acquainted with Mrs. Laurena Scantlen and know that she is the wife of James M. Scantlen and that on the 8th day of July, 1903 there was born to her a male child; that said child was living on March 4, 1905 and is said to have been named James Russell Scantlen.

                                                        William Kinch

Witnesses to mark

_____

_____

Subscribed and sworn to before me this   25   day of   March   1905.   C C Jones

                                                        Notary Public.

## Applications for Enrollment of Choctaw Newborn
## Act of 1905 Volume VIII

BIRTH AFFIDAVIT.

### DEPARTMENT OF THE INTERIOR.
### COMMISSION TO THE FIVE CIVILIZED TRIBES.

IN RE APPLICATION FOR ENROLLMENT, as a citizen of the Choctaw Nation, of James Russell Scantlen , born on the 8$^{th}$ day of July , 1903

Name of Father: James M Scantlen a citizen of the Choctaw Nation.
Name of Mother: Laurena Scantlen a citizen of the Choctaw Nation.

Postoffice Garland I.T.

### AFFIDAVIT OF MOTHER.

UNITED STATES OF AMERICA, Indian Territory,
Central DISTRICT.

I, Laurena Scantlen , on oath state that I am 27 years of age and a citizen by blood , of the Choctaw Nation; that I am the lawful wife of James M Scantlen , who is a citizen, by intermarriage of the Choctaw Nation; that a male child was born to me on 8$^{th}$ day of July , 1903; that said child has been named James Russell Scantlen , and was living March 4, 1905.

Laurena Scantlen

Witnesses To Mark:

Subscribed and sworn to before me this 25 day of March , 1905

C C Jones
Notary Public.

### AFFIDAVIT OF ATTENDING PHYSICIAN OR MID-WIFE.

UNITED STATES OF AMERICA, Indian Territory,
Western DISTRICT.

I, James M Scantlen , a————— , on oath state that I ~~attended on Mrs~~. am the husband , ~~wife~~ of Laurena Scantlen and was in attendance on her on the 8$^{th}$ day of July , 1903; that there was born to her on said date a male child; that said child was living March 4, 1905, and is said to have been named James Russell Scantlen and the I am he father of said child.

# Applications for Enrollment of Choctaw Newborn
## Act of 1905   Volume VIII

                                James M Scantlen

Witnesses To Mark:

{

Subscribed and sworn to before me this 23$^{rd}$   day of   March   , 1905

                                JB Campbell
                                Notary Public.

---

Choc New Born 454
    Notre Dame McClain   b. 11-21-03

                                                7-N.B. 454.

Muskogee, Indian Territory, May 9, 1905.

R. L. McClain,
    Bonanza, Arkansas.

Dear Sir:

    Receipt is hereby acknowledged of your letter of May 5, asking if you can have land reserved for your infant child until the Secretary of the Interior passes on her application for enrollment.

    In reply you are advised that the affidavits heretofore forwarded to the birth of your child, Notre Dame McClain have been filed with our records as an application for the enrollment of said child. No reservation of land or selection of allotment, however, can be made for children for whom application is made under the provisions of the act of Congress approved March 3, 1905, until their enrollment has been approved by the Secretary of the Interior.

                            Respectfully,

                                        Commissioner in Charge.

# Applications for Enrollment cf Choctaw Newborn
## Act of 1905   Volume VIII

7-2461

Muskogee, Indian Territory, March 31, 1905.

Rufus L. McClain,
    Bonanza, Arkansas.

Dear Sir:

    Receipt is hereby acknowledged of the affidavits of Mary I. McClain and D. A. Sims to the birth of Notre Dame McClain, daughter of Rufus L. and Mary I. McClain, November 21, 1903, and the same have been filed with our records as an application for the enrollment of said child.

                      Respectfully,

                                Chairman.

---

**BIRTH AFFIDAVIT.**

### DEPARTMENT OF THE INTERIOR.
### COMMISSION TO THE FIVE CIVILIZED TRIBES.

    **IN RE APPLICATION FOR ENROLLMENT,** as a citizen of the    Choctaw    Nation, of Notre Dame M$^c$Clain    , born on the  21  day of  November  , 1903

Name of Father: Rufus L. McClain       a citizen of the   Choctaw   Nation.
Name of Mother: Mary I. McClain       a citizen of the   Choctaw   Nation.

                    Postoffice    Bonanza, Ark.

---

**AFFIDAVIT OF MOTHER.**

**UNITED STATES OF AMERICA, Indian Territory,** }
     Central         **DISTRICT.** }

    I,    Mary I. M$^c$Clain   , on oath state that I am   26   years of age and a citizen by   Blood   , of the   Choctaw    Nation; that I am the lawful wife of  Rufus L. M$^c$Clain    , who is a citizen, by  Inter marriage    of the    Choctaw     Nation; that a   Female    child was born to me on  21  day of   November   , 1903; that said child has been named  Notre Dame M$^c$Clain    , and was living March 4, 1905.

                            Mary I M$^c$Clain

Witnesses To Mark:
{

## Applications for Enrollment of Choctaw Newborn
## Act of 1905   Volume VIII

Subscribed and sworn to before me this 24 day of March , 1905

W.F. Lester
Notary Public.

---

**AFFIDAVIT OF ATTENDING PHYSICIAN OR MID-WIFE.**

UNITED STATES OF AMERICA, Indian Territory, }
Central            DISTRICT.

I,  D.A. Sims    , a  Physician   , on oath state that I attended on Mrs.  Mary I M$^c$Clain   , wife of  Rufus L M$^c$Clain   on the  21  day of November   , 1903; that there was born to her on said date a  Female   child; that said child was living March 4, 1905, and is said to have been named  Notre Dame M$^c$Clain

D.A. Sims, M.D.

Witnesses To Mark:
{

Subscribed and sworn to before me this 24 day of March , 1905

W.F. Lester
Notary Public.

---

## AFFIDAVIT OF ATTENDING PHYSICIAN OR MIDWIFE

UNITED STATES OF AMERICA
INDIAN TERRITORY
Central       DISTRICT

I,   D. A. Sims    a    Physician
on oath state that I attended on Mrs.  Mary I M$^c$Clain   wife of   Rufus L McClain on the   21   day of  November   , 190 3 , that there was born to her on said date a Female   child, that said child is now living, and is said to have been named   Notre Dame M$^c$Clain

D.A. Sims      *M.D.*

Subscribed and sworn to before me this, the   17   day of February   190 5

WITNESSETH:                                        W.F. Lester      Notary Public.
Must be two witnesses  { Viola Karl
who are citizens         { Edwin S. Gregory

# Applications for Enrollment of Choctaw Newborn
## Act of 1905  Volume VIII

We hereby certify that we are well acquainted with D. A. Sims a Physician and know him to be reputable and of good standing in the community.

Viola Karl                                          Edwin S Gregory

**NEW-BORN AFFIDAVIT.**

Number..................

...Choctaw Enrolling Commission...

IN THE MATTER OF THE APPLICATION FOR ENROLLMENT, as a citizen of the Choctaw Nation, of  Notre Dame M$^c$Clain born on the 21 day of November 190 3

| | | |
|---|---|---|
| Name of father  Rufus L M$^c$Clain | a citizen of | Choctaw by Inter M. |
| Nation final enrollment No.  44 Inter M | | |
| Name of mother  Mary I. M$^c$Clain | a citizen of | Choctaw |
| Nation final enrollment No.  7137 | | |
| | Postoffice | Bonanza Ark |

**AFFIDAVIT OF MOTHER.**

UNITED STATES OF AMERICA
INDIAN TERRITORY
Central       DISTRICT

I       Mary I. M$^c$Clain       , on oath state that I am 26 years of age and a citizen by Blood of the Choctaw Nation, and as such have been placed upon the final roll of the Choctaw Nation, by the Honorable Secretary of the Interior my final enrollment number being 7137 ; that I am the lawful wife of Rufus L McClain InterM , who is a citizen of the Choctaw Nation, and as such has been placed upon the final roll of said Nation by the Honorable Secretary of the Interior, his final enrollment number being 44 Inter M and that a Female child was born to me on the 21 day of November 190 3; that said child has been named Notre Dame M$^c$Clain , and is now living.

Witnesseth.                                    Mary I. M$^c$Clain

Must be two Witnesses who are Citizens.    Viola Karl
                                            Edwin S Gregory

## Applications for Enrollment of Choctaw Newborn
## Act of 1905   Volume VIII

Subscribed and sworn to before me this   17   day of   Feb     190 5

                                                William F Lester
                                                             Notary Public.

My commission expires:
Feb first 1906

**BIRTH AFFIDAVIT.**

### DEPARTMENT OF THE INTERIOR.
### COMMISSION TO THE FIVE CIVILIZED TRIBES.

**IN RE APPLICATION FOR ENROLLMENT,** as a citizen of the   Choctaw   Nation, of   Notre Dame M$^c$Clain   , born on the   21   day of   November   , 1903

Name of Father: Rufus L M$^c$Clain       a citizen of the   Choctaw   Nation.
Name of Mother: Mary I McClain       a citizen of the   Choctaw   Nation.

                              Postoffice   Bonanza Ark

**AFFIDAVIT OF MOTHER.**

**UNITED STATES OF AMERICA, Indian Territory,**
    Central               **DISTRICT.**

      I,   Mary I McClain   , on oath state that I am   26   years of age and a citizen by   Blood   , of the   Choctaw   Nation; that I am the lawful wife of   Rufus L McClain   , who is a citizen, by   Intermarriage   of the   Choctaw   Nation; that a   girl   child was born to me on   21   day of   November   , 1903, that said child has been named   Notre Dame McClain   , and is now living.

Witnesses To Mark:
   {    Mary I. M$^c$Clain

      Subscribed and sworn to before me this   12   day of November   , 1904

                                           W.F. Lester
                                             Notary Public.

# Applications for Enrollment of Choctaw Newborn
## Act of 1905 Volume VIII

**AFFIDAVIT OF ATTENDING PHYSICIAN OR MID-WIFE.**

UNITED STATES OF AMERICA, Indian Territory, }
   Central              DISTRICT. }

    I,   D.A. Sims   , a   Physician   , on oath state that I attended on Mrs.   Mary I McClain   , wife of   Rufus L McClain   on the   21   day of November, 1903; that there was born to her on said date a   Girl   child; that said child is now living and is said to have been named Notre Dame McClain

                                              D. A. Sims, M.D.

Witnesses To Mark:
{

    Subscribed and sworn to before me this   12   day of   November   , 1904

                                            W.F. Lester
                                            Notary Public.

---

You will please notice that I failed to use one *(illegible)* the first *(illegible)*
                                        Yours Truly   W. F. Lester

---

Choc New Born 455
    Eloise Self   b. 9-17-04

                                                          Choctaw 4314

                          Muskogee, Indian Territory, March 31, 1905.

John H. Self,
    Stringtown, Indian Territory.

Dear Sir:

    Receipt is hereby acknowledge of the affidavits of Leona Self and J. A. Dabney to the birth of Eloise Self, daughter of John H. and Leona Self, September 17, 1904, and the same have been filed with our records as an application for the enrollment of said child.

                                         Respectfully,

                                                          Chairman.

Applications for Enrollment of Choctaw Newborn
Act of 1905 Volume VIII

## AFFIDAVIT OF ATTENDING PHYSICIAN OR MIDWIFE

UNITED STATES OF AMERICA  
INDIAN TERRITORY  
Central Judicial DISTRICT

I, J. A. Dabney a Practicing Physician on oath state that I attended on Mrs. Leona Self wife of John H Self on the 17th day of Sept , 190 4, that there was born to her on said date a female child, that said child is now living, and is said to have been named Eloise Self

J. A. Dabney M.D.

Subscribed and sworn to before me this, the 16th day of Jan 190 5

D.S. Kennedy
Notary Public.

WITNESSETH:

Must be two witnesses who are citizens and know the child.
- Oliver Thomas
- Joe B. Williams

We hereby certify that we are well acquainted with J. A. Dabney a Practicing Physician and know him to be reputable and of good standing in the community.

Oliver Thomas

Joe B. Williams

**NEW-BORN AFFIDAVIT.**

Number

## Choctaw Enrolling Commission.

IN THE MATTER OF THE APPLICATION FOR ENROLLMENT, as a citizen of the Choctaw Nation, of Eloise Self

born on the 17 day of Sept 190 4

Name of father John H Self a citizen of Choctaw
Nation final enrollment No 410
Name of mother Leona Self a citizen of Choctaw
Nation final enrollment No 12070

Postoffice Stringtown

# Applications for Enrollment of Choctaw Newborn
## Act of 1905   Volume VIII

### AFFIDAVIT OF MOTHER.

UNITED STATES OF AMERICA,  
INDIAN TERRITORY,  
Central     DISTRICT

I     Leona Self     on oath state that I am   29   years of age and a citizen by   Blood   of the   Choctaw   Nation, and as such have been placed upon the final roll of the   Choctaw   Nation, by the Honorable Secretary of the Interior my final enrollment number being   12070   ; that I am the lawful wife of   John H Self   , who is a citizen of the   Choctaw   Nation, and as such has been placed upon the final roll of said Nation by the Honorable Secretary of the Interior, his final enrollment number being   410   and that a   Female   child was born to me on the   17   day of   Sept   190 4; that said child has been named   Eloise   , and is now living.

WITNESSETH:     Leona Self

Must be two Witnesses who are Citizens.  
Oliver Thomas  
Joe B Williams

Subscribed and sworn to before me this   20$^{th}$   day of   Jan   190 5

D.S. Kennedy  
Notary Public.

My commission expires   Nov 1$^{st}$ 1905

---

**BIRTH AFFIDAVIT.**

### DEPARTMENT OF THE INTERIOR.
## COMMISSION TO THE FIVE CIVILIZED TRIBES.

IN RE APPLICATION FOR ENROLLMENT, as a citizen of the   Choctaw   Nation, of   Eloise Self   , born on the   17$^{th}$   day of   Sept   , 1904

Name of Father:   John H Self         a citizen of the   Choctaw   Nation.  
Name of Mother:   Leona Self         a citizen of the   Choctaw   Nation.

Postoffice   Stringtown, I.T.

---

### AFFIDAVIT OF MOTHER.

UNITED STATES OF AMERICA, Indian Territory,  
Central Judicial     DISTRICT.

I,   Leona Self   , on oath state that I am   29   years of age and a citizen by blood   , of the   Choctaw   Nation; that I am the lawful wife of   John H Self   , who is a citizen, by   Marriage   of the   Choctaw   Nation; that a   female

# Applications for Enrollment of Choctaw Newborn
## Act of 1905   Volume VIII

child was born to me on   17th   day of   Sept   , 1904; that said child has been named Eloise Self   , and was living March 4, 1905.

Leona Self

Witnesses To Mark:

{

Subscribed and sworn to before me this   27th   day of   Mch   , 1905

D.S. Kennedy<br>Notary Public.

---

**AFFIDAVIT OF ATTENDING PHYSICIAN OR MID-WIFE.**

UNITED STATES OF AMERICA, Indian Territory,
Central Judicial                DISTRICT.

I,   J. A. Dabney   , a   Physician   , on oath state that I attended on Mrs.   Leona Self   , wife of   John H Self   on the 17th   day of   Sept   , 1904; that there was born to her on said date a   female   child; that said child was living March 4, 1905, and is said to have been named   Eloise Self

J A Dabney

Witnesses To Mark:

{

Subscribed and sworn to before me this   25th   day of   Mch   , 1905

D.S. Kennedy<br>Notary Public.

---

Choc New Born 456
  Vernon Alvin Coon   b. 12-21-03

# Applications for Enrollment of Choctaw Newborn
## Act of 1905 Volume VIII

7-4338

Muskogee, Indian Territory, June 1, 1904.

A. D. Coon,
    Roff, Indian Territory.

Dear Sir:

    Receipt is hereby acknowledged of your letter of the 20th inst., enclosing the affidavits of Rhoda Coon and C. E. Logan, relative to the birth of your minor child, Alvin Coon, December 21, 1903, which it is presumed have been forwarded as an application for enrollment of said child as a citizen by blood of the Choctaw Nation of said child.

    You are informed that under the provisions of the Act of Congress approved July 1, 1902, the Commission is now without authority to receive or consider the original application for enrollment of any person whomsoever as a citizen of the Choctaw or Chickasaw Nation.

                        Respectfully,

                                        Chairman.

*my Choctaw Roll No 12129*

**BIRTH AFFIDAVIT.**

    **IN RE-APPLICATION FOR ENROLLMENT**, as a citizen of the Choctaw Nation, of Vernon Alvin Coon, born on the 21 day of December, 1903

Name of Father: Alva D Coon     a citizen of the Choctaw Nation.
Name of Mother: Rhoda Coon     a citizen of the Choctaw Nation.

                      Postoffice     Hart Ind. Terr.

**AFFIDAVIT OF MOTHER.**

UNITED STATES OF AMERICA, INDIAN TERRITORY,
    Southern District     District.

    I, Rhoda Coon, on oath state that I am 24 years of age and a citizen by Blood, of the Choctaw Nation; that I am the lawful wife of Alva D Coon, who is a citizen, by Intermarriage of the Choctaw Nation; that a Boy child was born to me on the 21 day of December, 1903, that said child has been named Vernon Alvin Coon, and is now living.

                                        Rhoda Coon

# Applications for Enrollment of Choctaw Newborn
# Act of 1905   Volume VIII

Witnesses To Mark:

{

Subscribed and sworn to before me this  20    day of    March    , 1905.

                                         Joseph Anderson
                                         Notary Public.

---

### AFFIDAVIT OF ATTENDING PHYSICIAN OR MID-WIFE.

UNITED STATES OF AMERICA, INDIAN TERRITORY,
Southern                            District.

    I,    Thena Morgan    , a    midwife    , on oath state that I attended on Mrs.   Rhoda Coon   , wife of   Alva D. Coon    on the  21  day of Dec , 190 3; that there was born to her on said date a   male    child; that said child is now living and is said to have been named   Vernon Alvin Coon

                                         Thena Morgan

Witnesses To Mark:

{

Subscribed and sworn to before me this  20    day of    March    , 1905.

                                         Joseph Anderson
                                         Notary Public.

---

United States of America,
Indian Territory
Southern District.

    In the matter of the application of A. D. Coon and Rhoda Coon for the enrollment of one child, Alvin Coon, born the 21st day of December 1903.

United States of America,
Indian Territory,
Southern District.

    Personally appeared before me the undersigned notary public in and for the Southern District of the Indian Territory, A. D. Coon and Rhoda Coon, the wife of the said A. D. Coon who being by me first duly sworn depose and say that on the 21st day of December 1903 there was born to them in the town of Roff, Indian Territory, a male child and that they named it Alvin.

                                         Rhoda Coon
                                         A D Coon

# Applications for Enrollment of Choctaw Newborn
## Act of 1905   Volume VIII

Subscribed and sworn to before me, this the 19th day of May 1904.

                                                        Jno Casteel
                                                        Notary Public.

United States of America,
Indian Territory,
Southern District,

     Personally appeared before me the undersigned notary public in and for the Southern District of the Indian Territory, Dr. C. E. Logan who being by me first duly sworn deposes and says that he was the attendind[sic] physician at the birth of a male child born to Rhoda Coon the wife of A. D. Coon on the 21st day of December 1903.

                                                        C.E. Logan M.D.

Subscribed and sworn to before me, this the 19th day of May 1904.

                                                        Jno Casteel
                                                        Notary Public.

---

Choc New Born 459
      Norma Jane Standley   b. 5-31-04

## AFFIDAVIT OF ATTENDING PHYSICIAN OR MIDWIFE

UNITED STATES OF AMERICA }
INDIAN TERRITORY
  Central      DISTRICT

     I,   J. S. Fulton   a   Practicing Physician on oath state that I attended on Mrs. Etna J Standley   wife of   Clarence P Standley on the   31   day of   May   , 190 4, that there was born to her on said date a   Female child, that said child is now living, and is said to have been named   Norma J Standley

                                       J.S. Fulton                M.D.
Subscribed and sworn to before me this, the   12$^{th}$   day of   **January**       190 5

                                         J[sic] W A Shoney
                                         Notary Public.

WITNESSETH:
Must be two witnesses { W. H. Marshall
who are citizens and
know the child.       C. C. Rose

## Applications for Enrollment of Choctaw Newborn
## Act of 1905   Volume VIII

We hereby certify that we are well acquainted with................................................................................
a ................................................................ and know .........................to be reputable and of good standing in the community.

                         C. C. Rose

                         W. H. Marshall

**BIRTH AFFIDAVIT.**

### DEPARTMENT OF THE INTERIOR.
### COMMISSION TO THE FIVE CIVILIZED TRIBES.

**IN RE APPLICATION FOR ENROLLMENT,** as a citizen of the   Choctaw   Nation, of Norma Jane Standley   , born on the  $31^{st}$   day of  May   , 1904

Name of Father:  Clarence Standley      a citizen of the   Choctaw   Nation.
Name of Mother:  Etna   "      a citizen of the   Choctaw   Nation.

                 Postoffice   Atoka I.T.

**AFFIDAVIT OF MOTHER.**

**UNITED STATES OF AMERICA, Indian Territory,**
     Central             **DISTRICT.**

I,  Etna Standley   , on oath state that I am  22   years of age and a citizen by Intermarriage   , of the   Choctaw   Nation; that I am the lawful wife of   Clarence Standley   , who is a citizen, by  blood   of the   Choctaw   Nation; that a female   child was born to me on  $31^{st}$   day of   May   , 1904; that said child has been named   Norma Jane Standley   , and was living March 4, 1905.

                       Etna J. Standley

Witnesses To Mark:

Subscribed and sworn to before me this  $18^{th}$   day of   March   , 1905

                       W.H. Angell
                           Notary Public.

## Applications for Enrollment of Choctaw Newborn
## Act of 1905   Volume VIII

### AFFIDAVIT OF ATTENDING PHYSICIAN OR MID-WIFE.

UNITED STATES OF AMERICA, Indian Territory, }
Central            DISTRICT.

I,   J.S. Fulton   , a   Physician   , on oath state that I attended on Mrs.   Etna Standley   , wife of   Clarence Standley   on the  31st  day of   May , 1904; that there was born to her on said date a ............... child; that said child was living March 4, 1905, and is said to have been named Norma Jane Standley

J.S. Fulton

Witnesses To Mark:
{

Subscribed and sworn to before me this   18th   day of   March   , 1905

N.S. Farmer
Notary Public.

---

**NEW-BORN AFFIDAVIT.**

Number...............

## Choctaw Enrolling Commission.

IN THE MATTER OF THE APPLICATION FOR ENROLLMENT, as a citizen of the   Choctaw   Nation, of   Norma J. Standley

born on the   31   day of   May   190 4

Name of father   Clarence P Standley        a citizen of   Choctaw   Nation final enrollment No  15332
Name of mother   Etna J Standley        a citizen of   white   Nation final enrollment No ——

Postoffice   Atoka I.T.

**AFFIDAVIT OF MOTHER.**

UNITED STATES OF AMERICA, }
    INDIAN TERRITORY,
Central       DISTRICT

I       Etna J Standley            on oath state that I am   22   years of age and a citizen by   white   of the  —— Nation, and as such have been placed upon the final roll of the  ——  Nation, by the Honorable Secretary of the Interior my final enrollment number being  —— ; that I am the lawful wife of   Clarence P Standley   , who is a citizen of the   Choctaw   Nation, and as such has been placed upon the final

## Applications for Enrollment of Choctaw Newborn
## Act of 1905   Volume VIII

roll of said Nation by the Honorable Secretary of the Interior, his final enrollment number being   15332   and that a   Female   child was born to me on the   31   day of   May 190 4; that said child has been named   Norma J Standley   , and is now living.

WITNESSETH:
Must be two   } W.H. Marshall
Witnesses who
are Citizens.   *(Name Illegible)*

Etna J   x   Standley
(her mark)

Subscribed and sworn to before me this   12$^{th}$   day of   Jan   190 5

W A Shoney
Notary Public.

My commission expires   Jan 11 1909

---

Choc New Born 458
    Sam Colbert   b. 7-10-03

7-NB-458

Muskogee, Indian Territory, June 7, 1905.

L. D. Horton,
    Boswell, Indian Territory.

Dear Sir:

    Receipt is hereby acknowledged of your letter of June 2, 1905, returning application for the enrollment of Sam Colbert corrected by having the seals affixed to the affidavits of the mother and the midwife.

Respectfully,

Chairman.

# Applications for Enrollment of Choctaw Newborn
## Act of 1905 Volume VIII

7-NB-458.

Muskogee, Indian Territory, May 26, 1905.

Aaron Colbert,
    Boswell, Indian Territory.

Dear Sir:

    There is returned herewith affidavit of Serena Colbert, mother, and Lena James, midwife to the birth of your infant child, Sam Colbert, from which the notary public, L. D. Horton, before whom they were executed, omitted his seal.

    Please have this seal affixed and return the application to this office.

    Respectfully,

    Chairman.

VR 26-4.

---

7-N.B. 458.

Muskogee, Indian Territory, May 5, 1905.

L. D. Horton,
    Boswell, Indian Territory.

Dear Sir:

    Receipt is hereby acknowledged of your letter of May 1, transmitting the affidavits of Serena Colbert and Lena James to the birth of Sam Colbert, son of Aaron and Serena Colbert, July 10, 1903, and the same have been filed with our records as an application for the enrollment of said child.

    The other application enclosed in your letter will be made the subject of a separate communication.

    Respectfully,

    Commissioner in Charge.

# Applications for Enrollment of Choctaw Newborn
## Act of 1905    Volume VIII

**COPY**

N. B. 458

Muskogee, Indian Territory, April 8, 1905.

Aaron Colbert,
    Boswell, Indian Territory.

Dear Sir:

    There is inclosed you herewith for execution application for the enrollment of your infant child, Sam Colbert, born July 10, 1903.

    The application heretofore filed with the Commission is incomplete in that it does not contain the affidavit of the attending physician or midwife. In case there was no physician or midwife in attendance, it will be necessary, for the child to be enrolled, that you secure the affidavits of two persons who have actual knowledge of the fact, that the child was born, was living on March 4, 1905, and that Serena Colbert was his mother.

    In having these affidavits executed care should be exercised to see that all names are written in full, as they appear in the body of the affidavit, and in the event that either of the persons signing the affidavit are unable to write, signatures by mark must be attested by two witnesses. Each affidavit must be executed before a Notary Public and the notarial seal and signature of the officer must be attached to each separate affidavit.

Respectfully,

SIGNED

*T. B. Needles.*

LM 8-16

Commissioner in Charge.

---

7-4370

Muskogee, Indian Territory, August 19, 1903.

Aron Colbert,
    Boswell, Indian Territory.

Dear Sir:

    Receipt is hereby acknowledged of the affidavits of Serane[sic] Carnes and Lorena B. McClure relative to the birth of your infant son, Sam Colbert, July 10, 1903, which appears to have been forwarded to this office as an application for enrollment of the above named child as a citizen of the Choctaw Nation.

# Applications for Enrollment of Choctaw Newborn
## Act of 1905  Volume VIII

Your attention is invited to Section 28 of the Act of Congress approved July 1, 1902 and ratified by the citizens of the Choctaw and Chickasaw Nations September 28, 1902, which is as follows:

"The names of all persons living on the date of the final ratification of this agreement entitled to be enrolled as provided in section 27 hereof shall be placed upon the rolls made by said Commission; and no child born thereafter to a citizen or freedman and no person intermarried thereafter to a citizen shall be entitled to enrollment or to participate in the distribution of the tribal property of the Choctaws and Chickasaws."

You will, therefore, understand that the Commission is now without authority to enroll infant children born to citizens of the Choctaw and Chickasaw Nations subsequent to September 25, 1902, the date of ratification of said Act of Congress.

Respectfully,

Commissioner in Charge.

---

**BIRTH AFFIDAVIT.**

### DEPARTMENT OF THE INTERIOR.
### COMMISSION TO THE FIVE CIVILIZED TRIBES.

IN RE APPLICATION FOR ENROLLMENT, as a citizen of the   Choctaw   Nation, of Sam Colbert   , born on the   10   day of   July   , 1903

Name of Father: Aaron Colbert           a citizen of the   Choctaw   Nation.
Name of Mother: Serena Colbert (Carnes)   a citizen of the   Choctaw   Nation.

Postoffice   Boswell, Ind. Ter.

---

### AFFIDAVIT OF MOTHER.

UNITED STATES OF AMERICA, Indian Territory,
    Central Judicial        DISTRICT.

I,   Serena Colbert (Carnes)   , on oath state that I am about 40 years of age and a citizen by   Blood   , of the   Choctaw   Nation; that I am the lawful wife of Aaron Colbert   , who is a citizen, by   Blood   of the   Choctaw   Nation; that a   male   child was born to me on   10   day of   July   , 1903; that said child has been named   Sam Colbert   , and was living March 4, 1905.

her
Serena x Colbert
mark

# Applications for Enrollment of Choctaw Newborn
## Act of 1905   Volume VIII

Witnesses To Mark:
{ L.D. Horton
  M.W. Thompson

    Subscribed and sworn to before me this   1   day of     May     , 1905

                           L.D. Horton
                                Notary Public.

---

### AFFIDAVIT OF ATTENDING PHYSICIAN OR MID-WIFE.

UNITED STATES OF AMERICA, Indian Territory,
Central Judicial         DISTRICT.

    I,   Lena James   , a   midwife   , on oath state that I attended on Mrs.   Serena Colbert (Carnes)   , wife of   Aaron Colbert   on the 10" day of July, 1903; that there was born to her on said date a   male   child; that said child was living March 4, 1905, and is said to have been named   Sam Colbert

                            her
                      Lena x James
Witnesses To Mark:        mark
{ L.D. Horton
  M.W. Thompson

    Subscribed and sworn to before me this   1   day of     May     , 1905

                             L.D. Horton
                                Notary Public.

---

BIRTH AFFIDAVIT.

### DEPARTMENT OF THE INTERIOR.
### COMMISSION TO THE FIVE CIVILIZED TRIBES.

---

    IN RE APPLICATION FOR ENROLLMENT, as a citizen of the   Choctaw   Nation, of   Sam Colbert   , born on the   10   day of   July   , 1903

Name of Father:  Aaron Colbert        a citizen of the   Choctaw   Nation.
Name of Mother:  Serena Colbert      a citizen of the   Choctaw   Nation.

                        Postoffice     Boswell, I.T.

# Applications for Enrollment of Choctaw Newborn
## Act of 1905   Volume VIII

### AFFIDAVIT OF MOTHER.

UNITED STATES OF AMERICA, Indian Territory,  
Central Judicial        DISTRICT.

I, Serena Colbert, on oath state that I am about 40 years of age and a citizen by blood, of the Choctaw Nation; that I am the lawful wife of Aaron Colbert, who is a citizen, by blood of the Choctaw Nation; that a male child was born to me on 10 day of July, 1903; that said child has been named Sam Colbert, and was living March 4, 1905.

                           her  
                        Serena x Colbert  
                          mark

Witnesses To Mark:  
{ Ellis Carnes  
  L.D. Horton

Subscribed and sworn to before me this 25 day of March, 1905

                      L.D. Horton  
                          Notary Public.

---

### AFFIDAVIT OF ATTENDING PHYSICIAN OR MID-WIFE.

UNITED STATES OF AMERICA, Indian Territory,  
Central Judicial        DISTRICT.

I, *Aaron Colbert, husband of Serena Colbert*, on oath state that I *am the father of the applicant, Sam Colbert and know that he was born to my wife, Serena Colbert* on the 10 day of July, 1903; that *he is a male* child; that said child was living March 4, 1905, and is ~~said to have been~~ named *Sam - That no midwife or physician attended her except a neighbor woman named Rena McClure whose residence I do not know, but might find her*

                         his  
                      Aaron x Colbert  
Witnesses To Mark:          mark  
{ Ellis Carnes  
  L.D. Horton

Subscribed and sworn to before me this 25 day of March, 1905

                      L.D. Horton  
                        Notary Public.

Applications for Enrollment of Choctaw Newborn
Act of 1905   Volume VIII

BIRTH AFFIDAVIT.

## DEPARTMENT OF THE INTERIOR,
### COMMISSION TO THE FIVE CIVILIZED TRIBES.

*IN RE Application for Enrollment,* as a citizen of the   The Choctaw   Nation, of   Sam Colbert  , born on the   10   day of   July 1903  , 1......

Name of Father: Aron[sic] Colbert          a citizen of the   Choctaw   Nation.
Name of Mother: Serane[sic] Carnes[sic]    a citizen of the   Choctaw   Nation.

Post-Office:   Boswell, Ind. Ter.

**AFFIDAVIT OF MOTHER.**

UNITED STATES OF AMERICA, }
  INDIAN TERRITORY.
  Central        District.  }

I,   Serane Carnes   , on oath state that I am   30   years of age and a citizen by   Birth  , of the   Choctaw   Nation; that I am the lawful wife of   Aron Colbert  , who is a citizen, by   Blood   of the   Choctaw   Nation; that a   Male   child was born to me on   10   day of   July, 1903  , 1........, that said child has been named   Sam Colbert  , and is now living.

                                      Serane x Carnes
WITNESSES TO MARK:
  { D.C. McClure
  { T.H Duncan

*Subscribed and sworn to before me this*   13   *day of*   August 1903  , 190.....

                              Thomas V McReynolds
                              My Com. expires Apr. 27th 1905
                              NOTARY PUBLIC.

**AFFIDAVIT OF ATTENDING PHYSICIAN OR MID-WIFE.**

UNITED STATES OF AMERICA, }
  INDIAN TERRITORY.
  Central        District.  }

I,   Lorena B. McClure   , a   Midwife   , on oath state that I attended on Mrs.   Serane Carnes  , wife of   Aron Colbert   on the   10   day of   July 1903  , 1........; that there was born to her on said date a   Male   child; that said child is now living and is said to have been named   Sam Colbert

# Applications for Enrollment of Choctaw Newborn
# Act of 1905   Volume VIII

|  | her |
|---|---|
| WITNESSES TO MARK: | Lorena B x M$^c$Clure |
| D.C. McClure | mark |
| THE Duncan | |

*Subscribed and sworn to before me this* 13 day of August 1903 , 190.....

Thomas V McReynolds
**NOTARY PUBLIC.**

---

Choc New Born 459
    Theodore McKinley Marston   b. 3-18-03
    Addie Marston   b. 3-18-03

$W^m O.B.$

**COMMISSIONERS:**
TAMS BIXBY,
THOMAS B. NEEDLES,
C.R. BRECKINRIDGE.

**DEPARTMENT OF THE INTERIOR,
COMMISSIONER TO THE FIVE CIVILIZED TRIBES.**

WM. O. BEALL
Secretary

REFER IN REPLY TO THE FOLLOWING:

7-NB-459.

ADDRESS ONLY THE
COMMISSION TO THE FIVE CIVILIZED TRIBES.

Muskogee, Indian Territory, May 25, 1905.

Bulah Marston,
    Atoka, Indian Territory.

Dear Sir:

    There are enclosed you herewith for execution applications for the enrollment of your infant children, Theodore McKinley Marston and Addie Marston.

    In the affidavits of January 13, 1905, the date of the children's birth is given as March 18, 1904, while in the affidavits of March 22 and 25, 1905, it is given as March 18, 1903. In the enclosed applications the date of birth is left blank. Please insert the correct date, and, when the affidavits are properly executed, return them to this office.

    In having these affidavits executed care should be exercised to see that all names are written in full, as they appear in the body of the affidavit, and in the event that either of the persons signing the affidavit are unable to write, signatures by mark must be

## Applications for Enrollment of Choctaw Newborn
## Act of 1905   Volume VIII

attested by two witnesses.  Each affidavit must be executed before a Notary Public and the notarial seal and signature of the officer must be attached to each separate affidavit.

Respectfully,

VR 25-10.                                                             Tams Bixby
                                                                                     Chairman.

---

**NEW-BORN AFFIDAVIT.**

Number..............

## Choctaw Enrolling Commission.

IN THE MATTER OF THE APPLICATION FOR ENROLLMENT, as a citizen of the Choctaw    Nation, of                              Theadore[sic] M. Marston   (a Twin)

born on the  18"   day of    March        1904

Name of father    Bulah Marston                    a citizen of     Choctaw
Nation final enrollment No  12230
Name of mother    Mary Marston                     a citizen of     ———
Nation final enrollment No    ———

Postoffice     Atoka I.T.

AFFIDAVIT OF MOTHER.

UNITED STATES OF AMERICA, ⎫
    INDIAN TERRITORY,             ⎬
    Central         DISTRICT       ⎭

   I      Mary Marston                           on oath state that I am  33  years of age and a ~~citizen~~ by   non citizen      of the  ———  Nation, and as such have been placed upon the final roll of the ................................................... Nation, by the Honorable Secretary of the Interior my final enrollment number being ...............; that I am the lawful wife of    Bulah Marston    , who is a citizen of the   Choctaw          Nation, and as such has been placed upon the final roll of said Nation by the Honorable Secretary of the Interior, his final enrollment number being  12230    and that a    male     child was born to me on the   18th  day of   March       1904 ; that said child has been named   Theodore M Marston      , and is now living.

Mary Marston

WITNESSETH:
  Must be two      ⎫ Jesse Gary
  Witnesses who  ⎬
  are Citizens.    ⎭ Nathan Davis

## Applications for Enrollment of Choctaw Newborn
## Act of 1905   Volume VIII

Subscribed and sworn to before me this   13   day of   January       190 5

A. E. Folsom
Notary Public.

My commission expires
9-Jan 1909

## AFFIDAVIT OF ATTENDING PHYSICIAN OR MIDWIFE

UNITED STATES OF AMERICA
INDIAN TERRITORY
Central    DISTRICT

I,   J S Fulton      a        Practicing Physician on oath state that I attended on Mrs.   Mary Marston   wife of    Bulah Marston on the   18th   day of   March   , 190 4, that there was born to her on said date a   Male child, that said child is now living, and is said to have been named   Theodore M Marston (a Twin)

J.S. Fulton           M.D.

Subscribed and sworn to before me this, the   14" day of   January      190 5

A. E. Folsom
Notary Public.

WITNESSETH:
Must be two witnesses who are citizens and know the child.
{ Jesse Gary
  Nathan Davis

We hereby certify that we are well acquainted with   D$^r$ J.S. Fulton a   Practicing Physician   and know   him   to be reputable and of good standing in the community.

9-Jan 1909

{ Jesse Gary
  Nathan Davis

BIRTH AFFIDAVIT.

## DEPARTMENT OF THE INTERIOR.
## COMMISSION TO THE FIVE CIVILIZED TRIBES.

IN RE APPLICATION FOR ENROLLMENT, as a citizen of the   Choctaw   Nation, of Theodore M$^c$Kinley Marston   , born on the   18$^{th}$   day of   March   , 1903

Name of Father: Bulah Marston          a citizen of the   Choc   Nation.
Name of Mother: Mary     "             a citizen of the   non citizen   Nation.

# Applications for Enrollment of Choctaw Newborn
## Act of 1905   Volume VIII

Postoffice   Atoka I.T.

---

**AFFIDAVIT OF MOTHER.**

UNITED STATES OF AMERICA, Indian Territory, }
Central                    DISTRICT.             }

I, Mary Marston , on oath state that I am 33 years of age and a citizen by Non Citizen , ~~of the~~ ~~Nation~~; that I am the lawful wife of Bulah Marston , who is a citizen, by blood of the Choctaw Nation; that a male child was born to me on 18$^{th}$ day of March , 1903; that said child has been named Theodore M$^c$Kinley Marston , and was living March 4, 1905.

Mary Marston

Witnesses To Mark:
{

Subscribed and sworn to before me this 22$^{nd}$ day of March , 1905

WH Angell
Notary Public.

---

**AFFIDAVIT OF ATTENDING PHYSICIAN OR MID-WIFE.**

UNITED STATES OF AMERICA, Indian Territory, }
Central                    DISTRICT.             }

I, J.S. Fulton , a physician , on oath state that I attended on Mrs. Mary Marston , wife of Bulah Marston on the 18$^{th}$ day of March , 1903; that there was born to her on said date a male child; that said child was living March 4, 1905, and is said to have been named Theodore M$^c$Kinley Marston

JS Fulton

Witnesses To Mark:
{

Subscribed and sworn to before me this 25$^{th}$ day of March , 1905

WH Angell
Notary Public.

Applications for Enrollment of Choctaw Newborn
Act of 1905   Volume VIII

**NEW-BORN AFFIDAVIT.**

Number..........

## Choctaw Enrolling Commission.

IN THE MATTER OF THE APPLICATION FOR ENROLLMENT, as a citizen of the Choctaw Nation, of  Adda Marston (a Twin)

born on the 18" day of March 1904

Name of father  Bulah Marston  a citizen of  Choctaw Nation final enrollment No 12230
Name of mother  Mary Marston  a ~~citizen~~ of  ———
Nation final enrollment No..........

Postoffice  Atoka I.T.

**AFFIDAVIT OF MOTHER.**

UNITED STATES OF AMERICA,
  INDIAN TERRITORY,
  Central       DISTRICT

I  Mary Marston  on oath state that I am 33 years of age and a ~~citizen~~ by  non citizen  of the ——— Nation, and as such have been placed upon the final roll of the ................................... Nation, by the Honorable Secretary of the Interior my final enrollment number being ..................; that I am the lawful wife of Bulah Marston  , who is a citizen of the Choctaw  Nation, and as such has been placed upon the final roll of said Nation by the Honorable Secretary of the Interior, his final enrollment number being  12230  and that a  female  child was born to me on the 18th day of  March  1904 ; that said child has been named  Adde[sic] Marston  , and is now living.

Mary Marston

WITNESSETH:
Must be two Witnesses who are Citizens.
  Jesse Gary
  Nathan Davis

Subscribed and sworn to before me this  13  day of  January  1905

A. E. Folsom
Notary Public.

My commission expires
9-Jan-1909

## Applications for Enrollment of Choctaw Newborn
## Act of 1905 Volume VIII

## AFFIDAVIT OF ATTENDING PHYSICIAN OR MIDWIFE

UNITED STATES OF AMERICA }
INDIAN TERRITORY
Central     DISTRICT

I,   J S Fulton    a    Practicing Physician on oath state that I attended on Mrs.   Mary Marston   wife of   Bulah Marston on the   18$^{th}$   day of   March   , 190 4, that there was born to her on said date a Female   child, that said child is now living, and is said to have been named   Adda Marston

J.S. Fulton    M.D.

Subscribed and sworn to before me this, the  14" day of  January   190 5

A. E. Folsom
Notary Public.

WITNESSETH:
Must be two witnesses who are citizens and know the child.   { Jesse Gary
Nathan Davis

We hereby certify that we are well acquainted with   D$^r$ J.S. Fulton   a   Practicing Physician   and know   him   to be reputable and of good standing in the community.

9-Jan-1909

{ Jesse Gary
Nathan Davis

---

**BIRTH AFFIDAVIT.**

### DEPARTMENT OF THE INTERIOR.
### COMMISSION TO THE FIVE CIVILIZED TRIBES.

**IN RE APPLICATION FOR ENROLLMENT,** as a citizen of the   Choctaw   Nation, of Addie Marston   , born on the  18$^{th}$   day of   March  , 1903

Name of Father: Bulah Marston          a citizen of the   Choc   Nation.
Name of Mother: Mary        "              a citizen of the  non citizen   Nation.

Postoffice    Atoka

# Applications for Enrollment of Choctaw Newborn
## Act of 1905   Volume VIII

**AFFIDAVIT OF MOTHER.**

UNITED STATES OF AMERICA, Indian Territory, }
    Central                DISTRICT. }

    I, Mary Marston, on oath state that I am 33 years of age and a ~~citizen by~~ Non Citizen, ~~of the Nat on~~; that I am the lawful wife of Bulah Marston, who is a citizen, by blood of the Choctaw Nation; that a female child was born to me on 18th day of March, 1903; that said child has been named Addie Marston, and was living March 4, 1905.

                                      Mary Marston

Witnesses To Mark:
{

    Subscribed and sworn to before me this 22nd day of March, 1905

                                      WH Angell
                                             Notary Public.

---

**AFFIDAVIT OF ATTENDING PHYSICIAN OR MID-WIFE.**

UNITED STATES OF AMERICA, Indian Territory, }
    Central                DISTRICT. }

    I, J S Fulton, a physician, on oath state that I attended on Mrs. Mary Marston, wife of Bulah Marston on the 18th day of March, 1903; that there was born to her on said date a female child; that said child was living March 4, 1905, and is said to have been named Addie Marston

                                        JS Fulton

Witnesses To Mark:
{

    Subscribed and sworn to before me this 25th day of March, 1905

                                       WH Angell
                                           Notary Public.

# Applications for Enrollment of Choctaw Newborn
## Act of 1905 Volume VIII

BIRTH AFFIDAVIT.

## DEPARTMENT OF THE INTERIOR.
## COMMISSION TO THE FIVE CIVILIZED TRIBES.

IN RE APPLICATION FOR ENROLLMENT, as a citizen of the Choctaw Nation, of Addie Marston, born on the 18th day of March, 1903

Name of Father: Bulah Marston     a citizen of the Choc Nation.
Name of Mother: Mary Marston     a citizen of the U.S. Nation.

Postoffice    Atoka, Ind. Ter.

### AFFIDAVIT OF MOTHER.

UNITED STATES OF AMERICA, Indian Territory,
    Central             DISTRICT.

I, Mary Marston, on oath state that I am 33 years of age and a citizen ~~by~~, of the United States Nation; that I am the lawful wife of Bulah Marston, who is a citizen, by blood of the Choctaw Nation; that a female child was born to me on 18th day of March, 1903; that said child has been named Addie Marston, and was living March 4, 1905.

                                                     Mary Marston

Witnesses To Mark:

Subscribed and sworn to before me this 27th day of May, 1905

                                                     WH Angell
                                                     Notary Public.

### AFFIDAVIT OF ATTENDING PHYSICIAN OR MID-WIFE.

UNITED STATES OF AMERICA, Indian Territory,
    Central             DISTRICT.

I, J S Fulton, a physician, on oath state that I attended on Mrs. Mary Marston, wife of Bulah Marston on the 18th day of March, 1903; that there was born to her on said date a female child; that said child was living March 4, 1905, and is said to have been named Addie Marston

                                                     JS Fulton

Witnesses To Mark:

## Applications for Enrollment of Choctaw Newborn
## Act of 1905   Volume VIII

Subscribed and sworn to before me this 29$^{th}$ day of    May    , 1905

WH Angell
Notary Public.

---

**BIRTH AFFIDAVIT.**

### DEPARTMENT OF THE INTERIOR.
### COMMISSION TO THE FIVE CIVILIZED TRIBES.

---

IN RE APPLICATION FOR ENROLLMENT, as a citizen of the    Choctaw    Nation, of Theodore M$^c$Kinley Marston    , born on the 18$^{th}$ day of March , 1903

Name of Father: Bulah Marston     a citizen of the Choc    Nation.
Name of Mother: Mary Marston     a citizen of the    U.S.    Nation.

Postoffice    Atoka, Ind. Ter.

---

**AFFIDAVIT OF MOTHER.**

UNITED STATES OF AMERICA, Indian Territory, }
    Central             DISTRICT.

I, Mary Marston , on oath state that I am 33 years of age and a citizen ~~by~~    , of the    United States    Nation; that I am the lawful wife of Bulah Marston    , who is a citizen, by blood    of the    Choctaw    Nation; that a female    child was born to me on    18$^{th}$    day of    March    , 1903; that said child has been named    Theodore M$^c$Kinley Marston    , and was living March 4, 1905.

Mary Marston

Witnesses To Mark:
{

Subscribed and sworn to before me this 27$^{th}$ day of    May    , 1905

WH Angell
Notary Public.

---

**AFFIDAVIT OF ATTENDING PHYSICIAN OR MID-WIFE.**

UNITED STATES OF AMERICA, Indian Territory, }
    Central             DISTRICT.

I, J F[sic] Fulton    , a    physician    , on oath state that I attended on Mrs. Mary Marston    , wife of Bulah Marston    on the 18$^{th}$    day of

## Applications for Enrollment of Choctaw Newborn
## Act of 1905   Volume VIII

March , 1903; that there was born to her on said date a    female    child; that said child was living March 4, 1905, and is said to have been named Theodore M$^c$Kinley Marston

J.S. Fulton

Witnesses To Mark:

{ Subscribed and sworn to before me this 29$^{th}$    day of    May    , 1905

WH Angell<br>Notary Public.

---

Choc New Born 460
       Joseph Riddle   b. 7-20-04
       Granted Feb 18, 1907

7-NB-460.                                                                                                           O.L.J.

### DEPARTMENT OF THE INTERIOR,
### COMMISSIONER TO THE FIVE CIVILIZED TRIBES.

-----

In the matter of the application for the enrollment of Joseph Riddle as a citizen of the Choctaw Nation.

### DECISION.

It appears from the record herein that on March 27, 1905, application was made to the Commission to the Five Civilized Tribes for the enrollment of Joseph Riddle as a citizen by blood of the Choctaw Nation under the provisions of the Act of Congress approved March 3, 1905 (33 Stats., 1060).

It further appears from the record herein and from the records in the possession of this office that said applicant was born on July 20, 1904; that he is the son of Cephus Riddle, whose name appears opposite No. 12768 upon the final roll of citizens by blood of the Choctaw Nation approved by the Secretary of the Interior March 6, 1903, and Susan Lewis, whose name appears opposite No. 4647 upon the final roll of Choctaw freedman approved by the Secretary of the Interior June 28, 1904; and that said applicant was living on March 4, 1905.

I am, therefore, of the opinion that Joseph Riddle should be enrolled as a citizen by blood of the Choctaw Nation under the provisions of the Act of Congress approved March 3, 1905 (33 Stats., 1060), and it is so ordered.

# Applications for Enrollment of Choctaw Newborn
## Act of 1905   Volume VIII

Tams Bixby   Commissioner.

Muskogee, Indian Territory.
FEB 18 1907

### Testimony of Susan Lewis

What is your name   Susan Lewis
"   "   "   P.O. Quinton, I T
How old are you   28
How many children have you
   Four boys & one girl
How are they enrolled
   They are enrolled as freedmen
Did you make application for joseph as a citz by blood of the Choc Nation   A Yes
Why didn't you make application as a freedman
   ~~Who is~~ His father is a citz by blood and wanted him enrolled that way
What is Joseph Riddles[sic] fathers[sic] name
   Cephus Riddle
Were you ever married to Cephus Riddle
   No Sir
Is Joseph Riddle still living   Yes Sir
Who is he living with   Living with me
You still desire for him to be enrolled as a citz by blood   Yes Sir
Where is Cephus Riddle
   He is at home
What is Cephus Riddles[sic] P.O.   Quinton

Susan Lewis

Subscribed and sworn to before me this 17th day of January 1907

J L Gary
Notary Public.

### Testimony of Coleman Riddle

What is your name   Coleman Riddle
How old are you   35   P.O. Quinton
Are you a citz by blood Choc Nation   Yes Sir
Who is Cephus Riddle   my brother
Is Cephus Riddle married   Yes
Has he any children by this wife   No
Is he the father of Joseph Riddle
   They all say he is but I don't know myself
Did Cephus ever say that Joseph was his child

## Applications for Enrollment of Choctaw Newborn
## Act of 1905 Volume VIII

No he never told me so
Do you think he is the father of Joseph
  Yes I think so
Is Joseph Riddle still living Yes
Who is Joseph living with A Susan
Who is the mother of Joseph A Susie Lewis

                                    Coleman Riddle

Subscribed and sworn to before me this 18th day of January 1907

                                    J L Gary
                                          Notary Public

**NEW-BORN AFFIDAVIT.**

                  Number............

### ...Choctaw Enrolling Commission...

      IN THE MATTER OF THE APPLICATION FOR ENROLLMENT, as a citizen of the Choctaw Nation, of Joseph Riddle

born on the 20 day of __July__ 190 4

Name of father   Cephus Riddle         a citizen of    Choctaw
Nation final enrollment No. ...............     Freedman
Name of mother   Susan Lewis        ~~a citizen of~~   Chickasaw
Nation final enrollment No. ...............

                                  Postoffice    Kinta I.T.

**AFFIDAVIT OF MOTHER.**

UNITED STATES OF AMERICA
INDIAN TERRITORY
   Western      DISTRICT

            I      Susan Lewis                 , on oath state that I am 27      years of age and a citizen by   Freedman    of the    Chickasaw Nation, and as such have been placed upon the final roll of the    Chickasaw  Nation, by the Honorable Secretary of the Interior my final enrollment number being ............; that I am the ~~lawful wife~~ of    Cephus Riddle    not married    , who is a citizen of the    Choctaw Nation, and as such has been placed upon the final roll of said Nation by the Honorable Secretary of the Interior, his final enrollment number being   3638    and that a     Male

# Applications for Enrollment of Choctaw Newborn
## Act of 1905 Volume VIII

child was born to me on the 20$^{th}$ day of July 190 4; that said child has been named Joseph Riddle , and is now ~~living,~~ ~~dead~~ living

Susan Lewis

Witnesseth.
Must be two Witnesses who are Citizens. } Andrew C. Bullard
Turner M$^c$Intosh

Subscribed and sworn to before me this 10 day of Feb 190 5

J. M. White
Notary Public.

My commission expires: Sept 2$^{th}$[sic] 1906

---

## AFFIDAVIT OF ATTENDING PHYSICIAN OR MIDWIFE

UNITED STATES OF AMERICA
INDIAN TERRITORY
  Western  DISTRICT

I, Mary Moore a *not married* Midwife on oath state that I attended on Mrs. Susan Lewis ~~wife~~ of Cephus Riddle on the 20 day of July , 190 4, that there was born to her on said date a male child, that said child is now living, and is said to have been named Joseph Riddle

her
Mary x Moore   ~~M. D.~~
mark

Subscribed and sworn to before me this, the 21st day of March 190 5

Wirt Franklin   Notary Public.

WITNESSETH:
Must be two witnesses who are citizens { Sims Colbert
JA Lynn

We hereby certify that we are well acquainted with Mary Moore a Midwife and know her to be reputable and of good standing in the community.

## Applications for Enrollment of Choctaw Newborn
## Act of 1905   Volume VIII

BIRTH AFFIDAVIT.

## DEPARTMENT OF THE INTERIOR.
## COMMISSION TO THE FIVE CIVILIZED TRIBES.

IN RE APPLICATION FOR ENROLLMENT, as a citizen of the    Choctaw    Nation, of Joseph Riddle    , born on the 20    day of    July  , 1904

Name of Father: Cephus Riddle    a citizen of the   Choctaw    Nation.
                                  Freedman
Name of Mother: Susan Lewis    ~~a citizen of the~~   Chickasaw   Nation.

Postoffice    Kinta, I.T.

### AFFIDAVIT OF MOTHER.

UNITED STATES OF AMERICA, Indian Territory, ⎱
    Western            DISTRICT.          ⎰

I,   Susan Lewis   , on oath state that I am  27   years of age and a citizen by Freedman   , of the    Chickasaw    Nation; that I am the ~~lawful wife~~ of   Cephus Riddle   not married    , who is a citizen, by blood   of the   Choctaw    Nation; that a   male   child was born to me on   20th   day of   July   , 1904; that said child has been named   Joseph Riddle   , and was living March 4, 1905.

                                    Susan Lewis
Witnesses To Mark:
 ⎰ Andrew C. Bullard
 ⎱ Turner M<sup>c</sup>Intosh

Subscribed and sworn to before me this  10  day of   Feb   , 1905

                                    J. M. White
                                        Notary Public.
My com expires Sept. 2th[sic] 1906

### AFFIDAVIT OF ATTENDING PHYSICIAN OR MID-WIFE.

UNITED STATES OF AMERICA, Indian Territory, ⎱
    Western            DISTRICT.          ⎰

I,   Mary Moore   , a   midwife   , on oath state that I attended on Mrs.   Susan Lewis   , ~~wife of~~ not married Cephus  Riddle    on the 20   day of   July   , 1904; that there was born to her on said date a   male   child; that said child was living March 4, 1905, and is said to have been named   Joseph Riddle

# Applications for Enrollment of Choctaw Newborn
## Act of 1905  Volume VIII

                                        her
Witnesses To Mark:          Mary x Moore
  { Sims Colbert             mark
    J. A. Lynn

Subscribed and sworn to before me this 21st day of    March   , 1905

                                      Wirt Franklin
                                          Notary Public.

---

7-NB-460.

                        Muskogee, Indian Territory, August 18, 1905.

Susan Lewis,
    Kinta, Indian Territory.

Dear Madam:

    In the matter of the application for the enrollment of your minor child Joseph Riddle as a citizen by blood of the Choctaw Nation it appears that said child claims his right to enrollment as such citizen through Cephus Riddle, who is alleged in your affidavit as to the birth of said child to be his father. It further appears that you were never married to the said Cephus Riddle.

    You are advised that before the rights of said child, as a citizen by blood of the Choctaw Nation can be finally determined, it will be necessary for you and the said Cephus Riddle to appear before the Commissioner to the Five Civilized Tribes at his office in Muskogee, Indian Territory, for the purpose of being examined under oath in regard to the parentage of your said son, Joseph Riddle. If you ever lived for any length of time with the said Cephus Riddle as his wife you should bring with you, when you appear at this Office, two disinterested persons who have a knowledge of the fact that you and the aid Cephus Riddle so lived together.

    Such appearance should be made made[s.c] with as little delay as possible.

                        Respectfully,

                        Acting Commissioner.

## Applications for Enrollment of Choctaw Newborn
## Act of 1905 Volume VIII

Choctaw N B 460

Muskogee, Indian Territory, October 13, 1905.

Guy A. Curry,
    Attorney at Law,
        Quinton, Indian Territory.

Dear Sir:

    Receipt is hereby acknowledged of your letter of October 10, stating that you have been retained as attorney in the matter of the application for the enrollment of Joseph Riddle, a minor child, as a citizen by blood of the Choctaw Nation, and asking the status of the case and if further evidence is needed.

    In reply to your letter you are advised that it appears from the record in this case that Joseph Riddle is the son of Susan Lewis, a Choctaw freedman, and she claims that the father of this child is Cephus Riddle, a citizen by blood of the Choctaw Nation, to whom she was not married. This office has not yet passed upon the case but in the event further evidence is necessary you will be notified.

                  Respectfully,

                              Commissioner.

---

7-4514.

17-1401.

Muskogee, Indian Territory, August 10, 1906.

Guy A. Curry,
    Quinton, Indian Territory.

Dear Sir:

    Receipt is hereby acknowledged of your letter of July 23, 1906, transmitting affidavits of Susan Lewis and Andrew C. Bullard to the birth of Joseph Riddle, child of Cephus and Susan Lewis, July 20, 1904.

                    Respectfully,

                              Commissioner.

# Applications for Enrollment of Choctaw Newborn
## Act of 1905  Volume VIII

7-NB-460

Muskogee, Indian Territory, February 4, 1907.

Cephus (or Wash) Riddle,
    Quinton, Indian Territory.

Dear Sir:

    In the matter of the application for the enrollment of your child, Joseph Riddle, as a citizen by blood of the Choctaw Nation, under the Act of Congress approved March 3, 1905, you are advised that it will be necessary for you to appear at this office at once for the purpose of testifying relative to the parentage of your child.

    This matter should receive your <u>immediate</u> attention.

        Respectfully,

                Commissioner.

---

7-NB-460

**COPY**

Muskogee, Indian Territory, February 27, 1907.

Mansfield, McMurray & Cornish,
    Attorneys for the Choctaw and Chickasaw Nations,
        South McAlester, Indian Territory.

Gentlemen:

    Inclosed herewith you will find a copy of the decision of the Commissioner to the Five Civilized Tribes, rendered February 18, 1907, granting the application for the enrollment of Joseph Riddle as a citizen by blood of the Choctaw Nation.

    You are further advised that the name of Joseph Riddle granted in said decision has been placed upon a schedule of citizens by blood of the Choctaw Nation to be submitted to the Secretary of the Interior for his approval. You will be notified of Departmental action thereon.

        Respectfully,
        SIGNED

                *Tams Bixby*
                Commissioner.

Registered.
Incl. 7-NB-460

# Applications for Enrollment of Choctaw Newborn
## Act of 1905   Volume VIII

7-NB-460

**COPY**

Muskogee, Indian Territory, February 27, 1907.

Gus[sic] A. Curry,
    Attorney at law,
        Quinton, Indian Territory.

Dear Sir:

Inclosed herewith you will find a copy of the decision of the Commissioner to the Five Civilized Tribes, rendered February 18, 1907, granting the application for the enrollment of Joseph Riddle as a citizen by blood of the Choctaw Nation.

You are further advised that the name of Joseph Riddle granted in said decision has been placed upon a schedule of citizens by blood of the Choctaw Nation to be submitted to the Secretary of the Interior for his approval. You will be notified of Departmental action thereon.

                Respectfully,
                SIGNED

                *Tams Bixby*
Registered.                Commissioner.
Incl. 7-NB-460

---

7-NB-460

Muskogee, Indian Territory, March 30, 1907.

Guy A. Curry,
    Quinton, Indian Territory.

Dear Sir:

Receipt is hereby acknowledged of your letter of March 13, 1907, in which you ask to be advised the action of the Secretary of the Interior in the case of Joseph Riddle as a citizen by blood of the Choctaw Nation.

In reply to your letter you are advised that on March 2, 1907, the Secretary of the Interior approved the enrollment of Joseph Riddle as a new born citizen of the Choctaw Nation under the Act of Congress approved March 3, 1905.

                Respectfully,

                            Acting Commissioner.

## Applications for Enrollment of Choctaw Newborn
## Act of 1905   Volume VIII

Muskogee, Indian Territory, July 31, 1907.

The Commissioner
    of Indian Affairs.

Sir:

Receipt is hereby acknowledged of Indian Office letter of July 2, 1907, (I.T. 55023-1907) authorizing this office to place the following notation opposite the name of Joseph Riddle as it appears on the roll of minor Choctaw freedmen at No. 119 "Duplication; see roll of new born citizens of the Choctaw Nation No. 1586; no allotment to be made under this number."

I have to advise that the name of Joseph Riddle appears at No. 1580 upon the roll of new born citizens of the Choctaw Nation instead of 1586 and the notation has been changed to show the correct number 1580.

I have to recommend that if the number in the notation above referred to placed upon the rolls in the Department and the Indian Office appears as 1586 that the same be changed to 1580 in order to correspond with the number of this citizen on the approved roll of new born citizens of the Choctaw Nation.

Respectfully,

Commissioner.

---

Choc New Born 461
    John Clifton Kirksey   b. 6-10-03
    Pearl Kirksey   b. 12-2-04

BIRTH AFFIDAVIT.

### DEPARTMENT OF THE INTERIOR.
### COMMISSION TO THE FIVE CIVILIZED TRIBES.

IN RE APPLICATION FOR ENROLLMENT, as a citizen of the   Choctaw   Nation, of John Clifton Kirksey, born on the 10th day of June, 1903

Name of Father: John A Kirksey     a citizen of the United States ~~Nation~~.
Name of Mother: Bettie M. Kirksey     a citizen of the   Choctaw   Nation.

Postoffice   Coaldale, Arkansas

# Applications for Enrollment of Choctaw Newborn
## Act of 1905   Volume VIII

**AFFIDAVIT OF MOTHER.**

UNITED STATES OF AMERICA, Indian Territory, }
Central        DISTRICT.

I, Bettie M Kirksey, on oath state that I am 19 years of age and a citizen by blood, of the Choctaw Nation; that I am the lawful wife of John A. Kirksey, who is a citizen, ~~by~~ of the United States ~~Nation~~; that a male child was born to me on 10th day of June, 1903; that said child has been named John Clifton Kirksey, and was living March 4, 1905.

         Bettie M Kirksey

Witnesses To Mark:
{

Subscribed and sworn to before me this 21st day of March, 1905

         Wirt Franklin
         Notary Public.

**AFFIDAVIT OF ATTENDING PHYSICIAN OR MID-WIFE.**

UNITED STATES OF AMERICA, Indian Territory, }
Central        DISTRICT.

I, Ada Williams, a mid-wife, on oath state that I attended on Mrs. Bettie M. Kirksey, wife of John A Kirksey on the 10th day of June, 1903; that there was born to her on said date a male child; that said child was living March 4, 1905, and is said to have been named John Clifton Kirksey

         Ada Williams

Witnesses To Mark:
{

Subscribed and sworn to before me this 27th day of March, 1905

         Wirt Franklin
         Notary Public.

Applications for Enrollment of Choctaw Newborn
Act of 1905   Volume VIII

# NEW BORN AFFIDAVIT

No _____

## CHOCTAW ENROLLING COMMISSION

IN THE MATTER OF THE APPLICATION FOR ENROLLMENT as a citizen of the Choctaw Nation, of   Pearl Kirksey   born on the   2   day of   December   190 4

Name of father   John Kirksey   a citizen of   Non   Nation, final enrollment No. ——   D.C. Justice
Name of mother   Bettie M Kirksey   a citizen of   Choctaw   Nation, final enrollment No.   6426

Coaldale, Ark.   Postoffice.

### AFFIDAVIT OF MOTHER

UNITED STATES OF AMERICA  
INDIAN TERRITORY  
DISTRICT   Central

I   Bettie M Kirksey (nee Justice)   , on oath state that I am   18   years of age and a citizen by   blood   of the   Choctaw   Nation, and as such have been placed upon the final roll of the   Choctaw   Nation, by the Honorable Secretary of the Interior my final enrollment number being   6426   ; that I am the lawful wife of   John Kirksey   , who is a citizen of the   non   Nation, and as such has been placed upon the final roll of said Nation by the Honorable Secretary of the Interior, his final enrollment number being —— and that a   Female   child was born to me on the   2 day of December 190 4; that said child has been named   Pearl Kirksey   , and is now living.

WITNESSETH:   Bettie M Kirksey  
Must be two witnesses  ⎰ Ada Williams  
who are citizens  ⎱ Samuel R Wilson

Subscribed and sworn to before me this, the   16   day of   February   , 190 5

James Bower  
Notary Public.

My Commission Expires:  
Sept 23-1907

Applications for Enrollment of Choctaw Newborn
Act of 1905   Volume VIII

# NEW BORN AFFIDAVIT

No ............

## CHOCTAW ENROLLING COMMISSION

IN THE MATTER OF THE APPLICATION FOR ENROLLMENT as a citizen of the Choctaw Nation, of   John Clifton Kirksey   born on the   10   day of   June   190 3

Name of father   John Kirksey   a citizen of   Non   Nation, final enrollment No. ——   D.C. Justice
Name of mother   Bettie M Kirksey   a citizen of   Choctaw   Nation, final enrollment No.   6426

Coaldale, Ark.   Postoffice.

### AFFIDAVIT OF MOTHER

UNITED STATES OF AMERICA  
   INDIAN TERRITORY  
DISTRICT   Central

I   Bettie M Kirksey (nee Justice)   , on oath state that I am   18   years of age and a citizen by   blood   of the   Choctaw   Nation, and as such have been placed upon the final roll of the   Choctaw   Nation, by the Honorable Secretary of the Interior my final enrollment number being   6426   ; that I am the lawful wife of   John Kirksey   , who is a citizen of the   non   Nation, and as such has been placed upon the final roll of said Nation by the Honorable Secretary of the Interior, his final enrollment number being —— and that a   Male   child was born to me on the   10   day of June 190 3; that said child has been named   John Clifton Kirksey   , and is now living.

WITNESSETH:   Bettie M Kirksey  
  Must be two witnesses   { Ada Williams  
  who are citizens     Samuel R Wilson

Subscribed and sworn to before me this, the   16   day of   February   , 190 5

James Bower  
      Notary Public.

My Commission Expires:  
   Sept 23-1907

# Applications for Enrollment of Choctaw Newborn
## Act of 1905   Volume VIII

### *Affidavit of Attending Physician or Midwife*

UNITED STATES OF AMERICA,  
   INDIAN TERRITORY,  
Central     DISTRICT

I, Sarah J Norman   a   midwife on oath state that I attended on Mrs. Bettie M Kirksey   wife of   John Kirksey on the 10 day of June , 190 3, that there was born to her on said date a male child, that said child is now living, and is said to have been named John Clifton Kirksey

          Sarah J Norman   M. D.

Subscribed and sworn to before me this the  16  day of  February   1905

          James Bower  
               Notary Public.

WITNESSETH:  
Must be two witnesses who are citizens and know the child.  
    Ada Williams  
    Samuel R Wilson

We hereby certify that we are well acquainted with   Sarah J Norman   a midwife   and know her   to be reputable and of good standing in the community.

Must be two citizen witnesses.  
    Ada Williams  
    Samuel R Wilson

---

### *Affidavit of Attending Physician or Midwife*

UNITED STATES OF AMERICA,  
   INDIAN TERRITORY,  
Central     DISTRICT

I, Ada Williams   a   midwife on oath state that I attended on Mrs. Bettie M Kirksey   wife of   John Kirksey on the 2 day of December , 190 4, that there was born to her on said date a Female child, that said child is now living, and is said to have been named Pearl Kirksey

          Ada Williams   M. D.

Subscribed and sworn to before me this the  16  day of  February   1905

          James Bower  
               Notary Public.

# Applications for Enrollment of Choctaw Newborn
## Act of 1905   Volume VIII

WITNESSETH:

Must be two witnesses who are citizens and know the child.
{ Ada Williams
  Samuel R Wilson

We hereby certify that we are well acquainted with   Ada Williams   a   midwife   and know   her   to be reputable and of good standing in the community.

Must be two citizen witnesses.
{ Samuel R Wilson
  Sarah J Norman

**BIRTH AFFIDAVIT.**

### DEPARTMENT OF THE INTERIOR.
## COMMISSION TO THE FIVE CIVILIZED TRIBES.

IN RE APPLICATION FOR ENROLLMENT, as a citizen of the   Choctaw   Nation, of   Pearl Kirksey   , born on the 2nd   day of   December   , 1904

Name of Father: John A Kirksey           a citizen of the United States ~~Nation~~.
Name of Mother: Bettie M. Kirksey        a citizen of the   Choctaw   Nation.

Postoffice   Coaldale, Arkansas

### AFFIDAVIT OF MOTHER.

UNITED STATES OF AMERICA, Indian Territory,
Central                    DISTRICT.

I,   Bettie M Kirksey   , on oath state that I am   19   years of age and a citizen by   blood   , of the   Choctaw   Nation; that I am the lawful wife of John A. Kirksey   , who is a citizen, ~~by~~ ............ of the United States ~~Nation~~; that a female   child was born to me on   2nd   day of   December   , 1904; that said child has been named   Pearl Kirksey   , and was living March 4, 1905.

Bettie M Kirksey

Witnesses To Mark:
{

Subscribed and sworn to before me this   21st   day of   March   , 1905

Wirt Franklin
Notary Public.

## Applications for Enrollment of Choctaw Newborn
## Act of 1905   Volume VIII

**AFFIDAVIT OF ATTENDING PHYSICIAN OR MID-WIFE.**

UNITED STATES OF AMERICA, Indian Territory, }
   Central               DISTRICT. }

    I,  Ada Williams  , a  mid-wife  , on oath state that I attended on Mrs. Bettie M. Kirksey  , wife of  John A Kirksey  on the  2nd day of December, 1904; that there was born to her on said date a  female  child; that said child was living March 4, 1905, and is said to have been named Pearl Kirksey

                                       Ada Williams

Witnesses To Mark:
{

    Subscribed and sworn to before me this  27th  day of  March  , 1905

                                     Wirt Franklin
                                     Notary Public.

---

Choc New Born 462
       Gertrude Irene Elliott   b. 7-30-03

                                           7-2566

                        Muskogee, Indian Territory, March 25, 1905.

T. W. Elliott,
    Braden, Indian Territory.

Dear Sir:

    Receipt is hereby acknowledged of your letter of March 20, 1905, enclosing former letter from the Commission from which we have been enabled to identify your wife upon our records as having been enrolled as Gertrude A. Reagan and the affidavits heretofore forwarded to the birth of Gertrude Irene Elliott, daughter of T. W. and Gertrude A. Elliott, July 30, 1903, have been filed with our records as an application for the enrollment of said child.

                        Respectfully,

                                           Chairman.

KB 1-24

## Applications for Enrollment of Choctaw Newborn
## Act of 1905   Volume VIII

**COPY**

Choctaw N.B. 462.

Muskogee, Indian Territory, April 26, 1905.

Turner W. Elliott,
    Braden, Indian Territory.

Dear Sir:

    Receipt is hereby acknowledged of your letter of April 20, transmitting the affidavits of Gertrude A. Elliott and joint affidavit of I. C. Talley and John J. Gill to the birth of Gertrude Irene Elliott, daughter of Turner W. and Gertrude A. Elliott, July 30, 1903, and the same have been filed with our records in the matter of the enrollment of said child.

    Reply to that portion of your letter in which you ask when you can file for this child, you are advised that no selection of allotment can be permitted for children for whom application has been made under the act of Congress approved March 3, 1905, until their enrollment has been approved by the Secretary of the Interior.

Respectfully,

*Tams Bixby*
SIGNED

Chairman.

N. B. 462

**COPY**

Muskogee, Indian Territory, April 8, 1905.

Turner W. Elliott,
    Poteau, Indian Territory.

Dear Sir:

    There is inclosed you herewith for execution application for the enrollment of your infant child, Gertrude Irene Elliott, born July 30, 1903.

    The affidavits heretofore filed with the Commission show the child was living on March 4, 1904. It is necessary, for the child to be enrolled, that she was living on March 4, 1905. You will please insert the mother's age in space provided for that purpose.

    In having these affidavits executed care should be exercised to see that all names are written in full, as they appear in the body of the affidavit, and in the event that either

## Applications for Enrollment of Choctaw Newborn
## Act of 1905   Volume VIII

of the persons signing the affidavit are unable to write, signatures by mark must be attested by two witnesses. Each affidavit must be executed before a Notary Public and the notarial seal and signature of the officer must be attached to each separate affidavit.

Respectfully,<br>
*T. B. Needles.*<br>
Commissioner in Charge.

SIGNED

LM 8-17

---

Muskogee, Indian Territory, March 7, 1905.

Turner W. Elliott,
    Poteau, Indian Territory

Dear Sir:

    You are advised that there have been received at this office the affidavits of Gertrude A. Elliott and Isham C. Tally to the birth of your infant daughter Gertrude Irene Elliott, July 30, 1903. It is stated in the affidavit of the mother that she is a citizen by blood of the Choctaw Nation and the wife of Turner W. Elliott a non citizen. You were requested to state the maiden name of your wife, the names of her parents, and other members of her family for whom application was made at the same time, stating the time and place application was made for her enrollment. Up to this time no reply to this letter has been received and you are requested to furnish the above information at one in order that disposition ay[sic] be made of the application for the enrollment of this child.

Respectfully,<br><br>
Commissioner in Charge.

---

**COPY**

7-2566

Muskogee, Indian Territory, December 15, 1904.

T. W. Elliott,
    Braden, Indian Territory.

Dear Sir:

    Receipt is hereby acknowledged of your letter of December 10, 1904, in which you state that the parents of your wife who is listed for enrollment under the name of Gertrude A. Reagan, were Phoebe and Robert Welch, and you request that if practicable her name be changed upon our records. You state that at the time she was listed for

## Applications for Enrollment of Choctaw Newborn
## Act of 1905   Volume VIII

enrollment she was living with her step-father Robert M. Reagan, by whom she was enrolled.

In reply to your letter you are informed that Gertrude A. Reagan has been enrolled by the Commission and her enrollment approved by the Department under the name of Gertrude A. Reagan, and under that name allotment of land has been made to her. It is therefore impracticable at this time to comply with your request to have her name changed upon our records.

Replying to that portion of your letter in which you ask if babies are going to be enrolled any time soon, you are informed that under the provisions of the Act of Congress approved July 1, 1902, which was ratified by the citizens of the Choctaw and Chickasaw Nations September 25, 1902, children born to recognized and enrolled citizens of the Choctaw and Chickasaw Nations subsequent to the date of the ratification of the Act of Congress above referred to are not entitled to enrollment.

The communication of the Commission of April 21, 1903, enclosed with your letter is herewith returned.

        Respectfully,

       SIGNED   *Tams Bixby*

Enc. KB 2-15.           Chairman.

---

**COPY**

Muskogee, Indian Territory, December 5, 1904.

Turner W. Elliott,
  Poteau, Indian Territory.

Dear Sir:

On March 7, 1903, there was received at this office the affidavits of Gertrude A. Elliott and I. C. Tally relative to the birth of your infant daughter Gertrude Irene Elliott July 30, 1903.

It is stated in the affidavit of the mother that her name is Gertrude A. Elliott, that she is seventeen years of age, and a citizen by blood of the Choctaw Nation.

You are requested to state her maiden name, the names of her parents, the time and place application was made for her enrollment, together with the names of the other members of the family to which she belongs for whom application was made at the same time, returning your reply in the enclosed envelope which requires no postage at your earliest convenience.

# Applications for Enrollment of Choctaw Newborn
## Act of 1905   Volume VIII

Respectfully,

SIGNED   *Tams Bixby*

Chairman.

Env.

**NEW-BORN AFFIDAVIT.**

Number..........

### ...Choctaw Enrolling Commission...

IN THE MATTER OF THE APPLICATION FOR ENROLLMENT, as a citizen of the Choctaw        Nation, of        Gertrude I. Elliott

born on the   30   day of   July     190 3

Name of father   Turner W. Elliott        a citizen of    white
Nation final enrollment No.   ———   *Daws*[sic] *Com Gertrude A. Reagan*
Name of mother   Gertrude A Elliott^        a citizen of    Choctaw
Nation final enrollment No.   7456

Postoffice    Braden I.T.

**AFFIDAVIT OF MOTHER.**

UNITED STATES OF AMERICA
INDIAN TERRITORY
   Central       DISTRICT

I      Gertrude A Elliott             , on oath state that I am   19   years of age and a citizen by   blood   of the   Choctaw       Nation, and as such have been placed upon the final roll of the   Choctaw   Nation, by the Honorable Secretary of the Interior my final enrollment number being   7456  ; that I am the lawful wife of   Turner W Elliott       , who is a citizen of the   white       Nation, and as such has been placed upon the final roll of said Nation by the Honorable Secretary of the Interior, his final enrollment number being ———  and that a   Female   child was born to me on the   30   day of   July     190 3; that said child has been named   Gertrude I Elliott   , and is now living.

Gertrude A Elliott

Witnesseth.

Must be two
Witnesses who
are Citizens.
}   E L Hickman

John S Merryman

Applications for Enrollment of Choctaw Newborn
Act of 1905   Volume VIII

Subscribed and sworn to before me this   25   day of   Feb       190 5

W.E. Harrell
MY COMMISSION EXPIRES AUG. 6, 1908.                Notary Public.
~~My commission expires~~:


## AFFIDAVIT OF ATTENDING PHYSICIAN OR MIDWIFE

UNITED STATES OF AMERICA
INDIAN TERRITORY
Central       DISTRICT

I,   Jno J Gill      a    Practicing Physician
on oath state that I attended on Mrs.  Gertrude A Elliott   wife of   Turner W Elliott
on the  30   day of  July  , 190 3, that there was born to her on said date a    Female   child, that said child is now living, and is said to have been named    Gertrude I Elliott

Jno J Gill           M.D.

WITNESSETH:
Must be two witnesses   { Robert A Welch
who are citizens and
know the child.          { Robert L Reagan

Subscribed and sworn to before me this, the    11      day of    Feb       190 5

J.D. Yandell       Notary Public.

We hereby certify that we are well acquainted with    Dr John J. Gill
a   Practicing Physician     and know   him    to be reputable and of good standing in the community.

{ Robert L. Reagan
{ Robert A Welch


BIRTH AFFIDAVIT.

## DEPARTMENT OF THE INTERIOR,
### COMMISSION TO THE FIVE CIVILIZED TRIBES.

**In Re Application for Enrollment,** as a citizen of the    Choctaw    Nation, of   Gertrude Irene Elliott  , born on the   30    day of   July    , 1903

Name of Father:  Turner W. Elliott           a citizen of the United States Nation.
Name of Mother:  Gertrude A. Elliott          a citizen of the   Choctaw   Nation.

# Applications for Enrollment of Choctaw Newborn
## Act of 1905   Volume VIII

Post-office Poteau, Indian Territory

### AFFIDAVIT OF MOTHER.

UNITED STATES OF AMERICA, }
   INDIAN TERRITORY,
   Central          District.

I, Gertrude A. Elliott, on oath state that I am Seventeen years of age and a citizen by blood, of the Choctaw Nation; that I am the lawful wife of Turner W Elliott, who is a citizen, by ............... of the United States Nation; that a female child was born to me on 30$^{th}$ day of July, 1903, that said child has been named Gertrude Irene Elliott, and is now living.

Gertrude A Elliott

WITNESSES TO MARK:

Subscribed and sworn to before me this 3$^{rd}$ day of March, 1904

My Comm expires Dec. 11 1906

Malcolm E Rosser
NOTARY PUBLIC.

### AFFIDAVIT OF ATTENDING PHYSICIAN OR MID-WIFE.

UNITED STATES OF AMERICA, }
   INDIAN TERRITORY,
   Central          District.

I, I. C. Tally, a Physician, on oath state that I attended on Mrs. Gertrude A. Elliott, wife of Turner W. Elliott on the 30$^{th}$ day of July, 1903; that there was born to her on said date a female child; that said child is now living and is said to have been named Gertrude Irene Elliott

Isham C. Talley

WITNESSES TO MARK:

Subscribed and sworn to before me this 4$^{th}$ day of March, 1904

C. L. Stone

My Commission expires Jan 1$^{st}$ 1906

NOTARY PUBLIC.

## Applications for Enrollment of Choctaw Newborn
## Act of 1905   Volume VIII

BIRTH AFFIDAVIT.

### DEPARTMENT OF THE INTERIOR.
### COMMISSION TO THE FIVE CIVILIZED TRIBES.

IN RE APPLICATION FOR ENROLLMENT, as a citizen of the Choctaw Nation, of Gertrude Irene Elliott, born on the 30" day of July, 1903

Name of Father: Turner W. Elliott     a citizen of the U.S. Nation.
Name of Mother: Gertrude A Elliott     a citizen of the Choctaw Nation.

Postoffice    Braden, Ind. Ter.

**AFFIDAVIT OF MOTHER.**

UNITED STATES OF AMERICA, Indian Territory,
Central     DISTRICT.

I, Gertrude A. Elliott, on oath state that I am 18 years of age and a citizen by Blood, of the Choctaw Nation; that I am the lawful wife of Turner W. Elliott, who is a citizen, ~~by~~ of the United States ~~Nation~~; that a Female child was born to me on 30" day of July, 1903; that said child has been named Gertrude Irene Elliott, and was living March 4, 1905.

Gertrude A Elliott

Witnesses To Mark:

Subscribed and sworn to before me this 20 day of April, 1905.

D M Larty

My Commission expires Jan 1st 1907     Notary Public.

**AFFIDAVIT OF ATTENDING PHYSICIAN OR MID-WIFE.**

UNITED STATES OF AMERICA, Indian Territory,
Central     DISTRICT.

We,

~~I~~, I.C. Talley and Jno J. Gill, a Physicians, on oath state that I attended on Mrs. Gertrude A Elliott, wife of Turner W Elliott on the 30th day of July, 1903; that there was born to her on said date a Female child; that said child was living March 4, 1905, and is said to have been named Gertrude Irene Elliott

I. C. Talley M.D.
Jno. J. Gill M.D.

# Applications for Enrollment of Choctaw Newborn
## Act of 1905  Volume VIII

Witnesses To Mark:

    Subscribed and sworn to before me this  24   day of     March     , 1905

                                  J T Maxey
                                  Notary Public.

My commission expires Jan 15- 1907

---

Choc New Born 463
    Noel May Anderson  b. 1-4-03

**BIRTH AFFIDAVIT.**

### DEPARTMENT OF THE INTERIOR.
### COMMISSION TO THE FIVE CIVILIZED TRIBES.

    **IN RE APPLICATION FOR ENROLLMENT,** as a citizen of the    Choctaw    Nation, of Noel May Anderson    , born on the  4th  day of  January  , 1903

Name of Father: Noel Anderson          a citizen of the  Choctaw   Nation.
Name of Mother: Mary Anderson       a citizen of the  Choctaw   Nation.

                      Postoffice    Gowen, Indian Territory.

**AFFIDAVIT OF MOTHER.**

**UNITED STATES OF AMERICA, Indian Territory,**
    Central                **DISTRICT.**

    I,  Mary Anderson    , on oath state that I am  24   years of age and a citizen by    marriage   , of the    Choctaw    Nation; that I am the lawful wife of   Noel Anderson    , who is a citizen, by  blood   of the    Choctaw    Nation; that a female     child was born to me on   4th  day of    January    , 1903; that said child has been named   Noel May Anderson    , and was living March 4, 1905.

                             Mary Anderson

Witnesses To Mark:

## Applications for Enrollment of Choctaw Newborn
## Act of 1905   Volume VIII

Subscribed and sworn to before me this   23rd   day of March   , 1905

                                      Wirt Franklin
                                      Notary Public.

---

#### AFFIDAVIT OF ATTENDING PHYSICIAN OR MID-WIFE.

**UNITED STATES OF AMERICA, Indian Territory,**
   Central                 **DISTRICT.**

I,   Sinie Grayson   , a   mid-wife   , on oath state that I attended on Mrs.   Mary Anderson   , wife of   Noel Anderson   on the 4th day of January , 1903; that there was born to her on said date a   female   child; that said child was living March 4, 1905, and is said to have been named   Noel May Anderson

                                     her
                              Sinie x Grayson
Witnesses To Mark:               mark
  { L Calfer
    *(Name Illegible)*

Subscribed and sworn to before me this   23rd   day of March   , 1905

                                      Wirt Franklin
                                      Notary Public.

---

Choc New Born 464
    Eller Cessie Flinchum   b. 7-21-04

---

                                                          Choctaw 3292

                     Muskogee, Indian Territory, March 31, 1905.

C. C. Flinchum,
    Calvin, Indian Territory.

Dear Sir:

    Receipt is hereby acknowledged of the affidavits of Susie Flinchum and Mrs. A. E. Wyrick to the birth of Eller Cecie[sic] Flinchum, daughter of C. C. and Susie Flinchum, July 21, 1904, and the same have been filed with our records as an application for the enrollment of said child.

## Applications for Enrollment of Choctaw Newborn
## Act of 1905   Volume VIII

You are requested to state your full name, your age, and the names of your parents, giving the matter your immediate attention

Respectfully,

Chairman.

---

**COPY**

Choctaw N.B.
464.

Muskogee, Indian Territory, April 7, 1905.

Mrs. J. A. Flinchum,
    Guertie, Indian Territory.

Dear Madam:

    Receipt is hereby acknowledged of your letter of March 28, in which you state that you had the child's mother execute a blank heretofore forwarded to you and sent it back and you trust the same was in proper form. You also ask if the mother can draw the money for this child, or if it will be necessary for the father to do so.

    In reply to your letter you are informed that affidavits have heretofore been filed with this Commission to the Five Civilized Tribes birth of Eller Cessie Flinchum, child of Columbus and Sissie Flinchum, and the same have been filed with our records as an application for the enrollment of said child. It is presumed that this is the child referred to in your letter although you do not mention the name of said child.

    Replying to that portion of your letter in which you ask who will be permitted to draw money for this child, you are advised that the payment of moneys to citizens of the Choctaw and Chickasaw Nations is a matter within the jurisdiction of the United States Indian Agent, and for information relative thereto you should address him at Muskogee, Indian Territory.

Respectfully,

SIGNED    *T. B. Needles.*
    Commissioner in Charge.

## Applications for Enrollment of Choctaw Newborn
## Act of 1905   Volume VIII

*(The letter below typed as given.)*

**COPY**

Calvin I.T.<br>Apr- 11th- 05

Commission to the five[sic] Civilized Tribes
   Muskogee, Ind Terr.

I received your letter and will send you my husbdand's name which is Columbus Flinchum. The son of ---James A. Flinchum & Julia A. Flinchum, and name is Susie A. Wyick my fathers names is John Wyick and my mothers name is Missie Wyick they are none citizon both of them, with Respect I remain,

Susie A. Flinchum.

---

**COPY**                                                                N.B. 464

Muskogee, Indian Territory, April 10, 1905.

Columbus Flinchum,
   Calvin, Indian Territory.

Dear Sir:

There is inclosed you herewith for execution application for the enrollment of your infant child, Eller Cessie Flinchum, born July 21, 1904.

In the affidavits heretofore filed with the Commission, the name of the father was given as "C. C. Flinchum," you will notice in the inclosed application it is "Columbus Flinchum" as it appears on the rolls.

The affidavits also show that the applicant claims through you. It is, therefore, necessary that the license and the certificate of your marriage to her mother, Susie Flinchum, be forwarded with the return of the inclosed application.

In having these affidavits executed care should be exercised to see that all names are written in full, as they appear in the body of the affidavit, and in the event that either of the persons signing the affidavit are unable to write, signatures by mark must be attested by two witnesses. Each affidavit must be executed before a Notary Public and the notarial seal and signature of the officer must be attached to each separate affidavit.

Respectfully,<br>SIGNED<br>*T. B. Needles.*<br>Commissioner in Charge.

LM 10-50

# Applications for Enrollment of Choctaw Newborn
## Act of 1905 Volume VIII

---

**COPY**                                                                                              7 NB 464

Muskogee, Indian Territory, April 19, 1905.

Susie A. Flinchum,
    Calvin, Indian Territory.

Dear Madam:

    Receipt is hereby acknowledged of your letter of April 11, 1905, enclosing affidavits of Susie Flinchum and Artie E. Wyrick to the birth of Eller Cessie Flinchum, daughter of Columbus and Susie Flinchum, July 21, 1904, and the same have been filed with our records as an application for the enrollment of said child.

    Receipt is also acknowledged of the marriage license and certificate between C. C. Flinchum and Susie Wyrick and the same have been filed with our records in the matter of the enrollment of said child.

                                      Respectfully,
                                      SIGNED

                                              *Tams Bixby*
                                              Chairman.

---

7-NB-464

Muskogee, Indian Territory, April 13, 1906.

Columbus C. Flinchum,
    Calvin, Indian Territory.

Dear Sir:

    Receipt is hereby acknowledged of your letter of April 7, 1906, in which you state that you were married under federal law September 20, 1903, and you ask if you can have your wife Susie Flinchum enrolled.

    In reply to your letter you are advised that under the act of Congress approved July 2, 1902, no person who married a citizen of the Choctaw or Chickasaw Nation subsequent to September 25, 1902, the date of the ratification of said act, is entitled to enrollment and allotment as an intermarried citizen of either of said nations.

                                      Respectfully,

                                      Acting Commissioner.

# Applications for Enrollment of Choctaw Newborn
## Act of 1905  Volume VIII

**BIRTH AFFIDAVIT.**

## DEPARTMENT OF THE INTERIOR.
## COMMISSION TO THE FIVE CIVILIZED TRIBES.

**IN RE APPLICATION FOR ENROLLMENT**, as a citizen of the   Choctaw   Nation, of Eller Cessie Flinchum   , born on the  21"  day of  July  , 1904

Name of Father: Columbus Flinchum   a citizen of the  Choctaw  Nation.
Name of Mother: Susie Flinchum   a citizen of the   U S   Nation.

Postoffice   Calvin Ind Ter

### AFFIDAVIT OF MOTHER.

**UNITED STATES OF AMERICA, Indian Territory,**
.................................................... **DISTRICT.**

I, Susie Flinchum  , on oath state that I am  20   years of age and a citizen by ———— , of the   United States   Nation; that I am the lawful wife of   Columbus Flinchum  , who is a citizen, by Blood   of the   Choctaw   Nation; that a Female   child was born to me on 21"   day of   July  , 1904; that said child has been named  Eller Cessie Flinchum   , and was living March 4, 1905.

Susie Flinchum

Witnesses To Mark:

Subscribed and sworn to before me this  14th  day of   April   , 1905

Henry L. Wallace
Notary Public.

### AFFIDAVIT OF ATTENDING PHYSICIAN OR MID-WIFE.

**UNITED STATES OF AMERICA, Indian Territory,**
.................................................... **DISTRICT.**

I,  Artie E Wyrick   , a  Mid Wife   , on oath state that I attended on Mrs.  Susie Flinchum   , wife of   Columbus Flinchum   on the  21"  day of  July  , 1904; that there was born to her on said date a   Female   child; that said child was living March 4, 1905, and is said to have been named  Eller Cessie Flinchum

Artie E Wyrick

## Applications for Enrollment of Choctaw Newborn
## Act of 1905 Volume VIII

Witnesses To Mark:
{

    Subscribed and sworn to before me this   14<sup>th</sup>   day of    April   , 1905

                                  Henry L. Wallace
                                  Notary Public.

---

**BIRTH AFFIDAVIT.**

### DEPARTMENT OF THE INTERIOR.
### COMMISSION TO THE FIVE CIVILIZED TRIBES.

---

**IN RE APPLICATION FOR ENROLLMENT,** as a citizen of the       Choctaw       Nation, of Eller Cessie      , born on the   21   day of   July   , 1904.

Name of Father: C. C. Flinchum        a citizen of the   Choctaw   Nation.
Name of Mother: Susy Flinchum        a citizen of the ........................ Nation.

                    Postoffice    Calvin I.T.

---

**AFFIDAVIT OF MOTHER.**

UNITED STATES OF AMERICA, Indian Territory, }
    Centrell[sic]        DISTRICT.

    I,   Susy Flinchum   , on oath state that I am   20   years of age and a citizen by Marriage   , of the   Choctaw   Nation; that I am the lawful wife of   C. C. Flinchum , who is a citizen, by blood    of the     Choctaw    Nation; that a   Girl   child was born to me on   21    day of   July   , 1904; that said child has been named   Eller Cessie   , and was living March 4, 1905.

                                Susie Flinchum

Witnesses To Mark:
{

    Subscribed and sworn to before me this   27   day of    March   , 1905

                                  Henry L. Wallace
                                      Notary Public.

## Applications for Enrollment of Choctaw Newborn
## Act of 1905  Volume VIII

### AFFIDAVIT OF ATTENDING PHYSICIAN OR MID-WIFE.

UNITED STATES OF AMERICA, Indian Territory, }
   Centrell[sic]        DISTRICT.
   Mrs.

I,   A. E. Wyrick   , a   Mid Wife   , on oath state that I attended on Mrs.   Susie Flinchum   , wife of   C. C. Flinchum   on the 21 day of July   , 1904; that there was born to her on said date a   Female   child; that said child was living March 4, 1905, and is said to have been named   Eller Cecie

Mrs A E Wyrick

Witnesses To Mark:
{

Subscribed and sworn to before me this  27$^{th}$  day of   March   , 1905

Henry L. Wallace
Notary Public.

---

No. 3764                    FORM NO. 598.

# MARRIAGE LICENSE.

UNITES STATES OF AMERICA, }
   THE INDIAN TERRITORY,    } ss:
   Central      DISTRICT.

To any Person Authorized by Law to Solemnize Marriage—Greeting:

*You are hereby commanded to solemnize the Rite and publish the* Banns of Matrimony *between Mr.*   C. C. Flinchum   *of*   Guertie   *in the Indian Territory, aged* 20 *years, and M* iss Susie Wyrick *of*   Guertie   *in the Indian Territory, aged* 18   *years, according to law, and do you officially sign and return this License to the parties therein named.*

WITNESS *my hand and official seal, this*  19  *day of*  Sept  A. D. 190 3

EJ Fannin
*Clerk of the United States Court.*

W C Donnelly
      *Deputy*

Applications for Enrollment of Choctaw Newborn
Act of 1905   Volume VIII

## CERTIFICATE OF MARRIAGE.

UNITES STATES OF AMERICA,  
THE INDIAN TERRITORY,   } ss:    I,    D. J. Austin  
_____ DISTRICT.          a    Minister

do hereby CERTIFY, that on the   20"   day of   September   A, D. 190 3; I did duly and according to law, as commanded in the foregoing License, solemnize the Rite and publish the BANNS OF MATRIMONY between the parties therein named.

Witness my hand this 21$^{st}$ day of Sept , A. D. 190 3

My credentials are recorded in the office of the Clerk of the United States Court in the Indian Territory, Central District, Book____Page____   So M$^c$Alester

D. J. Austin  
a   Minister

NOTE. -The License and Certificate of Marriage must be returned to the Office of the Clerk of the United States Court of the Indian Territory, from whence it was issued, within sixty days from the date thereof, or the party to whom the License was issued will be liable in the amount of One Hundred Dollars ($100.00).

No. 3764

## Certificate of Record of Marriages.

DEPARTMENT OF THE INTERIOR,  
Commission to the Five Civilized Tribes.

**FILED**

APR 19 1905    Tams Bixby   CHAIRMAN.

UNITED STATES OF AMERICA,  
INDIAN TERRITORY,   } SCT:  
Central   DISTRICT.

I,   E.J. Fannin   , Clerk of the United States Court in the Indian Territory and District aforesaid, do hereby CERTIFY, that the License for and Certificate of the Marriage of

Mr   C. C. Flinchum   and  
M iss Susie Wyrick   was

filed in my office in said Territory and District the  13 day of   Sept   A.D., 190 3 and duly recorded in Book  (?)  of Marriage Record, Page  585

WITNESS my hand and seal of said Court, at   So M$^c$Alester   , this (?) day of   Sept   , A.D. 1903

E. J. Fannin  
*Clerk.*

By  W C Donnelly   *Deputy.*

## Applications for Enrollment of Choctaw Newborn
## Act of 1905 Volume VIII

Choc New Born 465
    Henry Carl Bogle b. 8-17-04

**BIRTH AFFIDAVIT.**

### DEPARTMENT OF THE INTERIOR.
### COMMISSION TO THE FIVE CIVILIZED TRIBES.

**IN RE APPLICATION FOR ENROLLMENT,** as a citizen of the Choctaw Nation, of Henry Carl Bogle, born on the 17 day of Aug, 1904

Name of Father: David H Bogle     a citizen of the Choctaw Nation.
Name of Mother: Ada B Bogle     a citizen of the Choctaw Nation.

        Postoffice    Cheek I.T.

**AFFIDAVIT OF MOTHER.**

UNITED STATES OF AMERICA, Indian Territory,
    Southern      DISTRICT.

    I, Ada B. Bogle, on oath state that I am 22 years of age and a citizen by marriage, of the Choctaw Nation; that I am the lawful wife of David H Bogle, who is a citizen, by birth of the Choctaw Nation; that a male child was born to me on 17 day of Aug, 1904; that said child has been named Henry Carl Bogle, and was living March 4, 1905.

                              Ada B Bogle

Witnesses To Mark:
    Delia Hammond
    *(Name Illegible)*

    Subscribed and sworn to before me this 24th day of March, 1905

                            J.R. Pratley
                              Notary Public.

# Applications for Enrollment of Choctaw Newborn
## Act of 1905   Volume VIII

#### AFFIDAVIT OF ATTENDING PHYSICIAN OR MID-WIFE.

UNITED STATES OF AMERICA, Indian Territory, ⎱
   Southern             DISTRICT. ⎰

    I,   W. M. Kearney   , a   Physician   , on oath state that I attended on Mrs.   Ada B Bogle   , wife of   David H Bogle   on the   17   day of   Aug   , 1904; that there was born to her on said date a   male   child; that said child was living March 4, 1905, and is said to have been named   Henry Carl Bogle

                                        WM Kearney M.D.

Witnesses To Mark:
  ⎰ Delia Hammond
  ⎱ *(Name Illegible)*

    Subscribed and sworn to before me this   22   day of   March   , 1905

                                        E.S. Hammond
                                          Notary Public.

---

Choc New Born 466
        Delie Estel Mitts   b.  12-29-02
        James Isaac Mitts   b.  1-27-05

                                                      Choctaw 3650

                  Muskogee, Indian Territory March 31, 1905.

W. E. Mitts,
    Folsom, Indian Territory.

Dear Sir:

    Receipt is hereby acknowledged of the affidavits of Lucinda Mitts and R. P. Dickey to the birth of Delie Estle[sic] Mitts and James Isaac Mitts, children of W. E. and Lucinda Mitts, December 29, 1902, and January 27, 1905, and the same have been filed with our records as applications for the enrollment of these children.

                              Respectfully,

                                        Chairman.

## Applications for Enrollment of Choctaw Newborn
## Act of 1905   Volume VIII

*Affidavit of Attending Physician or Midwife*

UNITED STATES OF AMERICA,  
INDIAN TERRITORY,  
Central   DISTRICT

I,   R. P Dickey   a   Physician on oath state that I attended on Mrs. Lucinda Mitts   wife of   W. E. Mitts on the   29   day of   Dec  , 190 3[sic], that there was born to her on said date a   Female child, that said child is now living, and is said to have been named   Deali[sic] Estle Mitts

R.P. Dickey   M. D.

Subscribed and sworn to before me this the   23   day of   January   1905

J G Reeder

Notary Public.

WITNESSETH:

Must be two witnesses who are citizens and know the child. { May Vice  
Robert Vice

We hereby certify that we are well acquainted with   R.P. Dickey a   Physician   and know   him   to be reputable and of good standing in the community.

Must be two citizen witnesses. { May Vice  
Robert Vice

# Applications for Enrollment of Choctaw Newborn
## Act of 1905  Volume VIII

**NEW-BORN AFFIDAVIT.**

Number..............

## ...Choctaw Enrolling Commission...

IN THE MATTER OF THE APPLICATION FOR ENROLLMENT, as a citizen of the Choctaw Nation, of Deali Estle Mitts born on the 29 day of December 190 3[sic]

Name of father  W.E. Mitts       a citizen ~~of~~    married
~~Nation final enrollment No.~~...................
Name of mother  Lucinda Mitts    a citizen of   Choctaw
Nation final enrollment No. 10324
                                 Postoffice

### AFFIDAVIT OF MOTHER.

UNITED STATES OF AMERICA
INDIAN TERRITORY
   Central      DISTRICT

I Lucinda Mitts , on oath state that I am 25 years of age and a citizen by Blood of the Choctaw Nation, and as such have been placed upon the final roll of the Choctaw Nation, by the Honorable Secretary of the Interior my final enrollment number being 10324 ; that I am the lawful wife of W E Mitts , who is a citizen of the .................. Nation, and as such has been placed upon the final roll of said Nation by the Honorable Secretary of the Interior, his final enrollment number being .................. and that a Female child was born to me on the 29 day of December 190 3; that said child has been named Deali Estle Mitts , and is now living.

                                 Lucinda Mitts

Witnesseth.
  Must be two  ⎱ May Vice
  Witnesses who ⎰
  are Citizens.   Robert Vice

Subscribed and sworn to before me this 23 day of Jan 190 5

                      J. G. Reeder
                              Notary Public.

My commission expires:..................

## Applications for Enrollment of Choctaw Newborn
## Act of 1905 Volume VIII

BIRTH AFFIDAVIT.

## DEPARTMENT OF THE INTERIOR.
## COMMISSION TO THE FIVE CIVILIZED TRIBES.

IN RE APPLICATION FOR ENROLLMENT, as a citizen of the Choctaw Nation, of Delie Estle Mitts , born on the 29 day of December , 1902

Name of Father: W. E. Mitts     a citizen of the .................... Nation.
Name of Mother: Lucinda Mitts     a citizen of the Choctaw Nation.

Postoffice    Folsom Ind Ter

### AFFIDAVIT OF MOTHER.

UNITED STATES OF AMERICA, Indian Territory, }
    Cenral[sic]         DISTRICT. }

    I, Lucinda Mitts , on oath state that I am 26 years of age and a citizen by Blood , of the Choctaw Nation; that I am the lawful wife of W E Mitts , who is a citizen, by marrig[sic] of the Choctaw Nation; that a female child was born to me on 29 day of December , 1902; that said child has been named Delie Estle Mitts , and was living March 4, 1905.

                                   Lucinda Mitts

Witnesses To Mark:
   {

    Subscribed and sworn to before me this 25 day of March , 1905

                                   J G Reeder
                                        Notary Public.

### AFFIDAVIT OF ATTENDING PHYSICIAN OR MID-WIFE.

UNITED STATES OF AMERICA, Indian Territory, }
    Central         DISTRICT. }

    I, Dr R. P. Dickey , a Physician , on oath state that I attended on Mrs. Lucinda Mitts , wife of W E Mitts on the 29 day of December , 1902; that there was born to her on said date a female child; that said child was living March 4, 1905, and is said to have been named Delie Estle

                                   R.P. Dickey

Witnesses To Mark:
   {

# Applications for Enrollment of Choctaw Newborn
# Act of 1905   Volume VIII

Subscribed and sworn to before me this 25 day of    March    , 1905

J.G. Reeder
Notary Public.

---

**BIRTH AFFIDAVIT.**

## DEPARTMENT OF THE INTERIOR.
## COMMISSION TO THE FIVE CIVILIZED TRIBES.

---

IN RE APPLICATION FOR ENROLLMENT, as a citizen of the    Choctaw    Nation, of James Isaac Mitts    , born on the  27  day of  January  , 1905

Name of Father: W. E. Mitts           a citizen of the ........................ Nation.
Name of Mother: Lucinda Mitts         a citizen of the   Choctaw   Nation.

Postoffice    Folsom Ind Ter

---

### AFFIDAVIT OF MOTHER.

UNITED STATES OF AMERICA, Indian Territory, }
   Central              DISTRICT.

I, Lucinda Mitts    , on oath state that I am  26  years of age and a citizen by Blood    , of the   Choctaw    Nation; that I am the lawful wife of  W E Mitts    , who is a citizen, by marrige[sic]    of the    Choctaw    Nation; that a    Male    child was born to me on   27   day of    January    , 1905; that said child has been named   James Isaac Mitts    , and was living March 4, 1905.

Lucinda Mitts

Witnesses To Mark:
{

Subscribed and sworn to before me this  25 day of    March    , 1905

J G Reeder
Notary Public.

---

### AFFIDAVIT OF ATTENDING PHYSICIAN OR MID-WIFE.

UNITED STATES OF AMERICA, Indian Territory, }
   Central              DISTRICT.

I,  Dr R. P. Dickey    , a  Physician    , on oath state that I attended on Mrs.  Lucinda Mitts    , wife of   W E Mitts    on the  27  day of   January   ,

## Applications for Enrollment of Choctaw Newborn
## Act of 1905    Volume VIII

1905; that there was born to her on said date a ................... child; that said child was living March 4, 1905, and is said to have been named James Isaac Mitts

                                                R.P. Dickey

Witnesses To Mark:

{ Subscribed and sworn to before me this  25   day of     March       , 1905

                                                  J.G. Reeder
                                                 Notary Public.

---

Choc New Born 467
      Benjamin Edward Beams   b.  10-22-04

                                                                    7-3775

                        Muskogee, Indian Territory, April 1, 1905.

A. G. Beams,
      Kingston, Indian Territory.

Dear Sir:

      Receipt is hereby acknowledged of the affidavits of Belle C. Beams and E. F. Lewis to the birth of Benjimin[sic] Edward Beams, son of A. G. and Belle C. Beams, October 22, 1904, and the same have been filed with our records as an application for the enrollment of said child.

                        Respectfully,

                                            Chairman.

## Applications for Enrollment of Choctaw Newborn
## Act of 1905  Volume VIII

BIRTH AFFIDAVIT.

## DEPARTMENT OF THE INTERIOR.
## COMMISSION TO THE FIVE CIVILIZED TRIBES.

IN RE APPLICATION FOR ENROLLMENT, as a citizen of the Choctaw Nation, of Benjamin Edward Beams, born on the $22^d$ day of Oct, 1904

Name of Father: A. G. Beams  a citizen of the Choctaw Nation.
Name of Mother: Belle C. Beams  a citizen of the ................. Nation.

Postoffice  Kingston I.T.

### AFFIDAVIT OF MOTHER.

UNITED STATES OF AMERICA, Indian Territory,
Southern  DISTRICT.

I, Belle C. Beams, on oath state that I am 21 years of age and a citizen by marriage, of the Choctaw Nation; that I am the lawful wife of A.G. Beams, who is a citizen, by blood of the Choctaw Nation; that a male child was born to me on $22^d$ day of Oct, 1904; that said child has been named Benjamin Edward Beams, and was living March 4, 1905.

Belle C. Beams

Witnesses To Mark:
{

Subscribed and sworn to before me this $22^d$ day of March, 1905

D P Johnston
Notary Public.

### AFFIDAVIT OF ATTENDING PHYSICIAN OR MID-WIFE.

UNITED STATES OF AMERICA, Indian Territory,
Southern  DISTRICT.

I, E.F. Lewis, a physician, on oath state that I attended on Mrs. Belle C Beams, wife of A G Beams on the $22^d$ day of Oct, 1904; that there was born to her on said date a male child; that said child was living March 4, 1905, and is said to have been named Benjamin Edward Beams

E F Lewis MD

Witnesses To Mark:
{

# Applications for Enrollment of Choctaw Newborn
## Act of 1905  Volume VIII

Subscribed and sworn to before me this 25th day of March, 1905

D P Johnston
Notary Public.

---

Choc New Born 468
    Rason Battiest  b. 12-25-02

## DEPARTMENT OF THE INTERIOR.
## COMMISSION TO THE FIVE CIVILIZED TRIBES.

In the matter of the death of  Sallie A Battiest nee Drew  a citizen of the Choctaw  Nation, who formerly resided at or near  Bennington , Ind. Ter., and died on the  9th  day of  March  , 1904

**AFFIDAVIT OF RELATIVE.**

UNITED STATES OF AMERICA, Indian Territory, }
    Central           DISTRICT.              }

I,  Nicholas Battiest  , on oath state that I am  44  years of age and a citizen by  Blood  , of the  Choctaw  Nation; that my postoffice address is  Bennington  , Ind. Ter.; that I am  Husband  of  Sallie A Battiest nee Drew  who was a citizen, by  Blood  , of the  Choctaw  Nation and that said  Sallie A Battiest  died on the  9th  day of  March  , 1904

                                        his
                                Nicholas  x  Battiest
Witnesses To Mark:                       mark
  { Robert J Barnes
  { W O Byrd

Subscribed and sworn to before me this  4th  day of  November  , 1905.

W O Byrd
Notary Public.

# Applications for Enrollment of Choctaw Newborn
## Act of 1905   Volume VIII

### AFFIDAVIT OF ACQUAINTANCE.

UNITED STATES OF AMERICA, Indian Territory, }
Central         DISTRICT.

I, Robert J Barnes, on oath state that I am 30 years of age, and a citizen by Blood of the Choctaw Nation; that my postoffice address is Bennington, Ind. Ter.; that I was personally acquainted with Sallie A Battiest nee Drew who was a citizen, by Blood, of the Choctaw Nation; and that said Sallie A Battiest nee Drew died on the 9th day of March, 1904

Robert J Barnes

Witnesses To Mark:
{

Subscribed and sworn to before me this 4th day of November, 1905.

W O Byrd
Notary Public.

---

**BIRTH AFFIDAVIT.**

### DEPARTMENT OF THE INTERIOR.
### COMMISSION TO THE FIVE CIVILIZED TRIBES.

IN RE APPLICATION FOR ENROLLMENT, as a citizen of the Choctaw Nation, of Rason Battice[sic], born on the 25$^{th}$ day of Dec, 1902

Name of Father: Nicholas Battice      a citizen of the Choctaw Nation.
Name of Mother: Sallie A Drew (nee Battice)   a citizen of the ............ Nation.

Postoffice   Bennington I.T.

---

### AFFIDAVIT OF MOTHER.

UNITED STATES OF AMERICA, Indian Territory, }
Cent         DISTRICT.

I, Sallie A Battice, on oath state that I am 40 years of age and a citizen by blood, of the Choctaw Nation; that I am the lawful wife of Nicholas Battice, who is a citizen, by blood of the Choctaw Nation; that a male child was born to me on 25th day of December, 1902; that said child has been named Rason Battice, and was living March 4, 1905.

Sallie A Battice
his
By Nicholas x Battice
mark

# Applications for Enrollment of Choctaw Newborn
## Act of 1905  Volume VIII

Witnesses To Mark:
 { George Williams
   David Byington

Subscribed and sworn to before me this 27th day of Mch, 1905

B.W. Williams
Notary Public.

---

### AFFIDAVIT OF ATTENDING PHYSICIAN OR MID-WIFE.

UNITED STATES OF AMERICA, Indian Territory, }
Cent            DISTRICT.

I, Amanda Bully, a midwife, on oath state that I attended on Mrs. Sallie A Battice, wife of Nicholas Battice on the 25th day of December, 1902; that there was born to her on said date a Male child; that said child was living March 4, 1905, and is said to have been named Rason Battice

her
Amanda x Bully
mark

Witnesses To Mark:
 { George Williams
   David Byington

Subscribed and sworn to before me this 27th day of Mch, 1905

B.W. Williams
Notary Public.

---

### AFFIDAVIT OF MOTHER.

UNITED STATES OF AMERICA, Indian Territory, }
Central         DISTRICT.

I, Nicholas Battiest, on oath state that I am 42 years of age and a citizen by ~~Bennington~~ *Blood*, of the Choctaw Nation; that I am the lawful ~~wife of~~ husband of Sallie Battiest, deceased, who is a citizen, by blood of the Choctaw Nation; that a male child was born to me *her* on 25th day of December, 1902; that said child has been named Rason Battiest, and was living March 4, 1905.

his
By Nicholas x Battice
mark

Witnesses To Mark:
 { J.M. Burke
   W O Byrd

## Applications for Enrollment of Choctaw Newborn
## Act of 1905  Volume VIII

Subscribed and sworn to before me this 4th  day of    November    , 1905

W.O. Byrd<br>Notary Public.

---

**COPY**

N. B. 468

Muskogee, Indian Territory, April 10, 1905.

Nicholas Battice,
    Bennington, Indian Territory.

Dear Sir:

    There is inclosed you herewith for execution application for the enrollment of your infant child, Rason Battice, born December 25, 1902.

    In the affidavits heretofore filed with the Commission the mother's affidavit is signed "Sallie Battice by Nicholas Battice". It is necessary that the mother herself sign this affidavit.

    In having these affidavits executed care should be exercised to see that all names are written in full, as they appear in the body of the affidavit, and in the event that either of the persons signing the affidavit are unable to write, signatures by mark must be attested by two witnesses. Each affidavit must be executed before a Notary Public and the notarial seal and signature of the officer must be attached to each separate affidavit.

Respectfully,

SIGNED    *T. B. Needles.*

SEV 14-10. Commissioner in Charge.

## Applications for Enrollment of Choctaw Newborn
## Act of 1905   Volume VIII

*(The letter below typed as given.)*

(COPY)

Bennington, Ind. Ter.
April 26, 1905.

Hon. Commission to the
five Civilized tribes
Muskogee, Ind Ter.

I will try and explain why I signed for the mother of Rason Battice is that she is dead. The mother of Rason Battice is on the rolls as Sallie A. Drew, who is now dead I mailed to you with the proof death at the time I mailed the application for Rason Battice. I am on the rolls as Nicholas Battice, or Battiest, my name may be spelled Battiest I want ot be advised will it be necessary for me fill out the application sent me, or not, od correct the 1st one I sent.

Yours truly
his
Nicholas x Battice.
mark

---

CAS. E. McPHERREN            CADDO LAW AND
LAWYER                       COLLECTION AGENCY.

(COPY)

Caddo, I. T.   May 1, 1905.

Commission to the Five Civilized Tribes,
Muskogee, Indian Territory.

Gentlemen:

In reply to your letter of the 10th inst., regarding the signing of the affidavit of "Sallie A. Battice", I have to reply that Sallie A. Battice is the identical Sallie A. Drew Choctaw Roll No. 11300, and is the mother of Rason Battice.

The said Sallie A. Battice or Drew, died since her enrollment prior to the signing of the affidavit, she having also married Nicholas Battice Choctaw Roll No. 10153, prior to the signing of the affidavit hence the signature of Sallie A. Battice.

The said Rason Battice, is the identical child I have heretofore made inquiries about infant son of Nicholas Battice and Sallie A. Battice.

I am the guardian of Rason Battice and Moses Chubbee; if any corrections are to be made in the application of these two children please refer to me and I will give the matter my immediate attention.

## Applications for Enrollment of Choctaw Newborn
## Act of 1905 Volume VIII

Very respectfully,

MM                              Henry Byington.

(Notation in pencil--"Please find enclosed other papers as regard to the case. M B"

---

7 N.B. 468.

Muskogee, Indian Territory, May 8, 1905.

Henry Byington,
    Caddo, Indian Territory.

Dear Sir:

    Receipt is hereby acknowledged of your letter of May 1, enclosing communication from Nicholas Battice in which he states that he signed the affidavit for Sallie A. Battice for the reason that she is dead.

    In reference to this matter you are advised that if the mother of Rason Battice is dead it will be necessary to forward the affidavits of two disinterested persons who know of the birth of Rason Battice, that he is the child of Sallie A. Battice and that he was living on March 4, 1905.

    The communications enclosed with your letter are herewith returned.

Respectfully,

Commissioner in Charge.

DeB--1/5

---

*(The letter below typed as given.)*

7-1368.

(COPY)

Caddo, Ind. Ter.
June 3, 1905.

Hon. Commission to the Five Civilized Tribes,
    Muskogee, I. T.

    I enclose you two affidavits in support of the application of Resin Battiest. I think that the application is spelled Battice, and if there is any more corrections to be made, made, I will attend to that I have no time to go down to Bennington where these people live so I am in hopes these affidavits will be all right.

## Applications for Enrollment of Choctaw Newborn
## Act of 1905 Volume VIII

Yours truly,

Henry Byington.

---

7 NB 468

Muskogee, Indian Territory, June 8, 1905.

Henry Byington,
    Caddo, Indian Territory.

Dear Sir:

    Receipt is hereby acknowledged of your letter of June 3, 1905, enclosing affidavits of Henry and Lorena Byington to the birth of Rason Battiest, son of Nicholas and Sallie A. Battiest and the same have been filed with our records in the matter of the enrollment of said child.

    You are advised that the affidavits do not contain the date of the birth of said child and it will be necessary to have two affidavits giving the date of the birth of the child in the matter of his enrollment as a citizen by blood of the Choctaw Nation.

Respectfully,

Chairman.

---

Duplicate.

7-NB-468.

Muskogee, Indian Territory, June 9, 1905.

Nicholas Battiest,
    Bennington, Indian Territory.

Dear Sir:

    Referring to the application for the enrollment of your infant child, Rason Battiest, it is noted that the affidavits of Henry Byington and Lorena Byington, heretofore filed in this office in support of this application, fail to give the date of the applicant's birth.

    Before this matter can be finally determined it will be necessary for you to file in this office the affidavits of two persons who are disinterested and not related to the

# Applications for Enrollment of Choctaw Newborn
## Act of 1905  Volume VIII

applicant, who have knowledge of the facts; that the child was born, the date of his birth, that he was living on March 4, 1905, and that Sallie A. Battiest was his mother.

        Respectfully,

        Commissioner in Charge.

---

7-NB-468

        Muskogee, Indian Territory, July 29, 1905.

Henry Byington,
    Caddo, Indian Territory.

Dear Sir:

    Your attention is called to a communication addressed to you by the Commission to the Five Civilized Tribes under date of June 8, 1905, relative to the deficiency of the affidavits of Henry Byington and Lorena Byington, offered by you in support of the application for the enrollment of Ranson[sic] Battiest, infant child of Nicholas and Sallie A. Battiest.

    You were advised that said affidavits were deficient in that they did not show the date of birth of the child an you were requested to supply affidavits to the facts, that the child was born, the date of his birth, that he was living March 4, 1905, and that Sallie A. Battiest was her mother; that said Sallie A. Battiest, died, the date of her death, and to forward said affidavits immediately. No reply to this letter has been received.

    The matter should receive your prompt attention as no further action can be taken relative the enrollment of said child, until the evidence heretofore requested has been supplied.

        Respectfully,

        Commissioner.

## Applications for Enrollment of Choctaw Newborn
## Act of 1905   Volume VIII

7-NB-468

Muskogee, Indian Territory, July 29, 1905.

Nicholas Battiest,
    Bennington, Indian Territory.

Dear Sir:

Your attention is called to a communication addressed to you by the Commission to the Five Civilized Tribes, under date of June 9, 1905, in which you were requested to furnish additional evidence in the matter of the enrollment of your infant child, Ranson Battiest, born December 25, 1902.

In said letter you were advised that as it appeared from the affidavits heretofore filed in this case, that the mother, Sallie A. Battiest, formerly Drew, is dead, it would be necessary for the enrollment of the child that you file in this office the affidavits of two persons who are disinterested and not related to the application[sic], and who have actual knowledge of the facts, that the child was born, the date of his birth, that he was living March 4, 1905, and that Sallie A. Battiest was his mother. No reply to this letter has been received.

The matter should receive your immediate attention as no further action can be taken relative to the enrollment of your said child, until the evidence heretofore requested has been supplied.

Respectfully,

Commissioner.

---

*Substitute*

7-NB-468

Muskogee, Indian Territory, August 1, 1905.

Henry Byington,
    Caddo, Indian Territory.

Dear Sir:

Your attention is called to a communication addressed to you by the Commission to the Five Civilized Tribes under date of June 8, 1905, relative to the insufficiency of the affidavits of Henry Byington and Lorena Byington, offered by you in support of the application for the enrollment of Ranson Battiest, infant child of Nicholas and Sallie A. Battiest.

# Applications for Enrollment of Choctaw Newborn
## Act of 1905    Volume VIII

    You were advised that said affidavits were insufficient in that they did not show the date of birth of the child; and you were requested to supply affidavits to the facts, that the child was born, the date of his birth, that he was living March 4, 1905, and that Sallie A. Battiest was his mother; that said Sallie A. Battiest died, the date of her death, and to forward said affidavits immediately. No reply to this letter has been received.

    The matter should receive your prompt attention as no further action can be taken relative to the enrollment of said child until the evidence requested has been supplied.

                    Respectfully,

                                        Commissioner.

---

7-NB-1468.

                    Muskogee, Indian Territory, September 18, 1905.

Henry Byington,
    Caddo, Indian Territory.

Dear Sir:

    Receipt is hereby acknowledged of your letter of the 12th instant. You request to be advised as to whether the affidavit of Solomon Carnes, relative to the birth of Ranson Battiest minor son of Nicholas Battiest, has heretofore been filed with this office and if so if the evidence now on file is sufficient on which to base a decision in said case.

    In reply to your letter you are advised that on August 28, 1905, there were filed with this office the affidavits of Solomon Carnes and M. Bronaugh which set forth that Ranson Battiest, son of Nicholas Battiest is about three years old and is now living.

    You are advised that this office has heretofore several times requested proof of the death of the alleged mother of said child, Sallie A. Battiest, but to such requests no response has been received. It is necessary that the same be supplied.

    You are also advised that the name of said child appears in the different affidavits as Rason Battice and Ranson Battiest. The father of said child has been finally enrolled as Nicholas Battiest. The surname of said child must therefore follow that of his father.

    You are requested to furnish this office the affidavit of said Nicholas Battiest stating which of the above names is the correct name of said child.

    The affidavits of said Solomon Carnes and V. Bronaugh, above referred to, fail to set forth the name of the mother of the said Ranson Battiest and also fail to set forth the date of the birth of said child. Said affidavits are therefore defective.

## Applications for Enrollment of Choctaw Newborn
## Act of 1905   Volume VIII

It will be necessary for you to furnish this office, in the matter of the enrollment of said Ranson Battiest, the affidavits of two disinterested persons as to the birth of said child. Said affidavits must set forth said child's correct name, the date of his birth, the names of both parents and whether or not said child was living on March 4, 1905.

When the evidence above requested has been supplied the rights of said child as a citizen by blood of the Choctaw Nation can be finally determined.

                Respectfully,

                                          Acting Commissioner.

D C
Env.

---

7-3049
7-NB-468

                Muskogee, Indian Territory, November 8, 1905.

Henry Byington,
    Caddo, Indian Territory.

Dear Sir:

Receipt is hereby acknowledged of your letter of November 4, 1905, inclosing affidavits to the death of Sallie A. Battiest, formerly Drew, wife of Nicholas Battiest, which occurred March 9, 1904; also affidavits of Nicholas Battiest, Laymon Chubbee and Robert J. Barnes to the birth of Rayson[sic] Battiest, child of Nicholas and Sallie A. Battiest, December 25, 1902, and the same have been filed with the records of this office.

                Respectfully,

                                          Commissioner.

# Applications for Enrollment of Choctaw Newborn
## Act of 1905   Volume VIII

7-468

Muskogee, Indian Territory, February 26, 1906.

Henry Byington,
    Caddo, Indian Territory.

Dear Sir:

    Receipt is hereby acknowledged of your letter of February 20, 1906, asking the status of the application for the enrollment of Rayson Battiest.

    In reply to your letter you are advised that the name of Rayson Battiest has been placed upon a schedule of citizens by blood of the Choctaw Nation which has been forwarded the Secretary of the Interior, but this office has not yet been advised of Departmental action thereon.

                      Respectfully,

                                   Acting Commissioner.

---

7-NB-468.

Muskogee, Indian Territory, June 9, 1905.

Nicholas Battiest,
    Bennington, Indian Territory.

Dear Sir:

    Referring to the application for the enrollment of your infant child, it is noted that the affidavits of Henry Byington and Lorena Byington, heretofore filed in this office in support of this application, fail to give the date of the applicant's birth.

    Before this matter can be finally determined it will be necessary for you to file in this office the affidavits of two persons who are disinterested and not related to the applicant, who have knowledge of the facts; that the child was born, the date of his birth, that he was living on March 4, 1905 and that Sallie A. Battiest was his mother.

                      Respectfully,

                                   Chairman.

## Applications for Enrollment of Choctaw Newborn
## Act of 1905   Volume VIII

Central District,
Indian Territory.

  I, Solomon Carnes after having been first duly sworn state- I am 24 years old and my post office address is Bentley I.T. I am acquainted with Nicholas Battiest who lives near Bennington, Indian Territory I.T. I also know his minor son Ranson Battiest who is about three years old and know him to be now living. I am not of kin to the said Nicholas Battiest nor his said son and have no personal interest in the enrollment of his said son.

              Solomon Carnes

Subscribed and sworn to before me this the 24th day of August, 1905.

              L.D. Horton
              Notary Public.

---

Central District,
Indian Territory.

  I, V. Bronaugh after having been first duly sworn state- I am *(illegible)* years old and my post office address is Boswell I.T. I am acquainted with Nicholas Battiest who lives near Bennington, Indian Territory I.T. I also know his minor son Ranson Battiest who is about three years old and know him to be now living. I am not of kin to the said Nicholas Battiest nor his said son and have no personal interest in the enrollment of his said son.

              Solomon Carnes

Subscribed and sworn to before me this the 24th day of August, 1905.

              L.D. Horton
              Notary Public.

---

      INDIAN TERRITORY, CENTRAL DISTRICT.

| | |
|---|---|
| In the matter of the Enrollment ) | |
| ) | |
| of Rason Battiest, infant child ) | |
| ) | AFFIDAVIT. |
| of Nicholas Battiest and Sallie ) | |
| ) | |
| A. Battiest, nee Drew. ) | |

  Personally appeared before me, the undersigned authority, Laymon Chubbee, who being duly sworn makes the following statement:

## Applications for Enrollment of Choctaw Newborn
## Act of 1905 Volume VIII

My name is Laymon Chubbee, my P. O. address is Bennington, Indian Territory, and I am 50 years of age. I am a citizen of the Choctaw Nation by blood, and enrolled as such.

I am personally acquainted with Sallie A. Battiest, nee Drew, and also Nicholas Battiest. I know they were married and lived together as man and wife in Jackson County, Indian Territory, Choctaw Nation; that a male child was born to them on the 25th day of December, 1902, and that the child was named Rason Battiest. I know that Rason Battiest was living on the 4th day of March, 1905. This family are[sic] all Choctaw.

I am not related to Rason Battiest, and have no interest in the case.

Attest  
Robert H Barnes

his  
Laymon x Chubbee  
mark

Sworn and subscribed to before me, the undersigned authority, on this the 4th day of (Illegible) 1905.

W.O. Byrd  
Notary Public.

---

INDIAN TERRITORY, CENTRAL DISTRICT.

In the matter of the Enrollment )
)
of Rason Battiest, infant child )
) A F F I D AV IT.[sic]
of Nicholas Battiest and Sallie )
)
A. Battiest, nee Drew. )

-----

Personally appeared before me, the undersigned authority, Lorena Byington, who after being duly sworn makes the following statement:

My name is Lorena Byington, my postoffice address is Caddo, Indian Territory, and I am 34 years of age. I am a citizen by blood of the Choctaw Nation and enrolled as such.

I am personally acquainted with Sallie A. Battiest, nee Drew, and also Nicholas Battiest. I know they were married and lived together as man and wife in Jackson County, Choctaw Nation, Indian Territory; that a male child was born to them and that the child was named Rason Battiest. I know that Rason Battiest was living on the 4th day of March 1905. This family are all Choctaw Indians.

I am not related to Rason Battiest and have no interest in the case.

## Applications for Enrollment of Choctaw Newborn
## Act of 1905    Volume VIII

Witness to  
Mark    *Joel Byington*  
        *Henry Byington*

her  
Lorena x Byington  
       mark

Sworn and subscribed to before me this the 3 day of June ---1905.
*(Name Illegible)*  
Notary Public.

---

INDIAN TERRITORY, CENTRAL DISTRICT.

In the matter of the Enrollment  )  
                                 )  
of Rason Battiest, infant child  )  
                                 )   AFFIDAVIT.  
of Nicholas Battiest and Sallie  )  
                                 )  
A. Battiest, nee Drew.           )

---

Personally appeared before me, the undersigned authority, Robert J. Barnes, who being duly sworn makes the following statement:

My name is Robert J Barnes, my P. O. address is Bennington, Indian Territory, and I am 30 years of age. I am a citizen of the Choctaw Nation by blood, and enrolled as such.

I am personally acquainted with Sallie A. Battiest, nee Drew, and also Nicholas Battiest. I know they were married and lived together as man and wife in Jackson County, Indian Territory, Choctaw Nation; that a male child was born to them on the 25th day of December, 1902, and that the child was named Rason Battiest. I know that Rason Battiest was living on the 4th day of March, 1905. His family are all Choctaws.

I am not related to Rason Battiest, and have no interest in the case.

Robert J Barnes

Sworn and subscribed to before me, the undersigned authority, on this the 4th day of November, 1905.

W.O. Byrd  
Notary Public.

# Applications for Enrollment of Choctaw Newborn
## Act of 1905    Volume VIII

### INDIAN TERRITORY, CENTRAL DISTRICT.

In the matter of the Enrollment )
 )
of Rason Battiest, infant child )
 )     A F F I D AV IT.[sic]
of Nicholas Battiest and Sallie )
 )
A. Battiest, nee Drew. )

-----

Personally appeared before me, the undersigned authority, Lorena[sic] Byington, who after being duly sworn makes the following statement:

My name is ~~Lorena~~ Henry Byington, my postoffice address is Caddo, Indian Territory, and I am  54  years of age. I am a citizen by blood of the Choctaw Nation and enrolled as such.

I am personally acquainted with Sallie A. Battiest, nee Drew, and also Nicholas Battiest.  I know they were married and lived together as man and wife in Jackson County, Choctaw Nation, Indian Territory; that a male child was born to them and that the child was named Rason Battiest. I know that Rason Battiest was living on the 8th day of March 1905. This family are all Choctaw Indians.

I am not related to Rason Battiest and have no interest in the case.

                              Henry Byington

Sworn and subscribed to before me this the  3$^{rd}$   day of   June ---1905.
                              (Name Illegible)
                                   Notary Public.

---

Choc New Born 469
     Oda Monds  b. 3-17-04

## Applications for Enrollment of Choctaw Newborn
### Act of 1905   Volume VIII

Choctaw N B 280
469

Muskogee, Indian Territory, May 19, 1905.

Andrew L. McCarter,
  Owl, Indian Territory.

Dear Sir:

Receipt is hereby acknowledged of your letter of May 16, stating that some time ago you forwarded applications for the enrollment of Elberta G. McCarter and Oda Monds, but have heard nothing from them and you ask if they were received.

In reply to your letter you are advised that the affidavits heretofore forwarded to the birth of Elberta G. McCarter and Oda Monds have been filed with our records as applications for the enrollment of said children.

Respectfully,

Chairman.

**NEW-BORN AFFIDAVIT.**

Number............

## Choctaw Enrolling Commission.

IN THE MATTER OF THE APPLICATION FOR ENROLLMENT, as a citizen of the Choctaw Nation, of Oda Monds

born on the 17 day of March 190 4

Name of father   Richard Monds          a citizen of   Choctaw
Nation final enrollment No  11623
Name of mother   Mollie Monds           a citizen of   Choctaw
Nation final enrollment No  398

Postoffice   Owl I.T.

# Applications for Enrollment of Choctaw Newborn
## Act of 1905   Volume VIII

### AFFIDAVIT OF MOTHER.

UNITED STATES OF AMERICA,  
INDIAN TERRITORY,  
Central   DISTRICT

I   Mollie Monds   on oath state that I am   33   years of age and a citizen by   Marriage   of the   Choctaw   Nation, and as such have been placed upon the final roll of the   Choctaw   Nation, by the Honorable Secretary of the Interior my final enrollment number being   398   ; that I am the lawful wife of   Richard Monds   , who is a citizen of the   Choctaw   Nation, and as such has been placed upon the final roll of said Nation by the Honorable Secretary of the Interior, his final enrollment number being   11623   and that a   male   child was born to me on the   17   day of   March   190 4; that said child has been named   Oda Monds   , and is now living.

Mollie Monds

WITNESSETH:  
Must be two Witnesses who are Citizens.   John Zonala  
Mildred Zonola *(difficult to read handwriting)*

Subscribed and sworn to before me this   14   day of   Jan   190 5

John H Cross  
Notary Public.

My commission expires   Sept 24-1908

---

## AFFIDAVIT OF ATTENDING PHYSICIAN OR MIDWIFE

UNITED STATES OF AMERICA  
INDIAN TERRITORY  
Central   DISTRICT

I,   Elizabeth Goins   a   Midwife   on oath state that I attended on Mrs.   Mollie Monds   wife of   Richard Monds   on the   17   day of   March   , 190 4 , that there was born to her on said date a   Male   child, that said child is now living, and is said to have been named   Oda Monds

her  
Elizabeth x Goins       M.D.  
mark

Subscribed and sworn to before me this, the   14   day of   Jan   190 5

John H Cross  
Notary Public.

WITNESSETH:  
Must be two witnesses who are citizens and know the child.   John Zonala  
Mildred Zonola

# Applications for Enrollment of Choctaw Newborn
## Act of 1905  Volume VIII

We hereby certify that we are well acquainted with    Elizabeth Goins a    Midwife    and know    her    to be reputable and of good standing in the community.

{ John Zonala

{ Mildred Zonola

**BIRTH AFFIDAVIT.**

### DEPARTMENT OF THE INTERIOR.
### COMMISSION TO THE FIVE CIVILIZED TRIBES.

**IN RE APPLICATION FOR ENROLLMENT,** as a citizen of the    Choctaw    Nation, of Oda Monds    , born on the 17    day of    March   , 1904

Name of Father: Richard F Monds        a citizen of the   Choctaw    Nation.
Name of Mother: Mollie L. Monds        a citizen of the   Choctaw    Nation.

Postoffice    Owl I.T.

**AFFIDAVIT OF MOTHER.**

UNITED STATES OF AMERICA, Indian Territory, }
   Central                DISTRICT.  }

I,    Mollie L Monds    , on oath state that I am    34    years of age and a citizen by    Inter Marriage    , of the    Choctaw    Nation; that I am the lawful wife of Richard F. Monds        , who is a citizen, by    Blood    of the        Choctaw Nation; that a    Male    child was born to me on    17    day of    March    , 1904; that said child has been named    Oda Monds    , and was living March 4, 1905.

Mollie L Monds

Witnesses To Mark:
{

Subscribed and sworn to before me this 27   day of    March    , 1905

John H Cross
Notary Public.

## Applications for Enrollment of Choctaw Newborn
## Act of 1905    Volume VIII

**AFFIDAVIT OF ATTENDING PHYSICIAN OR MID-WIFE.**

UNITED STATES OF AMERICA, Indian Territory, }
  Central                DISTRICT.           }

   I,   Elizabeth Goins   , a   Midwife   , on oath state that I attended on Mrs.   Mollie L Monds   , wife of   Richard F Monds   on the 17 day of March   , 1904; that there was born to her on said date a   male   child; that said child was living March 4, 1905, and is said to have been named Oda Monds

                                       her
                             Elizabeth x Goins
Witnesses To Mark:            mark
  { Sam Self
  { M E Cross

   Subscribed and sworn to before me this 27   day of   March   , 1905

                              John H Cross
                              Notary Public.

---

Choc New Born 470
    Grubbs Anderson   b. 2-25-05

                                                   Choctaw 4731

                   Muskogee, Indian Territory, March 31, 1905.

Sibbie Smith,
    Scipio, Indian Territory.

Dear Madam:

   Receipt is hereby acknowledged of your affidavit and the affidavit of Margarette Anderson to the birth of Grubbs Anderson, son of Bill Anderson and Sibby Smithm[sic] February 25, 1905, and the same have been filed with our records as an application for the enrollment of said child.

                        Respectfully,

                                  Chairman.

# Applications for Enrollment of Choctaw Newborn
## Act of 1905   Volume VIII

BIRTH AFFIDAVIT.

## DEPARTMENT OF THE INTERIOR.
## COMMISSION TO THE FIVE CIVILIZED TRIBES.

---

IN RE APPLICATION FOR ENROLLMENT, as a citizen of the   Choctaw   Nation, of Grubbs Anderson   , born on the 25   day of   February   , 1905

Name of Father: Bill Anderson          a citizen of the   Choctaw   Nation.
Name of Mother: Sibby Smith          a citizen of the   Choctaw   Nation.

Postoffice   Scipio I.T.

---

### AFFIDAVIT OF MOTHER.

UNITED STATES OF AMERICA, Indian Territory,
   Central          DISTRICT.

I,   Sibby Smith   , on oath state that I am   19   years of age and a citizen by Blood   , of the   Choctaw   Nation; that I am *not* the lawful wife of   Bill Anderson, who is a citizen, by Blood   of the   Choctaw   Nation; that a   male   child was born to me on   25   day of   February   , 1905; that said child has been named Grubbs Anderson   , and was living March 4, 1905.

                                           her
                                  Sibby  x  Smith
Witnesses To Mark:                      mark
{ RB Coleman
{ *(Illegible)* Saylor

Subscribed and sworn to before me this   27   day of   March   , 1905

                                  RB Coleman
                                  Notary Public.

---

### AFFIDAVIT OF ATTENDING PHYSICIAN OR MID-WIFE.

UNITED STATES OF AMERICA, Indian Territory,
   Central          DISTRICT.

I,   Margarett Anderson   , a   Midwife   , on oath state that I attended on Mrs.   Sibby Smith   *not* , wife of ................. on the   25 day of February   , 1905; that there was born to her on said date a   male   child; that said child was living March 4, 1905, and is said to have been named Grubbs Anderson

155

## Applications for Enrollment of Choctaw Newborn
## Act of 1905 Volume VIII

Margarett Anderson

Witnesses To Mark:
{

    Subscribed and sworn to before me this 27 day of March , 1905

RB Coleman
Notary Public.

---

Choc New Born 471
    Gilber[sic] Byington b. 10-13-03

Choctaw 403

Muskogee, Indian Territory, March 31, 1905.

Joel Byington,
    Caney, Indian Territory.

Dear Sir:

    Receipt is hereby acknowledged of the affidavits of Emma Byington and Wilson Gibson to the birth of Gilbert Byington, son of Joel and Emma Byington, October 13, 1903, and the same have been filed with our records as an application for the enrollment of said child.

Respectfully,

Chairman.

## Applications for Enrollment of Choctaw Newborn
## Act of 1905  Volume VIII

**COPY**

7 NB 471

Muskogee, Indian Territory, April 21, 1905.

Joel Byington,
    Caddo, Indian Territory.

Dear Sir:

    Receipt is hereby acknowledged of your letter of April 15, 1905, asking if the enrollment of your child Gilbert Byington has been approved by the Secretary of the Interior.

    In reply to your letter you are informed that the affidavits heretofore forwarded to the birth of your son Gilbert Byington have been filed with our records as an application for the enrollment of said child, but his name has not yet been placed upon a schedule of citizens by blood of the Choctaw Nation prepared for forwarding to the Secretary of the Interior. You will be notified when his enrollment is approved by the Secretary of the Interior.

Respectfully,

SIGNED      *Tams Bixby*
    Chairman.

---

**BIRTH AFFIDAVIT.**

**DEPARTMENT OF THE INTERIOR.**
**COMMISSION TO THE FIVE CIVILIZED TRIBES.**

**IN RE APPLICATION FOR ENROLLMENT,** as a citizen of the Choctaw Nation, of Gilbert Byington, born on the 13 day of October, 1903

Name of Father: Joel Byington      a citizen of the Choctaw Nation.
Name of Mother: Emma Byington      a citizen of the Choctaw Nation.

Postoffice      Caney I.T.

---

**AFFIDAVIT OF MOTHER.**

UNITED STATES OF AMERICA, Indian Territory,
    Central      DISTRICT.

    I, Emma Byington, on oath state that I am 26 years of age and a citizen by blood, of the Choctaw Nation; that I am the lawful wife of Joel

# Applications for Enrollment of Choctaw Newborn
## Act of 1905   Volume VIII

Byington         , who is a citizen, by blood   of the    Choctaw      Nation; that a male     child was born to me on   13   day of    October    , 1903; that said child has been named    Gilbert Byington     , and was living March 4, 1905.

Emma Byington

Witnesses To Mark:
{ Cornelius Pistokach
{ Edward Hayes

   Subscribed and sworn to before me this  27   day of    March     , 1905

A Denton Phillips<br>Notary Public.

---

**AFFIDAVIT OF ATTENDING PHYSICIAN OR MID-WIFE.**

UNITED STATES OF AMERICA, Indian Territory, }
   Central              DISTRICT. }

   I,   Wilson Gibson      , a   midwife    , on oath state that I attended on Mrs.  Emma Byington    , wife of   Joel Byington    on the 13 day of  October , 1905; that there was born to her on said date a    male    child; that said child was living March 4, 1905, and is said to have been named  Gilbert Byington

Wilson Gibson

Witnesses To Mark:
{ Cornelius Pistokach
{ Edward Hayes

   Subscribed and sworn to before me this  27  day of    March     , 1905

A Denton Phillips<br>Notary Public.

---

Choc New Born 472
   Joel Burrel[sic] McGuire   b. 1-16-04

## Applications for Enrollment of Choctaw Newborn
## Act of 1905   Volume VIII

Choctaw Enrollment Commission
          Spiro I.T.
    Gentlemen Enclosed you will find a letter showing when I was approved by the Hon Secty of the Interior. I have not received my land certificate yet neither has my wife received her certificate therefor we do not know our enrollment number. Respt
                                              Emery O. McGuire

---

$W^m O.B.$

COMMISSIONERS:
TAMS BIXBY,
THOMAS B. NEEDLES,
C.R. BRECKINBRIDGE.
WM. O. BEALL
  Secretary

**DEPARTMENT OF THE INTERIOR,**
**COMMISSIONER TO THE FIVE CIVILIZED TRIBES.**

REFER IN REPLY TO THE FOLLOWING:
Choctaw 236

ADDRESS ONLY THE
COMMISSION TO THE FIVE CIVILIZED TRIBES.

                                    Muskogee, Indian Territory, November 26, 1904.

Emery O. McGuire,
    Utica, Indian Territory.

Dear Sir:

    You are hereby advised that your enrolment[sic] as an intermarried citizen of the Choctaw Nation was approved by the Secretary of the Interior November 16, 1904.

                          Respectfully,
                              T.B. Needles
                              Commissioner in Charge.

---

                                                            Choctaw 236

                                  Muskogee, Indian Territory, March 31, 1905.

Emery O. McGuire,
    Roberta, Indian Territory.

Dear Sir:

    Receipt is hereby acknowledged of the affidavits of Carrie McGuire and A. J. Wells to the birth of Joel Burrell McGuire, son of Emery O. and Carrie McGuire, January 16, 1904, and the same have been filed with our records as an application for the enrollment of said child.

                          Respectfully,

                                    Chairman.

Applications for Enrollment of Choctaw Newborn
Act of 1905   Volume VIII

# NEW BORN AFFIDAVIT

No ............

## CHOCTAW ENROLLING COMMISSION

IN THE MATTER OF THE APPLICATION FOR ENROLLMENT as a citizen of the Choctaw Nation, of     Joel B M$^c$Guire     born on the   16   day of    Jan      190 4

Name of father   Emery O M$^c$Guire       a citizen of    Choctaw     Nation, final enrollment No.    236
Name of mother   Carrie M$^c$Guire        a citizen of    Choctaw     Nation, final enrollment No............................

Utica I.T.                              Postoffice.

### AFFIDAVIT OF MOTHER

UNITED STATES OF AMERICA }
    INDIAN TERRITORY
DISTRICT    Central

I    Carrie M$^c$Guire      , on oath state that I am   26    years of age and a citizen by    Blood    of the    Choctaw     Nation, and as such have been placed upon the final roll of the   Choctaw    Nation, by the Honorable Secretary of the Interior my final enrollment number being................; that I am the lawful wife of   Emery O M$^c$Guire   , who is a citizen of the    Choctaw by marriage       Nation, and as such has been placed upon the final roll of said Nation by the Honorable Secretary of the Interior, his final enrollment number being................ and that a   Male    child was born to me on the  16 day of  Jan    190 4; that said child has been named   Joel B M$^c$Guire   , and is now living.

WITNESSETH:                              Carrie M$^c$Guire

Must be two witnesses  { H.G. Vanzant
who are citizens         Minnie Vanzant

Subscribed and sworn to before me this, the  27$^{th}$   day of    Feb    , 190 5

                                W.J. O'Donby
                                   Notary Public.
My Commission Expires:  Dec 17 1905

## Applications for Enrollment of Choctaw Newborn
## Act of 1905   Volume VIII

### *Affidavit of Attending Physician or Midwife*

UNITED STATES OF AMERICA, }
INDIAN TERRITORY,
Central     DISTRICT

I,   A.J. Wells   a   Physician on oath state that I attended on Mrs. Carrie M<sup>c</sup>Guire   wife of   Emery O. M<sup>c</sup>Guire on the 16<sup>th</sup> day of Jan , 190 4, that there was born to her on said date a   male child, that said child is now living, and is said to have been named   Joel B M<sup>c</sup>Guire

A. J. Wells       M. D.

Subscribed and sworn to before me this the 27<sup>th</sup>   day of   Feb   1905

W.J. O'Donby
Notary Public.

WITNESSETH:
Must be two witnesses who are citizens and know the child. { H.G. Vanzant
Minnie Vanzant

We hereby certify that we are well acquainted with   A.J. Wells a   Physician   and know   him   to be reputable and of good standing in the community.

Must be two citizen witnesses. { H.G. Vanzant
Minnie Vanzant

BIRTH AFFIDAVIT.

### DEPARTMENT OF THE INTERIOR.
### COMMISSION TO THE FIVE CIVILIZED TRIBES.

IN RE APPLICATION FOR ENROLLMENT, as a citizen of the   Choctaw   Nation, of Joel Burrell McGuire   , born on the 16<sup>th</sup>   day of Jan   , 1904
[sic]
Name of Father: Emery O M<sup>c</sup>Guire       a citizen of the   InbrimarriageNation.
Name of Mother: Carrie M<sup>c</sup>Guire       a citizen of the   Choctaw   Nation.

Postoffice   Roberta I.T.

# Applications for Enrollment of Choctaw Newborn
## Act of 1905   Volume VIII

**AFFIDAVIT OF MOTHER.**

UNITED STATES OF AMERICA, Indian Territory, }
Central        DISTRICT.

I, Carrie M<sup>c</sup>Guire, on oath state that I am 26 years of age and a citizen by Blood, of the Choctaw Nation; that I am the lawful wife of Emery O M<sup>c</sup>Guire, who is a citizen, by InbiMarriage[sic] of the Choctaw Nation; that a Male child was born to me cn 16$^{th}$ day of Jan, 1904; that said child has been named Joel Burrell M<sup>c</sup>Guire, and was living March 4, 1905.

Carrie McGuire

Witnesses To Mark:
{

Subscribed and sworn to before me this 25$^{th}$ day of march, 1905

W.J. O'Donby
Notary Public.

---

**AFFIDAVIT OF ATTENDING PHYSICIAN OR MID-WIFE.**

UNITED STATES OF AMERICA, Indian Territory, }
Central        DISTRICT.

I, A.J. Wells, a Physician, on oath state that I attended on Mrs. Carrie M<sup>c</sup>Guire, wife of Emery O M<sup>c</sup>Guire on the 16$^{th}$ day of Jan, 1904; that there was born to her on said date a male child; that said child was living March 4, 1905, and is said to have been named Joel Burrell M<sup>c</sup>Guire

A J Wells

Witnesses To Mark:
{

Subscribed and sworn to before me this 25$^{th}$ day of March, 1905

W.J. O'Donby
Notary Public.

---

Choc New Born 473
    Lillie May Camp b. 2-15-05

## Applications for Enrollment of Choctaw Newborn
## Act of 1905  Volume VIII

Choctaw 5330

Muskogee, Indian Territory, March 31, 1905.

John B. Camp,
    Copeland, Indian Territory.

Dear Sir:

    Receipt is hereby acknowledged of the affidavits of Levander Camp and J. F. Renegar to the birth of Lillie May Camp, daughter of John B. and Levander Camp, February 15, 1905, and the same have been filed with our records as an application for the enrollment of said child.

                  Respectfully,

                                      Chairman.

---

**BIRTH AFFIDAVIT.**

**DEPARTMENT OF THE INTERIOR.**
**COMMISSION TO THE FIVE CIVILIZED TRIBES.**

    **IN RE APPLICATION FOR ENROLLMENT,** as a citizen of the Choctaw Nation, of Lillie May Camp, born on the 15th day of February, 1905

Name of Father: John B Camp       a citizen of the United States Nation.
Name of Mother: Levander Camp     a citizen of the Choctaw Nation.

                  Postoffice     Copeland, I.T.

**AFFIDAVIT OF MOTHER.**

UNITED STATES OF AMERICA, Indian Territory,
    Central                 DISTRICT.

    I, Levander Camp, on oath state that I am _____ years of age and a citizen by blood, of the Choctaw Nation; that I am the lawful wife of John B Camp, who is a citizen, ~~by~~ _____ of the United States Nation; that a female child was born to me on 15th day of February, 1905; that said child has been named Lillie May Camp, and was living March 4, 1905.

                                  Levander Camp

Witnesses To Mark:

# Applications for Enrollment of Choctaw Newborn
## Act of 1905  Volume VIII

Subscribed and sworn to before me this 27th day of March , 1905

W L Richards
Notary Public.

---

**AFFIDAVIT OF ATTENDING PHYSICIAN OR MID-WIFE.**

UNITED STATES OF AMERICA, Indian Territory, }
Central                    DISTRICT.        }

I, J.F. Renegar , a physician , on oath state that I attended on Mrs. Levander Camp , wife of John B Camp on the 15$^{th}$ day of February , 1905; that there was born to her on said date a ................ child; that said child was living March 4, 1905, and is said to have been named Lillie May Camp

JF Renegar MD

Witnesses To Mark:
{

Subscribed and sworn to before me this 27th day of March , 1905

W L Richards
Notary Public.

---

Choc New Born 474
   Nowita Yarbrough  b. 4-16-03

Choctaw 3518

Muskogee, Indian Territory, March 31, 1905.

James Yarbrough,
   Durant, Indian Territory.

Dear Sir:

Receipt is hereby acknowledged of the affidavits of Annie Yarbrough and G. M. Rushing to the birth of Nowita Yarbrough, daughter of James and Annie Yarbrough, April 16, 1903, and the same have been filed with our records as an application for the enrollment of said child.

# Applications for Enrollment of Choctaw Newborn
# Act of 1905   Volume VIII

Respectfully,

Chairman.

---

7-NB-474.

Muskogee, Indian Territory, May 24, 1905.

James Yarbrough,
    Durant, Indian Territory.

Dear Sir:

    There is enclosed you herewith for execution application for the enrollment of your infant child, Nowita Yarbrough.

    In the application filed in this office on March 28, 1905, the mother gives the date of the applicants[sic] birth as April 16, 1903, while the physician gives it as April 16, 1902. In the application filed on the 26th ultimo, both parties give the date of birth as April 16, 1903. In the enclosed application the date of the applicants[sic] birth is left blank, in which you will please supply the correct date and when the affidavits are properly executed, return the application to this office.

    In having these affidavits executed care should be exercised to see that all names are written in full, as they appear in the body of the affidavit, and in the event that either of the persons signing the affidavit are unable to write, signatures by mark must be attested by two witnesses. Each affidavit must be executed before a Notary Public and the notarial seal and signature of the officer must be attached to each separate affidavit.

Respectfully,

VR 24-3.                                                                                                        Chairman.

---

7 N.B. 474.

Muskogee, Indian Territory, May 29, 1905.

James Yarbrough,
    Durant, Indian Territory.

Dear Sir:

    Receipt is hereby acknowledged of the affidavits of Annie Yarbrough and G. M. Rushing, M.D., to the birth of Nowita Yarbrough, daughter of James and Annie

## Applications for Enrollment of Choctaw Newborn
## Act of 1905   Volume VIII

Yarbrough, April 16, 1903, and the same have been filed with our records in the matter of the enrollment of said child.

Respectfully,

Chairman.

---

7-NB-474

Muskogee, Indian Territory, August 8, 1905.

James Yarbrough,
    Durant, Indian Territory.

Dear Sir:

Receipt is hereby acknowledged of your letter of August 4, 1905, addressed to W. M. Baker has been by him referred to this office for appropriate action. Therein you ask if your child Nowita Yarbrough has been approved.

In reply to your letter you are advised that the name of Nowita Yarbrough has been placed upon a schedule of citizens by blood of the Choctaw Nation which has been forwarded the Secretary of the Interior for approval and you will be notified when her enrollment is approved by the Department.

Respectfully,

Acting Commissioner.

---

**NEW-BORN AFFIDAVIT.**

Number............

## Choctaw Enrolling Commission.

IN THE MATTER OF THE APPLICATION FOR ENROLLMENT, as a citizen of the Choctaw Nation, of Nowita Yarbrough

born on the 16$^{th}$ day of April 190 3

Name of father   Jas Yarbrough        a citizen of    Choctaw
Nation final enrollment No   191
Name of mother   Annie Yarbrough     a citizen of    Choctaw
Nation final enrollment No   9994

## Applications for Enrollment of Choctaw Newborn
## Act of 1905   Volume VIII

Postoffice    Durant I.T.

**AFFIDAVIT OF MOTHER.**

UNITED STATES OF AMERICA,
INDIAN TERRITORY,
Central   DISTRICT

I    Annie Yarbrough    on oath state that I am   25   years of age and a citizen by   Blood   of the   Choctaw   Nation, and as such have been placed upon the final roll of the   Choctaw   Nation, by the Honorable Secretary of the Interior my final enrollment number being   9994   ; that I am the lawful wife of   Jas Yarbrough   , who is a citizen of the   Choctaw   Nation, and as such has been placed upon the final roll of said Nation by the Honorable Secretary of the Interior, his final enrollment number being   191   and that a   Female   child was born to me on the 16$^{th}$   day of   April   190 3; that said child has been named   Nowita Yarbrough   , and is now living.

Annie Yarbrough

WITNESSETH:

Must be two Witnesses who are Citizens.   Thos J Sexton
C A Robinson

Subscribed and sworn to before me this   16   day of   January   190 5

L.B. Wilkins
Notary Public.

My commission expires   26 Nov 1906

---

## AFFIDAVIT OF ATTENDING PHYSICIAN OR MIDWIFE

UNITED STATES OF AMERICA
INDIAN TERRITORY
Central   DISTRICT

I,   G. M. Rushing   a   Practicing Physician on oath state that I attended on Mrs.   Annie Yarbrough   wife of   Jas Yarbrough   on the   16   day of April   , 190 3, that there was born to her on said date a   Female   child, that said child is now living, and is said to have been named   Nowita Yarbrough

G.M. Rushing   M.D.

Subscribed and sworn to before me this, the   16   day of   Jan   190 5

James Bower
Notary Public.

WITNESSETH:

Must be two witnesses who are citizens and know the child.   Thos J Sexton
C. A. Robinson

## Applications for Enrollment of Choctaw Newborn
## Act of 1905   Volume VIII

We hereby certify that we are well acquainted with G. M. Rushing a Practicing Physician and know him to be reputable and of good standing in the community.

Thos J Sexton

C.A. Robinson

**BIRTH AFFIDAVIT.**

### DEPARTMENT OF THE INTERIOR.
### COMMISSION TO THE FIVE CIVILIZED TRIBES.

IN RE APPLICATION FOR ENROLLMENT, as a citizen of the Choctaw Nation, of Nowita Yarbrough, born on the 16 day of April, 1903

Name of Father: James Yarbrough   a citizen of the Choctaw Nation.
Name of Mother: Annie Yarbrough   a citizen of the Choctaw Nation.

Postoffice   Durant I.T.

**AFFIDAVIT OF MOTHER.**

UNITED STATES OF AMERICA, Indian Territory, DISTRICT.

I, Annie Yarbrough, on oath state that I am 27 years of age and a citizen by Blood, of the Choctaw Nation; that I am the lawful wife of James Yarbrough, who is a citizen, by Intermarriage of the Choctaw Nation; that a Female child was born to me on 16$^{th}$ day of April, 1903; that said child has been named Nowita Yarbrough, and was living March 4, 1905.

Annie Yarbrough

Witnesses To Mark:

Subscribed and sworn to before me this 25 day of May, 1905

Notary Public.

## Applications for Enrollment of Choctaw Newborn
## Act of 1905   Volume VIII

### AFFIDAVIT OF ATTENDING PHYSICIAN OR MID-WIFE.

UNITED STATES OF AMERICA, Indian Territory,
Central        DISTRICT.

I, G. M. Rushing, a Physician, on oath state that I attended on Mrs. Annie Yarbrough, wife of James Yarbrough on the 16$^{th}$ day of April, 1903; that there was born to her on said date a Female child; that said child was living March 4, 1905, and is said to have been named Nowita Yarbrough

G.M. Rushing M.D.

Witnesses To Mark:

Subscribed and sworn to before me this 25 day of May, 1905

T.B. Wilkins
Notary Public.

BIRTH AFFIDAVIT.

### DEPARTMENT OF THE INTERIOR.
## COMMISSION TO THE FIVE CIVILIZED TRIBES.

IN RE APPLICATION FOR ENROLLMENT, as a citizen of the Choctaw Nation, of Nowita Yarbrough, born on the 16 day of April, 1903

Name of Father: James Yarbrough        a citizen of the Choctaw Nation.
Name of Mother: Annie Yarbrough        a citizen of the Choctaw Nation.

Postoffice   Durant Ind Ter

### AFFIDAVIT OF MOTHER.

UNITED STATES OF AMERICA, Indian Territory,
Central        DISTRICT.

I, Annie Yarbrough, on oath state that I am 27 years of age and a citizen by Blood, of the Choctaw Nation; that I am the lawful wife of James Yarbrough, who is a citizen, by Marriage of the Choctaw Nation; that a Female child was born to me on 16$^{th}$ day of April, 1903; that said child has been named Nowita Yarbrough, and was living March 4, 1905.

Annie Yarbrough

Witnesses To Mark:

# Applications for Enrollment of Choctaw Newborn
## Act of 1905   Volume VIII

Subscribed and sworn to before me this   25 day of   Mach[sic]   , 1905

                         T.B. Wilkins
                         Notary Public.

**AFFIDAVIT OF ATTENDING PHYSICIAN OR MID-WIFE.**

UNITED STATES OF AMERICA, Indian Territory, }
    Central                   DISTRICT. }

I,   G. M. Rushing   , a   Practicing Physician   , on oath state that I attended on Mrs.   Annie Yarbrough   , wife of   James Yarbrough   on the   16th   day of   April   , 1902[sic]; that there was born to her on said date a   Female   child; that said child was living March 4, 1905, and is said to have been named   Nowita Yarbrough

                         G.M. Rushing M.D.

Witnesses To Mark:

{ Subscribed and sworn to before me this   25   day of   March   , 1905

                         T.B. Wilkins
                         Notary Public.

---

Choc New Born 475
    Frank Williams Pusley   b. 2-26-04

                                      7-3271.

                   Muskogee, Indian Territory, February 7, 1903.

Lyman Pusley,
    Guertie, Indian Territory.

Dear Sir:

    Receipt is hereby acknowledged of your letter of January 28, 1903, in which you ask if you can have your infant child, nine days old, enrolled; and request that a blank application for its enrollment be sent you.   A blank of such description is herewith enclosed.

## Applications for Enrollment of Choctaw Newborn
## Act of 1905  Volume VIII

Further replying to your communication, you are advised that the Commission is without authority to enroll as citizens of the Choctaw and Chickasaw Nations children born subsequent to September 25, 1902; as the act of Congress approved July 1, 1902, which was ratified by the citizens of the Choctaw and Chickasaw Nations at a special election held September 25, 1902, provides as follows:

"The names of all persons living on the date of the final ratification of this agreement entitled to be enrolled as provided in section 27 hereof shall be placed upon the rolls made by said Commission; and no child born thereafter to a citizen or freedman and no person intermarried thereafter to a citizen shall be entitled to enrollment or to participate in the distribution of the tribal property of the Choctaws and Chickasaws."

Respectfully,

Acting Chairman.

---

Choctaw 3271

Muskogee, Indian Territory, March 31, 1905.

Lyman Pusley,
Guertie, Indian Territory.

Dear Sir:

Receipt is hereby acknowledged of the affidavits of Lizzie Pusley and Cassie Jackson to the birth of Frank William Pusley, child of Lyman and Lizzie Pusley, July 26, 1904, and the same have been filed with our records as an application for the enrollment of said child.

Respectfully,

Chairman.

# Applications for Enrollment of Choctaw Newborn
## Act of 1905  Volume VIII

**NEW-BORN AFFIDAVIT.**

Number..................

## ...Choctaw Enrolling Commission...

IN THE MATTER OF THE APPLICATION FOR ENROLLMENT, as a citizen of the Choctaw Nation, of  Frank William Pusley

born on the 26 day of ____July____ 190 4

Name of father   Lyman Pusley          a citizen of   Choctaw
Nation final enrollment No.   9433
Name of mother   Lizzie Pusley         a citizen of   Choctaw
Nation final enrollment No.   9434

Postoffice   Guertie

### AFFIDAVIT OF MOTHER.

UNITED STATES OF AMERICA
INDIAN TERRITORY
Central       DISTRICT

I   Lizzie Pusley   , on oath state that I am 25 years of age and a citizen by blood of the Choctaw Nation, and as such have been placed upon the final roll of the Choctaw Nation, by the Honorable Secretary of the Interior my final enrollment number being 9434 ; that I am the lawful wife of Lyman Pusley , who is a citizen of the Choctaw Nation, and as such has been placed upon the final roll of said Nation by the Honorable Secretary of the Interior, his final enrollment number being 9433 and that a Male child was born to me on the 26 day of July 190 4; that said child has been named Frank William Pusley , and is now living.

Lizzie Pusley

Witnesseth.

Must be two Witnesses who are Citizens.   Osbon Pusley
John Pusley

Subscribed and sworn to before me this  _2 day of Jan  190 5

Ben F. Gillum
Notary Public.

My commission expires:
Jan 24/06

## Applications for Enrollment of Choctaw Newborn
## Act of 1905  Volume VIII

## AFFIDAVIT OF ATTENDING PHYSICIAN OR MIDWIFE

UNITED STATES OF AMERICA
INDIAN TERRITORY
Central    DISTRICT

I,   Cassey Jackson    a    Midwife    on oath state that I attended on Mrs.  Lizzie Pusley   wife of   Lyman Pusley   on the   26   day of   July   , 190 4 , that there was born to her on said date a   male   child, that said child is now living, and is said to have been named   Frank William Pusley

                                                       her
                                  Mrs Cassey x Jackson
                                           mark

Subscribed and sworn to before me this, the    12    day of   January    190 5

WITNESSETH:                                         Ben F. Gillum    Notary Public.
Must be two witnesses  { John Pusley
who are citizens          Osbon Pusley

We hereby certify that we are well acquainted with    Cassey Jackson   a    Midwife    and know   her    to be reputable and of good standing in the community.

_____                John Pusley

_____                Osbon Pusley

---

BIRTH AFFIDAVIT.

### DEPARTMENT OF THE INTERIOR.
### COMMISSION TO THE FIVE CIVILIZED TRIBES.

IN RE APPLICATION FOR ENROLLMENT, as a citizen of the    Choctaw    Nation, of    Frank William Pusley    , born on the   26th   day of   July   , 1904

Name of Father:  Lyman Pusley         a citizen of the   Choctaw    Nation.
Name of Mother:  Lizzie Pusley          a citizen of the   Choctaw    Nation.

                            Postoffice    Guertie, I. T.

# Applications for Enrollment of Choctaw Newborn
# Act of 1905   Volume VIII

### AFFIDAVIT OF MOTHER.

UNITED STATES OF AMERICA, Indian Territory, }
Central        DISTRICT.

I, Lizzie Pusley, on oath state that I am 24 years of age and a citizen by Blood, of the Choctaw Nation; that I am the lawful wife of Lyman Pusley, who is a citizen, by Blood of the Choctaw Nation; that a male child was born to me on 26 day of July, 1904; that said child has been named Frank William Pusley, and was living March 4, 1905.

Lizzie Pusley

Witnesses To Mark:
{

Subscribed and sworn to before me this 25 day of Mch, 1905

Ben F. Gillum
Notary Public.

### AFFIDAVIT OF ATTENDING PHYSICIAN OR MID-WIFE.

UNITED STATES OF AMERICA, Indian Territory, }
Central        DISTRICT.

I, Cassie Jackson, a midwife, on oath state that I attended on Mrs. Lizzie Pusley, wife of Lyman Pusley on the 26 day of July, 1904; that there was born to her on said date a male child; that said child was living March 4, 1905, and is said to have been named Frank William Pusley

her
Cassie x Jackson
mark

Witnesses To Mark:
{ AW Raydon
  (Name Illegible)

Subscribed and sworn to before me this 25 day of Mch, 1905

Ben F. Gillum
Notary Public.

## Applications for Enrollment of Choctaw Newborn
## Act of 1905   Volume VIII

Choc New Born 476
    Agnes Carney   b. 12-20-03

**BIRTH AFFIDAVIT.**

### DEPARTMENT OF THE INTERIOR.
### COMMISSION TO THE FIVE CIVILIZED TRIBES.

IN RE APPLICATION FOR ENROLLMENT, as a citizen of the   Choctaw   Nation, of Agnes Carney   , born on the   20th   day of   December   , 1903

Name of Father: Nolis Carney (Norris Carney)   a citizen of the   Choctaw   Nation.
Name of Mother: Cillen Wilson   a citizen of the   Choctaw   Nation.

Postoffice   Chambers, I.T.

**AFFIDAVIT OF MOTHER.**

UNITED STATES OF AMERICA, Indian Territory, }
    Central   DISTRICT. }

    I,   Cillen Wilson   , on oath state that I am   about 20   years of age and a citizen by   blood   , of the   Choctaw   Nation; that I am  *not* the lawful wife of Nolis Carney (Norris Carney)   , who is a citizen, by   blood   of the   Choctaw   Nation; that a   female   child was born to me on   the 20th   day of   December   , 1903; that said child has been named   Agnes Carney   , and was living March 4, 1905.

                her
          Cillen x Wilson
Witnesses To Mark:      mark
{ Columbus Campelube
{ David M. Mackey

    Subscribed and sworn to before me this   16th   day of   March   , 1905

                Wirt Franklin
                Notary Public.

**AFFIDAVIT OF ATTENDING PHYSICIAN OR MID-WIFE.**

UNITED STATES OF AMERICA, Indian Territory, }
    Central   DISTRICT. }

    I,   Louisiana Carney   , a   mid-wife   , on oath state that I attended on Mrs.   Cillen Wilson   *not*  , wife of   Nolis Carney (Norris Carney)   on the 20th

# Applications for Enrollment of Choctaw Newborn
## Act of 1905 Volume VIII

day of December , 1903; that there was born to her on said date a female child; that said child was living March 4, 1905, and is said to have been named Agnes Carney

Witnesses To Mark:
   { David M Mackey
    Columbus Campelube

Louisiana x Carney
her     mark

Subscribed and sworn to before me this 16th day of March , 1905

Wirt Franklin
Notary Public.

---

Choc New Born 477
   Thelma Henley b. 4-27-03

7-5722

Muskogee, Indian Territory, March 31, 1905.

B. Frank Henley,
   Amber, Indian Territory.

Dear Sis:

Receipt is hereby acknowledged of the affidavits of Edna A. Henley and P. E. Connoway to the birth of Thelma Henley, daughter of B. Frank and Edna A. Henley, April 27, 1903, and the same have been filed with our records as an application for the enrollment of said child.

Respectfully,

Chairman.

## Applications for Enrollment of Choctaw Newborn
## Act of 1905   Volume VIII

BIRTH AFFIDAVIT.

## DEPARTMENT OF THE INTERIOR.
## COMMISSION TO THE FIVE CIVILIZED TRIBES.

IN RE APPLICATION FOR ENROLLMENT, as a citizen of the Choctaw Nation, of Thelma Henley, born on the 27 day of April, 1903

Name of Father: B Frank Henley   a citizen of the United States Nation.
Name of Mother: Edna A Henley   a citizen of the Choctaw Nation.

Postoffice   Amber, I.T.

### AFFIDAVIT OF MOTHER.

UNITED STATES OF AMERICA, Indian Territory,  
Southern   DISTRICT.

I, Edna A Henley, on oath state that I am Thirty four years of age and a citizen by blood, of the Choctaw Nation; that I am the lawful wife of B. Frank Henley, who is a citizen, ~~by~~ .................. of the United States ~~Nation~~; that a female child was born to me on 27 day of April, 1903; that said child has been named Thelma Henley, and was living March 4, 1905.

Edna A Henley

Witnesses To Mark:

Subscribed and sworn to before me this 27 day of March, 1905

M. D. Carson

My commission expires November 25, 1905.   Notary Public.
Southern Dist I.T.

### AFFIDAVIT OF ATTENDING PHYSICIAN OR MID-WIFE.

UNITED STATES OF AMERICA, Indian Territory,  
Southern   DISTRICT.

I, Dr. P. K. Connoway, a Physician, on oath state that I attended on Mrs. Edna A Henley, wife of B. Frank Henley on the 27 day of April, 1903; that there was born to her on said date a female child; that said child was living March 4, 1905, and is said to have been named Thelma Henley

PK Connoway M.D.

## Applications for Enrollment of Choctaw Newborn
## Act of 1905   Volume VIII

Witnesses To Mark:

{

Subscribed and sworn to before me this  27   day of      March        , 1905

M. D. Carson
My commission expires November 25, 1905.                 Notary Public.
Southern Dist I.T.

**BIRTH AFFIDAVIT.**

# DEPARTMENT OF THE INTERIOR,
### COMMISSION TO THE FIVE CIVILIZED TRIBES.

*IN RE Application for Enrollment*, as a citizen of the       Choctaw        Nation, of   Thelma Henley   , born on the    27    day of   April    , 1903

Name of Father:  B. Frank Henley          a citizen of the    U.S.      ~~Nation~~.
Name of Mother:  Edna E[sic] Henley       a citizen of the    Choctaw    Nation.

Post-Office:        ~~Chi~~  Minco Ind Ter

**AFFIDAVIT OF MOTHER.**

UNITED STATES OF AMERICA, ⎫
   **INDIAN TERRITORY.**           ⎬
  Southern        District.      ⎭

I,   Edna A Henley      , on oath state that I am   31   years of age and a citizen by   blood   and adoption  , of the   Choctaw    Nation; that I am the lawful wife of    B. Frank Henley   , who is a citizen, ~~by~~ .................. of the   U S    Nation; that a    female child was born to me on    27    day of   April    , 1903, that said child has been named Thelma Henley    , and is now living.

Edna A Henley

**WITNESSES TO MARK:**

{

*Subscribed and sworn to before me this*   3$^{rd}$    *day of*   July    , *1903*

M.D. Carson
*NOTARY PUBLIC.*
Southern Dist I.T.

## Applications for Enrollment of Choctaw Newborn
## Act of 1905  Volume VIII

**AFFIDAVIT OF ATTENDING PHYSICIAN OR MID-WIFE.**

UNITED STATES OF AMERICA,  
    **INDIAN TERRITORY.**  
Southern       District.

    I,   Philip K Connoway  , a   Physician    , on oath state that I attended on Mrs.   Edna E Henley  , wife of   B. Frank Henley   on the   27   day of   April  , 190 3; that there was born to her on said date a   female   child; that said child is now living and is said to have been named   Thelma Henley

                                        Philip K Connoway

**WITNESSES TO MARK:**

    *Subscribed and sworn to before me this*   3$^{rd}$   *day of*   July   , 1903

                                        M.D. Carson  
                                        *NOTARY PUBLIC.*  
                                      Southern Dist I.T.

---

Choc New Born 478  
        Waneta Jeane Cotton   b. 9-23-04

*(The affidavit below typed as given.)*

To whome it may Concern:

                        This is to certify that I Florence Bond was personally acquainted with Heidee Cotton diceased wife of Pink Cotton the mother of Waneta Jeane Cotton & that I was present at the time Waneta Jeanne Cotton was Born Sept 23$^{rd}$ 1904 & I do certify that Heidee Cotton was the mother of Waneta Jeanne Cotton who is now & was living March 4$^{th}$ 1905

                                        Florence Bond

Subscribed & sworn to before me this the 14 of April 1905

                                    S.W. Frost  
    My Com Expires                      Notary Public.  
    Feb 3$^{d}$ 1906

## Applications for Enrollment of Choctaw Newborn
## Act of 1905   Volume VIII

*(The affidavit below typed as given.)*

To whome it may Concern

This is to certify that I, Lizzie Jackson, Indian Territory was personally acquainted with Haidee Cotton deceased wife of Pink Cotton & that I was present at the time Waneta Jeanne Cotton was born Sept 23$^{rd}$ 1904 & I do certify that Haidee Cotton was the mother of Waneta Jeanne Cotton, who is now & was living March 4$^{th}$ 1905

Lizzie Jackson

Subscribed and sworn to before me this the 14$^{th}$ of April 1905

J L Mentzer

My Com expires Feb 1- 1908

*No 43*

**BIRTH AFFIDAVIT.**

### DEPARTMENT OF THE INTERIOR.
### COMMISSION TO THE FIVE CIVILIZED TRIBES.

**IN RE APPLICATION FOR ENROLLMENT,** as a citizen of the Choctaw Nation, of Waneta Jeanne Cotton , born on the 23 day of Sept , 1904

Name of Father: Pink Cotton   a citizen of the Choctaw Nation.
Name of Mother: Haidee Cotton   a citizen of the Choctaw Nation.

Postoffice   Hickory I.T.

**AFFIDAVIT OF MOTHER.**

UNITED STATES OF AMERICA, Indian Territory,
    Southern        DISTRICT.

I, Haidee Cotton , on oath state that I am 36 years of age and a citizen by Intermarriage , of the Choctaw Nation; that I am the lawful wife of Pink Cotton , who is a citizen, by Blood of the Choctaw Nation; that a Female child was born to me on 23 day of Sept , 1904, that said child has been named Waneta Jeanne Cotton , and is now living.

Haidee Cotton

Witnesses To Mark:

## Applications for Enrollment of Choctaw Newborn
## Act of 1905   Volume VIII

Subscribed and sworn to before me this  27  day of  December  , 1904

J L Mentzer
Notary Public.

---

#### AFFIDAVIT OF ATTENDING PHYSICIAN OR MID-WIFE.

UNITED STATES OF AMERICA, Indian Territory, }
Southern           DISTRICT.

I,    J A Deen        , a   physician        , on oath state that I attended on Mrs.  Mrs Haidee Cotton   , wife of   Pink Cotton    on the   23    day of Sept , 1904; that there was born to her on said date a    Female    child; that said child is now living and is said to have been named Waneta Jeanne Cotton

J A Deen

Witnesses To Mark:
{

Subscribed and sworn to before me this  26   day of  Dec   , 1904

*(Name Illegible)*
Notary Public.

---

BIRTH AFFIDAVIT.

#### DEPARTMENT OF THE INTERIOR.
## COMMISSION TO THE FIVE CIVILIZED TRIBES.

IN RE APPLICATION FOR ENROLLMENT, as a citizen of the     Choctaw     Nation, of Waneta Jeanne Cotton    , born on the  23   day of  Sept   , 1904

Name of Father:  Pink Cotton            a citizen of the Chocktaw[sic]Nation.
Name of Mother:  Haidee Cotton          a citizen of the   Chocktaw   Nation.

Postoffice   Hickory I.T.

---

#### AFFIDAVIT OF MOTHER.

UNITED STATES OF AMERICA, Indian Territory, }
Southern           DISTRICT.

I,   Pink Cotton    , on oath state that I am   28    years of age and a citizen by blood   , of the    Choctaw     Nation; that I am the lawful ~~wife~~ *Husband* of Haidee Cotton    , who is a citizen, by  Intermarriage    of the      Chocktaw      Nation;

# Applications for Enrollment of Choctaw Newborn
## Act of 1905   Volume VIII

that a    female    child was born to ~~me~~ *Haidee Cotton my wife who is now dead* on 23 day of    September   , 1904; that said child has been named   Waneta Jeanne   , and was living March 4, 1905.

Pink Cotton

Witnesses To Mark:
{

Subscribed and sworn to before me this   27$^{th}$   day of   March   , 1905

*(Name Illegible)*
Notary Public.

---

**AFFIDAVIT OF ATTENDING PHYSICIAN OR MID-WIFE.**

UNITED STATES OF AMERICA, Indian Territory, ⎫
Southern                    DISTRICT.    ⎭

I,   J.A. Deen    , a   Physician   , on oath state that I attended on Mrs.   Haidee Cotton   , wife of   Pink Cotton   on the 23$^{rd}$   day of   Sept   , 1904; that there was born to her on said date a    female    child; that said child was living March 4, 1905, and is said to have been named   Waneta Jeanne

J A Deen

Witnesses To Mark:
{

Subscribed and sworn to before me this   27$^{th}$   day of   March   , 1905

*(Name Illegible)*
Notary Public.

---

**COPY**

N. B. 478

Muskogee, Indian Territory, April 10, 1905.

Pink Cotton,
    Hickory, Indian Territory.

Dear Sir:

    It appears from the affidavits heretofore filed with the Commission that the mother of the applicant, Waneta Jeanne Cotton, is dead. It is therefore necessary that you secure the affidavits of two persons who have actual knowledge of the fact that the child

## Applications for Enrollment of Choctaw Newborn
## Act of 1905   Volume VIII

was born, date of her birth, that she was living on March 4, 1905 and that Haidee Cotton was her mother.

Please give this matter your immediate attention.

SIGNED

Respectfully,

*T. B. Needles.*
Commissioner in Charge.

---

7-263

Muskogee, Indian Territory, April 21, 1905.

Pink Cotton,
    Hickory, Indian Territory.

Dear Sir:

Receipt is hereby acknowledged of your letter of April 14, 1905, enclosing affidavits of Florence Bond and Lizzie Jackson to the birth of Waneta Jeanne Cotton, daughter of Pink and Haidee Cotton, September 23, 1904, and the same have been filed with our records as an application for the enrollment of said child.

Respectfully,

Chairman.

---

Choc New Born 479
    Ollie May Jones   b. 5-15-04

BIRTH AFFIDAVIT.

### DEPARTMENT OF THE INTERIOR.
### COMMISSION TO THE FIVE CIVILIZED TRIBES.

**IN RE APPLICATION FOR ENROLLMENT,** as a citizen of the   Choctaw   Nation, of Ollie May Jones   , born on the  15  day of  May , 1904

Name of Father: Perry Jones      a citizen of the  Choctaw  Nation.
Name of Mother: Marthey E Jones      a citizen of the  Choctaw  Nation.

# Applications for Enrollment of Choctaw Newborn
## Act of 1905 Volume VIII

Postoffice  Palmer, Indian Territory

---

### AFFIDAVIT OF MOTHER.

UNITED STATES OF AMERICA, Indian Territory, }
Southern                DISTRICT.         }

I, Marthey E Jones , on oath state that I am 33 years of age and a citizen by Marriage , of the Choctaw Nation; that I am the lawful wife of Perry Jones , who is a citizen, by Blood of the Choctaw Nation; that a Female child was born to me on 15$^{th}$ day of May , 1904; that said child has been named Ollie May Jones , and was living March 4, 1905.

                                                her
                               Marthey x E. Jones

Witnesses To Mark:                   mark
{ H.S. Oliver
{ D A Taylor

Subscribed and sworn to before me this 25 day of March , 1905

My Commission Expires June 27, 1907        A D Goodenough
                                      Notary Public.

---

### AFFIDAVIT OF ATTENDING PHYSICIAN OR MID-WIFE.

State of Texas
~~UNITED STATES OF AMERICA, Indian Territory,~~ }
County of Dallus[sic]        DISTRICT. }

I, W H Powell , a M. D. , on oath state that I attended on Mrs. Marthey E Jones , wife of Perry Jones on the 15 day of May , 1904; that there was born to her on said date a Female child; that said child was living March 4, 1905, and is said to have been named Ollie May Jones

                               W.H. Powell M.D.

Witnesses To Mark:
{

Subscribed and sworn to before me this 27$^{th}$ day of March , 1905

                               H.C. Jarrel
                               Notary Public.

## Applications for Enrollment of Choctaw Newborn
## Act of 1905   Volume VIII

Choctaw 295.

Muskogee, Indian Territory, March 31, 1905.

A. D. Goodenough,
    Palmer, Indian Territory.

Dear Sir:

    Receipt is hereby acknowledged of your letter of March 28$^{th}$, enclosing the affidavits of Marthey E. Jones and H. A.[sic] Powell to the birth of Ollie May Jones, daughter of Perry and Marthey E. Jones, May 15, 1904, and the same have been filed with our records as an application for the enrollment of said child.

        Respectfully,

                Chairman.

---

<u>Choc New Born 480</u>
    Ruby Mowdy   b. 3-6-04

---

**BIRTH AFFIDAVIT.**

### DEPARTMENT OF THE INTERIOR.
### COMMISSION TO THE FIVE CIVILIZED TRIBES.

**IN RE APPLICATION FOR ENROLLMENT,** as a citizen of the Choctaw Nation, of Ruby Mowdy, born on the 6th day of March, 1904

Name of Father:  Frank M Mowdy      a citizen of the  Choctaw  Nation.
Name of Mother: Viola Mowdy        a citizen of the  Choctaw  Nation.

           Postoffice   Coalgate Indian Territory

# Applications for Enrollment of Choctaw Newborn
## Act of 1905  Volume VIII

### AFFIDAVIT OF MOTHER.

UNITED STATES OF AMERICA, Indian Territory, }
Central        DISTRICT.

I, Viola Mowdy , on oath state that I am 30 years of age and a citizen by blood , of the Choctaw Nation; that I am the lawful wife of Frank M Mowdy , who is a citizen, by Inter marriage of the Choctaw Nation; that a female child was born to me on 6th day of March , 1904; that said child has been named Ruby Mowdy , and was living March 4, 1905.

Viola Mowdy

Witnesses To Mark:
{
Subscribed and sworn to before me this 27th day of March , 1905

Geo. A Frasher
Notary Public.

### AFFIDAVIT OF ATTENDING PHYSCIAN OR MID-WIFE.

UNITED STATES OF AMERICA, Indian Territory, }
Central        DISTRICT.

I, S. S. McCullough , a Physcian[sic] , on oath state that I attended on Mrs. Viola Mowdy , wife of Frank M Mowdy on the 6th day of March , 1904; that there was born to her on said date a female child; that said child was living March 4, 1905, and is said to have been named Ruby Mowdy

SS McCullough M.D.

Witnesses To Mark:
{
Subscribed and sworn to before me this 27th day of March , 1905

Geo. A Frasher

---

Choc New Born 481
    Zona Washington  b. 2-15-05

## Applications for Enrollment of Choctaw Newborn
## Act of 1905   Volume VIII

**BIRTH AFFIDAVIT.**

### DEPARTMENT OF THE INTERIOR.
### COMMISSION TO THE FIVE CIVILIZED TRIBES.

IN RE APPLICATION FOR ENROLLMENT, as a citizen of the Choctaw Nation, of Zona Washington, born on the 15th day of February, 1905

Name of Father: Levi Washington     a citizen of the Choctaw Nation.
Name of Mother: Lytie Washington     a citizen of the Choctaw Nation.

Postoffice     Wister, Ind. Ter.

**AFFIDAVIT OF MOTHER.**

UNITED STATES OF AMERICA, Indian Territory,
Central     DISTRICT.

    I, Lytie Washington, on oath state that I am about 30 years of age and a citizen by blood, of the Choctaw Nation; that I am the lawful wife of Levi Washington, who is a citizen, by blood of the Choctaw Nation; that a female child was born to me on 15th day of February, 1905; that said child has been named Zona Washington, and was living March 4, 1905.

                                      her
                              Lytie x Washington
Witnesses To Mark:                    mark
    Peter Maytubby Jr
    Victor M Locke J.P.

    Subscribed and sworn to before me this 28th day of March, 1905

                              Wirt Franklin
                                   Notary Public.

**AFFIDAVIT OF ATTENDING PHYSICIAN OR MID-WIFE.**

UNITED STATES OF AMERICA, Indian Territory,
Central     DISTRICT.

    I, Mollie McCurtain, a mid-wife, on oath state that I attended on Mrs. Lytie Washington, wife of Levi Washington on the 15th day of February, 1905; that there was born to her on said date a female child; that said child was living March 4, 1905, and is said to have been named Zona Washington

                                her
                           Mollie x McCurtain
                               mark

# Applications for Enrollment of Choctaw Newborn
## Act of 1905 Volume VIII

Witnesses To Mark:
  { Peter Maytubby Jr
  { Victor M Locke J.P.

Subscribed and sworn to before me this 28th day of March , 1905

                               Wirt Franklin
                               Notary Public.

---

Choc New Born 482
    Myrtle Lela Taylor  b. 12-25-04

**BIRTH AFFIDAVIT.**

### DEPARTMENT OF THE INTERIOR.
### COMMISSION TO THE FIVE CIVILIZED TRIBES.

**IN RE APPLICATION FOR ENROLLMENT,** as a citizen of the Choctaw Nation, of Myrtle Lela Taylor , born on the 25 day of December , 1904

Name of Father: Phelen Taylor        a citizen of the Choctaw Nation.
Name of Mother: Jencey Gipson      a citizen of the Choctaw Nation.

                   Postoffice    Bethel I.T.

### AFFIDAVIT OF MOTHER.

**UNITED STATES OF AMERICA, Indian Territory,** }
    Central            **DISTRICT.** }

    I, Jincey Gipson , on oath state that I am 28 years of age and a citizen by blood , of the Choctaw Nation; that I am the lawful wife of Phelen Taylor , who is a citizen, by blood of the Choctaw Nation; that a female child was born to me on the 25$^{th}$ day of December , 1904; that said child has been named Myrtle Lela Taylor . and was living March 4, 1905.

                               her
                         Jincey x Gipson
Witnesses To Mark:           mark
  { Phelen Taylor
  { Carl Patterson

## Applications for Enrollment of Choctaw Newborn
## Act of 1905   Volume VIII

Subscribed and sworn to before me this 24th day of March , 1905

Carl Patterson
Notary Public.

---

**AFFIDAVIT OF ATTENDING PHYSICIAN OR MID-WIFE.**

UNITED STATES OF AMERICA, Indian Territory,  
Central   DISTRICT.

I, Lizzie Jefferson , a mid-wife , on oath state that I attended on Mrs. Jincey Gipson , wife of Phelen Taylor on the 25 day of December , 1904; that there was born to her on said date a female child; that said child was living March 4, 1905, and is said to have been named Myrtle Lela Taylor

Lizzie Jefferson

Witnesses To Mark:
{

Subscribed and sworn to before me this 24th day of March , 1905

Carl Patterson
Notary Public.

---

Choc New Born 483
    Stella Frances Onubby  b. 10-7-04

Choctaw 1688.

Muskogee, Indian Territory, April 18, 1905.

Robert L. Onubby,
    Leflore, Indian Territory.

Dear Sir:

Receipt is hereby acknowledged of your letter of April 12, enclosing license and certificate of your marriage to Emma Grillette and the same have been filed in support of the application for the enrollment of your child, Stella Frances Onubby.

## Applications for Enrollment of Choctaw Newborn
## Act of 1905   Volume VIII

Respectfully,

Chairman.

**COPY**

N. B. 483

Muskogee, Indian Territory, April 8, 1905.

Robert L. Onubby,
    LeFlore, Indian Territory.

Dear Sir:

    You are hereby advised that before the application for the enrollment of your infant child, Stella Frances Onubby, can be finally disposed of, it will be necessary for you to furnish the Commission with either the original or a certified copy of the license and certificate of your marriage to Emma Onubby.

    Please give this matter your immediate attention.

Respectfully,

SIGNED

*T. B. Needles.*
Commissioner in Charge.

---

**BIRTH AFFIDAVIT.**

### DEPARTMENT OF THE INTERIOR.
### COMMISSION TO THE FIVE CIVILIZED TRIBES.

**IN RE APPLICATION FOR ENROLLMENT,** as a citizen of the Choctaw Nation, of Stella Frances Onubby, born on the 7$^{th}$ day of October, 1904

Name of Father: Robert L Onubby    a citizen of the Choctaw Nation.
Name of Mother: Emma Onubby    a citizen of the Choctaw Nation.

Postoffice    LeFlore Ind Ter

# Applications for Enrollment of Choctaw Newborn
## Act of 1905   Volume VIII

### AFFIDAVIT OF MOTHER.

UNITED STATES OF AMERICA, Indian Territory, }
............................................................ DISTRICT. }

I, Emma Onubby, on oath state that I am 26 years of age and a citizen by——, of the U.S.A. Nation; that I am the lawful wife of Robert L Onubby, who is a citizen, by blood of the Choctaw Nation; that a Female child was born to me on 7th day of October, 1904; that said child has been named Stella Frances Onubby, and was living March 4, 1905.

Emma Onubby

Witnesses To Mark:
{

Subscribed and sworn to before me this 28th day of March, 1905

Lacey P Bobo<br>Notary Public.

---

### AFFIDAVIT OF ATTENDING PHYSICIAN OR MID-WIFE.

UNITED STATES OF AMERICA, Indian Territory, }
Central                    DISTRICT. }

I, Mattie F. Dunlap, a mid-wife, on oath state that I attended on Mrs. Emma Onubby, wife of Robert L Onubby on the 7th day of October, 1904; that there was born to her on said date a Female child; that said child was living March 4, 1905, and is said to have been named Stella Frances Onubby

Mattie F Dunlap

Witnesses To Mark:
{
Subscribed and sworn to before me this 28th day of March, 1905

Lacey P Bobo<br>Notary Public.

*Robert L Onubby is Choc By Blood - Roll #4748*

# Applications for Enrollment of Choctaw Newborn
## Act of 1905  Volume VIII

Marriage License

{ Choctaw Nation }
{ Sugar Loaf County }

To any person authorized by Law to solemnize Marriage; Greeting:--
You are hereby commanded to Solemnize the Rite and Publish the Banns of Matrimony between Mr. Robert L. Onubby a citizen of the Choctaw Nation of Leflore, I.T. age 27 years, and Miss Emma Grilliette a citizen of the United States of Leflore, I.T. age 26 years, according to the Laws of the Choctaw Nation, and do you officially sign and return this License to the parties therein named.
Witness my hand and seal of office this 24 day of November A.D. 1903.

Robert E. Lee,<br>Clerk of Sugar Loaf County, C.N.

Certificate of Marriage

I, Henry J Sexton a County Judge of Sugar Loaf County Choctaw Nation do hereby certify that one the 29 day of November, A.D. 1903, I did duly and according to the Laws of the Choctaw Nation, as commanded in the foregoing License, solemnize the Rite and publish the Banns of matrimony between the parties therein named.
Witness my hand this 29 day of November A.D. 1903.
My credentials or commissions are recorded in the office of the Clerk of the Court of Sugar Loaf County Choctaw Nation, in Book vol "C" Page 81.

Henry J Sexton<br>County Judge, Sugar Loaf County

"Certificate of Record of Marriages"

{ Choctaw Nation }
{ Sugar Loaf County }

I, Robert E. Lee, clerk of the court of Sugar Loaf County, do hereby certify that the License for certificate of the marriage of Mr. Robert L. Onubby and Miss Emma Grilliette was filed in my office the 2 day of December A.D. 1903, and duly recorded in Book vol "C" page 104.
Witness my hand and seal of office this 2 day of December A.D. 1903

Robert E Lee<br>Clerk of Sugar Loaf County

---

## AFFIDAVIT OF ATTENDING PHYSICIAN OR MIDWIFE

UNITED STATES OF AMERICA
INDIAN TERRITORY
  Central        DISTRICT

I,    A. R. Sisk    a    Physician on oath state that I attended on Mrs. Emma Onubby    wife of    Robert L. Onubby on the   7   day of   October  , 190 4, that there was born to her on said date a    Female child, that said child is now living, and is said to have been named    Stella Onubby

## Applications for Enrollment of Choctaw Newborn
### Act of 1905   Volume VIII

                                                            A.R. Sisk          M.D.

Subscribed and sworn to before me this, the    17    day of Feb    190 5

WITNESSETH:                                    Robert E Lee    Notary Public.
Must be two witnesses   { Mack H LeFlore      My Com expires Jan 11-1906
who are citizens        { Wm J Burns

We hereby certify that we are well acquainted with     A R Sisk a    Physician    and know    him    to be reputable and of good standing in the community.

_____                  John Holloway

_____                  Oscar Davis

**NEW-BORN AFFIDAVIT.**

                       Number_____

### ...Choctaw Enrolling Commission...

IN THE MATTER OF THE APPLICATION FOR ENROLLMENT, as a citizen of the Choctaw       Nation, of        Stella Onubby

born on the    7    day of \_\_\_\_October\_\_\_\_ 190 5[sic]

Name of father    Robert L Onubby         a citizen of     Choctaw
Nation final enrollment No.  4748
Name of mother    Emma Onubby          a citizen of _____
Nation final enrollment No..._____

                                                          Postoffice    LeFlore I.T.

### AFFIDAVIT OF MOTHER.

UNITED STATES OF AMERICA
INDIAN TERRITORY
     Central       DISTRICT

          I       Emma Onubby             , on oath state that I am    27      years of age and a citizen by _____ of the_____ Nation, and as such have been placed upon the final roll of the_____Nation, by the Honorable Secretary of the Interior my final enrollment number being_____ ; that I am the lawful wife of    Robert L. Onubby      , who is a citizen of the     Choctaw Nation, and as such has been placed upon the final roll of said Nation by the Honorable Secretary of the Interior, his final enrollment number being    4748    and that a     Female

# Applications for Enrollment of Choctaw Newborn
## Act of 1905   Volume VIII

child was born to me on the   7   day of   October   190 4; that said child has been named Stella Onubby   , and is now living.

Emma Onubby

Witnesseth.
  Must be two  ⎫  Wm J Burns
  Witnesses who ⎬
  are Citizens. ⎭  Mack H LeFlore

Subscribed and sworn to before me this   17   day of   Feb   190 5

W S Harris<br>Notary Public.

My commission expires:   7/8/??

---

Choc New Born 484
      Lela Anderson   b. 5-21-04
      Leo Bennett Anderson   b. 11-26-02

Muskogee, Indian Territory, July 25, 1905.

Chief Clerk,
    Choctaw Land Office,
        Atoka, Indian Territory.

Dear Sir:

    Refer to duplicate Choctaw New Born Roll Card No. 484, in the possession of your office and change the name of the father of the applicant thereon to read, "Houston D. Anderson" instead of "Houston Anderson", and the name of the mother of applicant thereon to read, "Jane A. Moore", instead of "Jane Moore"; and change notation on said card, which now reads:
    "Jane Moore mother of Nos. 1 and 2, is identified as Jane Burns, No. 2, on Choctaw roll card No. 3000", to read:

"Jane Anderson . . . . . . . . . . . . . . ."

Respectfully,

Commissioner.

## Applications for Enrollment of Choctaw Newborn
## Act of 1905   Volume VIII

*(The above letter given again.)*

---

7-3000

Muskogee, Indian Territory, May 1, 1905.

Houston Anderson,
    Summerfield, Indian Territory.

Dear Sir:

    Receipt is hereby acknowledged of the affidavits of Jane Anderson nee Burns and Mertha[sic] Collin[sic] to the birth of Leo Bennett and Lela Anderson, children of Houston and Jane Anderson, November 26, 1902 and May 21, 1904, and the same have been filed with our records as applications for the enrollment of said children.

    Receipt is also acknowledged of the affidavits of Jane Anderson nee Burns and Davis U. Bell to the death of Lela Anderson, daughter of Houston and Jane Anderson, March 26, 1905, and the same have been filed with our records as evidence of the death of said child.

                                   Respectfully,

                                                Chairman.

---

*Substitute*

Muskogee, Indian Territory, July 26, 1905.

Chief Clerk,
    Choctaw Land Office,
        Atoka, Indian Territory.

Dear Sir:

    Refer to duplicate Choctaw New Born Roll Card No. 484, in the possession of your office and change the name of the father of the applicant thereon to read, "Houston D. Anderson instead of "Houston Anderson", and the name of the mother of applicant thereon to read, "Jane Anderson" instead of "Jane Moore"; and change notation on said card, which now reads:

    "Jane Moore, mother of Nos. 1 and 2, is identified as Jane Burns, No. 2, on Choctaw roll card No. 3000."

# Applications for Enrollment of Choctaw Newborn
## Act of 1905 Volume VIII

to read:

"Jane Anderson, mother of Nos. 1 and 2, is identified as Jane Burns, No. 2 on Choctaw roll card No. 3000."

Respectfully,

Commissioner.

---

*(The above letter given again.)*

---

**COPY**                  N. B. 484

Muskogee, Indian Territory, April 8, 1905.

Houston Anderson,
    Summerfield, Indian Territory.

Dear Sir:

There is inclosed you herewith for execution application for the enrollment of your infant children, Leo Bennett Anderson and Lela Anderson, born May 26, 1902 and May 21, 1904, respectively.

In the affidavits heretofore filed by you with the Commission that of the physician or midwife was left blank. Before the Commission can finally dispose of this case, it will be necessary that you secure these affidavits.

In having these affidavits executed care should be exercised to see that all names are written in full, as they appear in the body of the affidavit, and in the event that either of the persons signing the affidavit are unable to write, signatures by mark must be attested by two witnesses. Each affidavit must be executed before a Notary Public and the notarial seal and signature of the officer must be attached to each separate affidavit.

Respectfully,<br>SIGNED<br>T. B. Needles.<br>Commissioner in Charge.

LM 8-19.

## Applications for Enrollment of Choctaw Newborn
## Act of 1905  Volume VIII

**COPY**

Wister, Ind Ter Mar 30, 1905

Chf. Clk. Enrolling Div.
    Com to the Five Civ Tribes
        Muskogee, I. T.                        Dear Sir

    There are enclosed herewith affidavits regarding the birth of Leo Bennett Anderson and Lela Anderson by their mother Jane Moore-nee Burns, Choc. B.B. Roll #8794.

    Houston Anderson the father of aforesaid children if a Choc. By Blood and the divorced husband of Jane Moore-- nee Burns. Jane Moore-- nee Burns, wishes the Commission to send to Melvina Bacon Talihina, I. T. a blank birth proof with instructions for her to appear before a Notary Public to make affidavit as mid-wife in re application for enrollment of Leo Bennett Anderson; also, to send to Levina Anderson, Talihina, I. T. a blank birth proof with above instruction as midwife in re application for Enrollment of Lela Anderson.

    There is also herewith enclosed "Death proof" of aforesaid Lela Anderson pending enrollment.

                    Very Respt.-
                    (Signed) Lacey P. Bobo.
                    Clk. in Charge,
                          Choc. Locating Party.

---

**BIRTH AFFIDAVIT.**

**DEPARTMENT OF THE INTERIOR.**
**COMMISSION TO THE FIVE CIVILIZED TRIBES.**

---

**IN RE APPLICATION FOR ENROLLMENT,** as a citizen of the    Choctaw    Nation, of Leo Bennett Anderson    , born on the 26 day of Nov , 1902

Name of Father: Houston Anderson        a citizen of the Choctaw Nation.
Name of Mother: Jane Anderson, nee Burns    a citizen of the Choctaw Nation.

                        Postoffice    Summerfield I.T.

# Applications for Enrollment of Choctaw Newborn
## Act of 1905 Volume VIII

### AFFIDAVIT OF MOTHER.

UNITED STATES OF AMERICA, Indian Territory, }
Central        DISTRICT. }

I, Jane Anderson nee Burns , on oath state that I am 26 years of age and a citizen by blood , of the Choctaw Nation; that I am the lawful wife of Houston Anderson , who is a citizen, by blood of the Choctaw Nation; that a male child was born to me on 26 day of November , 1902; that said child has been named Leo Bennett Anderson , and was living March 4, 1905.

                                Jane Anderson, nee Burns

Witnesses To Mark:
{

Subscribed and sworn to before me this 25 day of April , 1905

                                Robert E Lee
                                Notary Public.

My com expires Jan 11-1906

---

### AFFIDAVIT OF ATTENDING PHYSICIAN OR MID-WIFE.

UNITED STATES OF AMERICA, Indian Territory, }
Central District       DISTRICT. }

I, Mertha[sic] Collin , a midwife , on oath state that I attended on Mrs. Jane Anderson nee Burns , wife of Houston Anderson on the 26 day of November , 1902; that there was born to her on said date a male child; that said child was living March 4, 1905, and is said to have been named Leo Bennett Anderson
                                her
                        Mertha x Collin
                                mark

Witnesses To Mark:
{ Davis W Bell
{ John Sevier

Subscribed and sworn to before me this 26 day of April , 1905

                                Robert E Lee
                                Notary Public.

My com expires Jan 11-1906

*Find enrollment no of Jane Anderson being No 8794*

## Applications for Enrollment of Choctaw Newborn
## Act of 1905   Volume VIII

BIRTH AFFIDAVIT.

### DEPARTMENT OF THE INTERIOR.
### COMMISSION TO THE FIVE CIVILIZED TRIBES.

**IN RE APPLICATION FOR ENROLLMENT,** as a citizen of the     Choctaw     Nation, of Leo Bennett Anderson    , born on the  26$^{th}$   day of  May[sic]   , 1902

Name of Father:  Houston Anderson         a citizen of the   Choctaw    Nation.
Name of Mother:  Jane Moore, nee Burns    a citizen of the   Choctaw    Nation.

Postoffice     Summerfield I.T.

### AFFIDAVIT OF MOTHER.

UNITED STATES OF AMERICA, Indian Territory,
................................................ DISTRICT.

I,  Jane Moore - nee Burns    , on oath state that I am  26    years of age and a citizen by    blood    , of the   Choctaw    Nation; that I am the lawful wife of Houston Anderson    , who is a citizen, by  blood    of the     Choctaw Nation; that a    male    child was born to me on   26$^{th}$    day of  November   , 1902; that said child has been named    Leo Bennett Anderson  , and was living March 4, 1905.

Jane Moore

Witnesses To Mark:

Subscribed and sworn to before me this  28$^{th}$   day of   March     , 1905

Lacey P Bobo
Notary Public.

BIRTH AFFIDAVIT.

### DEPARTMENT OF THE INTERIOR.
### COMMISSION TO THE FIVE CIVILIZED TRIBES.

**IN RE APPLICATION FOR ENROLLMENT,** as a citizen of the     Choctaw     Nation, of Lela Anderson    , born on the  21$^{st}$   day of  May   , 1904

Name of Father:  Houston Anderson         a citizen of the   Choctaw    Nation.
Name of Mother:  Jane Moore - nee Burns   a citizen of the   Choctaw    Nation.

Postoffice     Summerfield Ind Ter.

# Applications for Enrollment of Choctaw Newborn
## Act of 1905   Volume VIII

### AFFIDAVIT OF MOTHER.

UNITED STATES OF AMERICA, Indian Territory,  
............................................... DISTRICT.

I, Jane Moore - nee Burns, on oath state that I am 26 years of age and a citizen by blood, of the Choctaw Nation; that I am the ~~lawful~~ *divorced* wife of Houston Anderson, who is a citizen, by blood of the Choctaw Nation; that a Female child was born to me on 21$^{st}$ day of May, 1904; that said child has been named Lela Anderson, and was living March 4, 1905.

Jane Moore

Witnesses To Mark:

Subscribed and sworn to before me this 28$^{th}$ day of March, 1905

Lacey P Bobo  
Notary Public.

*Mrs Jane Moore is enrolled as Jane Burns, Choc. B.B. Roll #8794*

---

**BIRTH AFFIDAVIT.**

### DEPARTMENT OF THE INTERIOR.
### COMMISSION TO THE FIVE CIVILIZED TRIBES.

IN RE APPLICATION FOR ENROLLMENT, as a citizen of the Choctaw Nation, of Lela Anderson, born on the 21 day of May, 1904

Name of Father: Houston Anderson    a citizen of the Choctaw Nation.  
Name of Mother: Jane Anderson, nee Burns    a citizen of the Choctaw Nation.

Postoffice   Summerfield I.T.

---

### AFFIDAVIT OF MOTHER.

UNITED STATES OF AMERICA, Indian Territory,  
Central           DISTRICT.

I, Jane Anderson nee Burns, on oath state that I am 26 years of age and a citizen by blood, of the Choctaw Nation; that I am the lawful wife of Houston Anderson, who is a citizen, by blood of the Choctaw Nation; that a female child was born to me on 21 day of May, 1904; that said child has been named Lela Anderson, and was living March 4, 1905.

## Applications for Enrollment of Choctaw Newborn
## Act of 1905   Volume VIII

                                      Jane Anderson, nee Burns

Witnesses To Mark:
{

    Subscribed and sworn to before me this 26 day of   April   , 1905

                                      Robert E Lee

My com expires Jan 11-1906                     Notary Public.

---

**AFFIDAVIT OF ATTENDING PHYSICIAN OR MID-WIFE.**

UNITED STATES OF AMERICA, Indian Territory, }
  Central                      DISTRICT. }

    I, Mertha Collin, a midwife, on oath state that I attended on Mrs. Jane Anderson nee Burns, wife of Houston Anderson on the 21 day of May, 1904; that there was born to her on said date a female child; that said child was living March 4, 1905, and is said to have been named Lela Anderson

                                      her
                              Mertha x Collin

Witnesses To Mark:                   mark
{ Davis W Bell
{ John Sevier

    Subscribed and sworn to before me this 26 day of   April   , 1905

                                    Robert E Lee
                                    Notary Public.

My com expires Jan 11-1906
*Find enrollment no of Jane Anderson being No 8794*

---

Choc New Born 485
    L. B. Bird   b. 6-12-03

## Applications for Enrollment of Choctaw Newborn
## Act of 1905 Volume VIII

7-NB-485.

Muskogee, Indian Territory, May 26, 1905.

Billy Bird,
    Roff, Indian Territory.

Dear Sir:

    There is enclosed you herewith for execution application for the enrollment of your infant child, L. B. Bird.

    In the physician's affidavit of the 26th ultimo, and the mother's affidavit of the 1st instant, the date of the applicant's birth is given as June 12, 1903, while the mother's affidavit of March 27, 1905, gives the date of birth as June 12, 1904. In the enclosed application the date of birth is left blank. Please insert the correct date and when the affidavits are properly executed, return them to this office.

    In having these affidavits executed care should be exercised to see that all names are written in full, as they appear in the body of the affidavit, and in the event that either of the persons signing the affidavit are unable to write, signatures by mark must be attested by two witnesses. Each affidavit must be executed before a Notary Public and the notarial seal and signature of the officer must be attached to each separate affidavit.

Respectfully,

VR 26-7.                                                                  Chairman.

---

N. B. 485

Muskogee, Indian Territory, April 8, 1905.

Billy Bird,
    Roff, Indian Territory.

Dear Sir:

    There is inclosed you herewith for execution application for the enrollment of your infant child, L. B. Bird, born June 12, 1904.

    The application heretofore filed with the Commission is incomplete in that it does not contain the affidavit of the physician or midwife. You will notice from the inclosed application that the affidavit of the one in attendance is also required.

## Applications for Enrollment of Choctaw Newborn
## Act of 1905    Volume VIII

In case there was no one in attendance, it will be necessary that you secure the affidavits of two persons who have actual knowledge of the fact that the child was born, was living on March 4, 1905, and that Edna Bird was his mother.

In having these affidavits executed care should be exercised to see that all names are written in full, as they appear in the body of the affidavit, and in the event that either of the persons signing the affidavit are unable to write, signatures by mark must be attested by two witnesses. Each affidavit must be executed before a Notary Public and the notarial seal and signature of the officer must be attached to each separate affidavit.

                                  Respectfully,
                                  SIGNED
                                *T. B. Needles.*
LM 8-18.                       Commissioner in Charge.

---

                                              7 N.B. 485.

                      Muskogee, Indian Territory, June 5, 1905.

Billy Bird,
    Roff, Indian Territory.

Dear Sir:

Receipt is hereby acknowledged of the affidavits of Edna Bird and G. B. Fondren to the birth of L. B. Bird, son of Billy and Edna Bird, June 12, 1903, and the same have been filed with our records in the matter of the enrollment of said child.

                                Respectfully,

                                         Commissioner in Charge.

---

7-NB-485

                    Muskogee, Indian Territory, August 12, 1905.

Mrs. Edna Bird,
    Roff, Indian Territory.

Dear Madam:

Receipt is hereby acknowledged of your letter of August 3, 1905, addressed to Jeff Ward which has been referred to this office for reply. Therein you ask to be advised when the enrollment of your child L. B. Bird is approved.

## Applications for Enrollment of Choctaw Newborn
## Act of 1905   Volume VIII

In reply to your letter you are advised that the name of your child L. B. Bird has been placed upon a schedule of citizens by blood of the Choctaw Nation which has been forwarded the Secretary of the Interior and you will be notified when his enrollment is approved by the Department.

Respectfully,

Acting Commissioner.

**BIRTH AFFIDAVIT.**

### DEPARTMENT OF THE INTERIOR.
## COMMISSION TO THE FIVE CIVILIZED TRIBES.

**IN RE APPLICATION FOR ENROLLMENT,** as a citizen of the Choctaw Nation, of L. B. Bird, born on the 12th day of June, 1903.

Name of Father: Billy Bird     a citizen of the Choctaw Nation.
Name of Mother: Edna Bird     a citizen of the Choctaw Nation.

Postoffice   Roff Ind. Ter

### AFFIDAVIT OF MOTHER.

UNITED STATES OF AMERICA, Indian Territory, }
Southern      DISTRICT. }

I, Edna Bird, on oath state that I am 20 years of age and a citizen by intermarriage, of the Choctaw Nation; that I am the lawful wife of Billy Bird, who is a citizen, by blood of the Choctaw Nation; that a male child was born to me on 12th day of June, 1903; that said child has been named L. B. Bird, and was living March 4, 1905.

Edna Bird

Witnesses To Mark:
{

Subscribed and sworn to before me this 1st day of May, 1905.

H.C. Miller
Notary Public.

## Applications for Enrollment of Choctaw Newborn
## Act of 1905 Volume VIII

**BIRTH AFFIDAVIT.**

### DEPARTMENT OF THE INTERIOR.
### COMMISSION TO THE FIVE CIVILIZED TRIBES.

IN RE APPLICATION FOR ENROLLMENT, as a citizen of the Choctaw Nation, of L. B. Bird, born on the 12 day of June, 1903

Name of Father: Billie Bird        a citizen of the Choctaw Nation.

Name of Mother: Edna Bird       a citizen of the *non* ............ Nation.

Postoffice    Roff, I.T.

**AFFIDAVIT OF MOTHER.**

UNITED STATES OF AMERICA, Indian Territory, } ............ DISTRICT.

I, Edna Bird, on oath state that I am ....... years of age and a citizen by ............, *non* of the ............ Nation; that I am the lawful wife of Billie Bird, who is a citizen, by blood of the Choctaw Nation; that a male child was born to me on 12 day of June, 1903; that said child has been named L. B. Bird, and was living March 4, 1905.

Witnesses To Mark:
{ ............
  ............ }

Subscribed and sworn to before me this ....... day of ............, 1905.

............
                                                              Notary Public.

**AFFIDAVIT OF ATTENDING PHYSICIAN OR MID-WIFE.**

UNITED STATES OF AMERICA, Indian Territory, }
    Southern                DISTRICT.

I, G.B. Fondren, a Physician, on oath state that I attended on Mrs. Edna Bird, wife of Billie Bird on the 12 day of June, 1903; that there was born to her on said date a male child; that said child was living March 4, 1905, and is said to have been named L. B. Bird

                                   G. B. Fondren

# Applications for Enrollment of Choctaw Newborn
## Act of 1905   Volume VIII

Witnesses To Mark:

{

    Subscribed and sworn to before me this  26  day of   April   , 1905

                              H.G. Rowley
                                Notary Public.

My com. expires Mch. 9-1909

---

**BIRTH AFFIDAVIT.**

## DEPARTMENT OF THE INTERIOR.
## COMMISSION TO THE FIVE CIVILIZED TRIBES.

---

    IN RE APPLICATION FOR ENROLLMENT, as a citizen of the    CHOCTAW    Nation, of   L. B. Bird   , born on the  12   day of  June  , 1904

Name of Father: Billy Bird          a citizen of the   CHOCTAW    Nation.
Name of Mother: Edna Bird         a citizen of the   CHOCTAW    Nation.

                        Postoffice    Roff, I.T.

---

### AFFIDAVIT OF MOTHER.

UNITED STATES OF AMERICA, Indian Territory, }
    Southern                       DISTRICT. }

    I,   Edna Bird   , on oath state that I am  20  years of age and a citizen by intermarriage  , of the   CHOCTAW   Nation; that I am the lawful wife of  Billy Bird  , who is a citizen, by blood   of the   CHOCTAW   Nation; that a   male   child was born to me on  12th   day of  June   , 1904; that said child has been named   L. B. Bird   , and was living March 4, 1905.

                              Edna Bird

Witnesses To Mark:

{

    Subscribed and sworn to before me this  27$^{th}$  day of   March   , 1905

                                H.C. Miller
                                Notary Public.

## Applications for Enrollment of Choctaw Newborn
## Act of 1905   Volume VIII

BIRTH AFFIDAVIT.

### DEPARTMENT OF THE INTERIOR.
### COMMISSION TO THE FIVE CIVILIZED TRIBES.

IN RE APPLICATION FOR ENROLLMENT, as a citizen of the Choctaw Nation, of L. B. Bird, born on the 12$^{th}$ day of June, 1903

Name of Father: Billy Bird     a citizen of the Choctaw Nation.
Name of Mother: Edna Bird     a citizen of the Choctaw Nation.

Postoffice   Roff Ind. Ter

**AFFIDAVIT OF MOTHER.**

UNITED STATES OF AMERICA, Indian Territory,
Central     DISTRICT.

I, Edna Bird, on oath state that I am 20 years of age and a citizen by intermarriage, of the Choctaw Nation; that I am the lawful wife of Billy Bird, who is a citizen, by blood of the Choctaw Nation; that a male child was born to me on 12$^{th}$ day of June, 1903; that said child has been named L. B. Bird, and was living March 4, 1905.

                                          Edna Bird

Witnesses To Mark:
{

Subscribed and sworn to before me this 1$^{st}$ day of June, 1905

My commission expires        Andrew J Turner
Mar-17-1909                       Notary Public.

**AFFIDAVIT OF ATTENDING PHYSICIAN OR MID-WIFE.**

UNITED STATES OF AMERICA, Indian Territory,
Central     DISTRICT.

I, G.B. Fondren, a Physician, on oath state that I attended on Mrs. Edna Bird, wife of Billie Bird on the 12$^{th}$ day of June, 1903; that there was born to her on said date a male child; that said child was living March 4, 1905, and is said to have been named L. B. Bird

                                  G. B. Fondren M.D.

Witnesses To Mark:
{

## Applications for Enrollment of Choctaw Newborn
## Act of 1905   Volume VIII

Subscribed and sworn to before me this  1ˢᵗ  day of   June    , 1905

Andrew J Turner<br>Notary Public.

---

Choc New Born 486
      Leola Lynn   b. 2-24-05

7-243

Muskogee, Indian Territory, March 27, 1905.

J. Y. Lynn,
    Oakland, Indian Territory.

Dear Sir:

    Receipt is hereby acknowledged of the affidavits of Alice L. Lynn and T. A. Laylock to the birth of Leola Lynn daughter of J. Y. and Alice L. Lynn, February 24, 1905, and the same have been filed with our records as an application for the enrollment of said child.

                Respectfully,

                              Chairman.

---

**COPY**.

N.B. 486

Muskogee, Indian Territory, April 3, 1905.

J. Y. Lynn,
    Oakland, Indian Territory.

Dear Sir:

    There is inclosed you herewith for execution application for the enrollment of your infant child, Leola Lynn, born February 24, 1905.

    In the affidavits heretofore filed with the Commission the name of the mother appeared as Alice L. Lynn. In the inclosed application it is Elsie L. Lynn as it appears on the approved Choctaw roll.

## Applications for Enrollment of Choctaw Newborn
## Act of 1905 Volume VIII

In having these affidavits executed care should be exercised to see that all names are written in full, as they appear in the body of the affidavit, and in the event that either of the persons signing the affidavit are unable to write, signatures by mark must be attested by two witnesses. Each affidavit must be executed before a Notary Public and the notarial seal and signature of the officer must be attached to each separate affidavit.

Respectfully,

LM 3-4

~~GENOIS~~ Tams Bixby
Chairman.

---

**COPY**

7-N B 486

Muskogee, Indian Territory, April 12, 1905.

J. Y. Lynn,
    Oakland, Indian Territory.

Dear Sir:

Receipt is hereby acknowledged of the affidavits of Elsie L. Lynn and Thomas A. Blaylock to the birth of Leola Lynn, daughter of J. Y. and Elsie L. Lynn, February 24, 1905, and the same have been filed with our records as an application for the enrollment of said child.

Respectfully,
SIGNED    *T. B. Needles.*
Commissioner in Charge.

---

**BIRTH AFFIDAVIT.**

**DEPARTMENT OF THE INTERIOR.**
**COMMISSION TO THE FIVE CIVILIZED TRIBES.**

---

**IN RE APPLICATION FOR ENROLLMENT**, as a citizen of the Choctaw Nation, of Leola Lynn, born on the 24 day of Feb, 1905

*by intermarriage*

Name of Father: J. Y. Lynn      a citizen of the Choctaw Nation.
Name of Mother: Alcie L. Lynn      a citizen of the Choctaw Nation.

Postoffice    Oakland Ind. Ter.

# Applications for Enrollment of Choctaw Newborn
## Act of 1905   Volume VIII

**AFFIDAVIT OF MOTHER.**

UNITED STATES OF AMERICA, Indian Territory,　}
　Southern　　　　　　DISTRICT.

    I,　Alcie L. Lynn　, on oath state that I am　23　years of age and a citizen by blood　, of the　Choctaw　Nation; that I am the lawful wife of　J. Y. Lynn　, who is a citizen, by intermarriage　of the　Choctaw　Nation; that a　female　child was born to me on　24　day of　February　, 1905; that said child has been named　Leola Lynn　, and was living March 4, 1905.

                                    Alcie L. Lynn

Witnesses To Mark:
{ *(Name Illegible)*
  Viola Hipp

    Subscribed and sworn to before me this　20　day of　March　, 1905

                                    F.E. Kennemer
                                    Notary Public.

---

**AFFIDAVIT OF ATTENDING PHYSICIAN OR MID-WIFE.**

UNITED STATES OF AMERICA, Indian Territory,　}
　Southern　　　　　　DISTRICT.

    I,　T.A. Blaylock　, a　Physician　, on oath state that I attended on Mrs.　Alcie L. Lynn　, wife of　J. Y. Lynn　on the　24　day of　Feb　, 1905; that there was born to her on said date a　female　child; that said child was living March 4, 1905, and is said to have been named Leola Lynn

                                  T.A. Blaylock M.D.

Witnesses To Mark:
{ *(Name Illegible)*
  J.S. Welch

    Subscribed and sworn to before me this　20　day of　March　, 1905

                                    F.E. Kennemer
                                    Notary Public.

## Applications for Enrollment of Choctaw Newborn
## Act of 1905   Volume VIII

BIRTH AFFIDAVIT.

### DEPARTMENT OF THE INTERIOR.
### COMMISSION TO THE FIVE CIVILIZED TRIBES.

IN RE APPLICATION FOR ENROLLMENT, as a citizen of the Choctaw Nation, of Leola Lynn, born on the 24 day of February, 1905

Name of Father: J. Y. Lynn           a citizen of the Choctaw Nation.
Name of Mother: Elsie L. Lynn    a citizen of the Choctaw Nation.

Postoffice   Oakland Ind. Ter.

### AFFIDAVIT OF MOTHER.

UNITED STATES OF AMERICA, Indian Territory, }
........................................................ DISTRICT.

I, Elsie L. Lynn, on oath state that I am 23 years of age and a citizen by Blood, of the Choctaw Nation; that I am the lawful wife of J. Y. Lynn, who is a citizen, by Intermarriage of the Choctaw Nation; that a female child was born to me on 24 day of February, 1905; that said child has been named Leola Lynn, and was living March 4, 1905.

Elsie L. Lynn

Witnesses To Mark:
{ F.S. Hyso
{ J H Lynn

Subscribed and sworn to before me this 10 day of March, 1905

F.E. Kennemer
Notary Public.

### AFFIDAVIT OF ATTENDING PHYSICIAN OR MID-WIFE.

UNITED STATES OF AMERICA, Indian Territory, }
Southern                          DISTRICT.

I, Thos. A. Blaylock, a Physician, on oath state that I attended on Mrs. Elsie L. Lynn, wife of J. Y. Lynn on the 24 day of February, 1905; that there was born to her on said date a female child; that said child was living March 4, 1905, and is said to have been named Leola Lynn

Thos. A. Blaylock M.D.

## Applications for Enrollment of Choctaw Newborn
## Act of 1905   Volume VIII

Witnesses To Mark:

{

Subscribed and sworn to before me this 7$^{th}$ day of April , 1905

Geo E Rider<br>
Notary Public.

---

Choc New Born 487
  Mary Elizabeth Smith  b. 9-24-03

Choctaw 4513.

Muskogee, Indian Territory, March 31, 1905.

Hill T. Smith,
  Canadian, Indian Territory.

Dear Sir:

   Receipt is hereby acknowledged of the affidavits of Pearl Smith and J. A. Adams to the birth of Elizabeth Smith, daughter of Hill T. and Pearl Smith, September 24, 1903, and the same have been filed with our records as an application for the enrollment of said child.

   Receipt is also acknowledged of the marriage license and certificate between Hill T. Smith and Miss Pearl Brooks, of November 2, 1902, which have been filed with said affidavits.

Respectfully,

Chairman.

---

## AFFIDAVIT OF ATTENDING PHYSICIAN OR MIDWIFE

UNITED STATES OF AMERICA
INDIAN TERRITORY
  Western        DISTRICT

   I,   J A Adams    a        Physician
on oath state that I attended on Mrs.  Pearl Smith   wife of   Hill T. Smith
on the   24$^{th}$    day of September    , 190 3 , that there was born to her on said date a

## Applications for Enrollment of Choctaw Newborn
## Act of 1905  Volume VIII

female child, that said child is now living, and is said to have been named Mary Elizabeth Smith

               J A Adams      M.D.

     Subscribed and sworn to before me this, the    17      day of Feby     190 5

WITNESSETH:           Milton Heistein     Notary Public.

Must be two witnesses who are citizens { F.R. Smith

       Robt F Turner

    We hereby certify that we are well acquainted with    J A Adams   a physician    and know   him    to be reputable and of good standing in the community.

    F.R. Smith             _____

    Robt F Turner           _____

           _____

### NEW-BORN AFFIDAVIT.

       Number..................

### ...Choctaw Enrolling Commission...

        _____

    IN THE MATTER OF THE APPLICATION FOR ENROLLMENT, as a citizen of the Choctaw     Nation, of     Mary Elizabeth Smith

born on the 24   day of ___September___ 190 3

Name of father    Hill T Smith        a citizen of    Choctaw
Nation final enrollment No.   12514
Name of mother   Pearl Smith         a citizen of    Choctaw
Nation final enrollment No. ―

              Postoffice    Canadian I.T.

### AFFIDAVIT OF MOTHER.

UNITED STATES OF AMERICA
INDIAN TERRITORY
............................. DISTRICT

     I     Pearl Smith           , on oath state that I am 20    years of age and a citizen by blood   of the   U.S.      Nation, and as such have been placed upon the final roll of the ―   Nation, by the Honorable Secretary of the Interior my final enrollment number being ― ; that I am the lawful wife of Hill T.

## Applications for Enrollment of Choctaw Newborn
## Act of 1905   Volume VIII

Smith          , who is a citizen of the    Choctaw         Nation, and as such has been placed upon the final roll of said Nation by the Honorable Secretary of the Interior, his final enrollment number being    12514    and that a    Girl    child was born to me on the    24   day of    September    190 3; that said child has been named    Mary Elizabeth Smith    , and is now living.

Pearl Smith

Witnesseth.
  Must be two ⎫ F.R. Smith
  Witnesses who ⎬
  are Citizens. ⎭ Robt F Turner

    Subscribed and sworn to before me this    17$^{th}$    day of    Feb    190 5

Milton Heistein<br>Notary Public.

My commission expires:
    Jany 27$^{th}$ 1909

**Applications for Enrollment of Choctaw Newborn
Act of 1905   Volume VIII**

No. 1590

## Certificate of Record of Marriages.

UNITED STATES OF AMERICA,
INDIAN TERRITORY,       SCT:
Central        DISTRICT.

I,      E.J. Fannin      , Clerk of the United States Court in the Indian Territory and District aforesaid, do hereby CERTIFY, that the License for and Certificate of the Marriage of

Mr.   Hill F[sic] Smith      and

Miss Pearl Brooks      was

filed in my office in said Territory and District the 8" day of November A.D., 190 2 and duly recorded in Book 2 of Marriage Record, Page 177

WITNESS my hand and seal of said Court, at *(Illegible)* , this 8th day of November , A.D. 190 2

E. J. Fannin
*Clerk.*
By   T F Varner   *Deputy.*

MAR 29 1905

DEPARTMENT OF THE INTERIOR,
Commission to the Five Civilized Tribes.
**FILED**

APR 1 1905

*Tm Bly* CHAIRMAN.

Applications for Enrollment of Choctaw Newborn
Act of 1905   Volume VIII

No. 1590                       FORM NO. 598

# MARRIAGE LICENSE.

UNITES STATES OF AMERICA,  
   THE INDIAN TERRITORY,  } ss:  
   Central          DISTRICT.

To any Person Authorized by Law to Solemnize Marriage—Greeting:

*You are hereby commanded to solemnize the Rite and publish the* Banns of Matrimony *between Mr.*   Hill F.[sic] Smith   *of*   Canadian   in the Indian Territory, aged   26   years, and *M* iss Pearl Brooks   *of*   Cowlington   in the Indian Territory, aged   17   years, *according to law, and do you officially sign and return this License to the parties therein named.*

WITNESS my hand and official seal, this   29   day of   October   A. D. 190 2

                       E.J. Fannin  
                       *Clerk of the United States Court.*

By T.T. Varner  
      Deputy

---

## CERTIFICATE OF MARRIAGE.

UNITES STATES OF AMERICA,  
   THE INDIAN TERRITORY,  } ss:        I,        *(Name Illegible)*  
   Central          DISTRICT.        a    Minister of the Gospel

do hereby CERTIFY, that on the   25   day of   November   A, D. 190 2; I did duly and according to law, as commanded in the foregoing License, solemnize the Rite and publish the BANNS OF MATRIMONY between the parties therein named.

Witness my hand this   25   day of   November   , A. D. 190 2

My credentials are recorded in the office of the Clerk of the United States Court in the Indian Territory, Central District, Book   A   Page   159

                    *(Name Illegible)*

                    a   Minister of the Gospel

# Applications for Enrollment of Choctaw Newborn
## Act of 1905   Volume VIII

NOTE. -The License and Certificate of Marriage must be returned to the Office of the Clerk of the United States Court of the Indian Territory, from whence it was issued, within sixty days from the date thereof, or the party to whom the License was issued will be liable in the amount of One Hundred Dollars ($100.00).

**BIRTH AFFIDAVIT.**

## DEPARTMENT OF THE INTERIOR.
## COMMISSION TO THE FIVE CIVILIZED TRIBES.

IN RE APPLICATION FOR ENROLLMENT, as a citizen of the   Choctaw   Nation, of Mary Elizabeth Smith   , born on the   $24^{th}$   day of   Sept   , 1903

Name of Father: Hill T Smith            a citizen of the   Choctaw   Nation.
Name of Mother: Pearl Smith           a citizen of the   U.S.   Nation.

Postoffice   Canadian I.T.

**AFFIDAVIT OF MOTHER.**

UNITED STATES OF AMERICA, Indian Territory,
   Western                DISTRICT.

I,   Pearl Smith   , on oath state that I am   20   years of age and a citizen by marriage of the   Choctaw   Nation; that I am the lawful wife of   Hill T Smith   , who is a citizen, by blood   of the   Choctaw   Nation; that a   female   child was born to me on   24th   day of   September   , 1903; that said child has been named Mary Elizabeth Smith   , and was living March 4, 1905.

                                        Pearl Smith
Witnesses To Mark:

Subscribed and sworn to before me this 27th   day of   March   , 1905

                        Milton Heistein
                            Notary Public.

**AFFIDAVIT OF ATTENDING PHYSICIAN OR MID-WIFE.**

UNITED STATES OF AMERICA, Indian Territory,
   Western                DISTRICT.

I,   J A Adams        , a   Physician   , on oath state that I attended on Mrs.   Pearl Smith   , wife of   Hill T Smith   on the 24th day of Sept   , 1903; that there was born to her on said date a   girl   child; that said child was living March 4, 1905, and is said to have been named Mary Elizabeth Smith

# Applications for Enrollment of Choctaw Newborn
## Act of 1905   Volume VIII

J.A. Adams, M.D.

Witnesses To Mark:

{ Subscribed and sworn to before me this 27th day of March , 1905

Milton Heistein
Notary Public.

---

Choc New Born 488
    Jennings Bryan Le Flore   b. 12-22-02
    Ann Ruth Le Flore   b. 11-1-04

7-5449

Muskogee, Indian Territory, April 1, 1905.

W. W. Leflore,
    Jackson, Indian Territory.

Dear Sir:

    Receipt is hereby acknowledged of the affidavits of Daisy LeFlore and J. W. Phillips to the birth of Jennings Bryan LeFlore and Anna Ruth LeFlore, children of William W. and Daisy LeFlore, December 22, 1902, and November 1, 1904, and the same have been filed with our records as an application for the enrollment of said children.

Respectfully,

Chairman.

---

**BIRTH AFFIDAVIT.**

**DEPARTMENT OF THE INTERIOR.**
**COMMISSION TO THE FIVE CIVILIZED TRIBES.**

IN RE APPLICATION FOR ENROLLMENT, as a citizen of the   Choctaw   Nation, of Jennings Bryan LeFlore   , born on the 22 day of December , 1902

Name of Father: William W. LeFlore      a citizen of the   Choctaw   Nation.
Name of Mother: Daisy LeFlore      a citizen of the   Choctaw   Nation.

## Applications for Enrollment of Choctaw Newborn
## Act of 1905  Volume VIII

Postoffice    Jackson, Ind. Ter.

---

### AFFIDAVIT OF MOTHER.

UNITED STATES OF AMERICA, Indian Territory, }
Central                                  DISTRICT. }

I, Daisy LeFlore, on oath state that I am 24 years of age and a citizen by Intermarriage, of the Choctaw Nation; that I am the lawful wife of William W. LeFlore, who is a citizen, by Blood of the Choctaw Nation; that a male child was born to me on 22 day of December, 1902; that said child has been named Jennings Bryan LeFlore, and was living March 4, 1905.

Daisy LeFlore

Witnesses To Mark:
{

Subscribed and sworn to before me this 25 day of March, 1905

G W Adair
Notary Public.

---

### AFFIDAVIT OF ATTENDING PHYSICIAN OR MID-WIFE.

UNITED STATES OF AMERICA, Indian Territory, }
Central                                  DISTRICT. }

I, J. W. Phillips, a Physician, on oath state that I attended on Mrs. Daisy LeFlore, wife of William W LeFlore on the $22^{nd}$ day of December, 1902; that there was born to her on said date a male child; that said child was living March 4, 1905, and is said to have been named Jennings Bryan LeFlore

J.W. Phillips, M.D.

Witnesses To Mark:
{

Subscribed and sworn to before me this 27 day of March, 1905

G W Adair
Notary Public.

# Applications for Enrollment of Choctaw Newborn
## Act of 1905   Volume VIII

**BIRTH AFFIDAVIT.**

### DEPARTMENT OF THE INTERIOR.
### COMMISSION TO THE FIVE CIVILIZED TRIBES.

IN RE APPLICATION FOR ENROLLMENT, as a citizen of the Choctaw Nation, of Anna Ruth LeFlore, born on the 1st day of November, 1904

Name of Father: William W. LeFlore    a citizen of the Choctaw Nation.
Name of Mother: Daisy LeFlore    a citizen of the Choctaw Nation.

Postoffice    Jackson, Ind. Ter.

### AFFIDAVIT OF MOTHER.

UNITED STATES OF AMERICA, Indian Territory,
   Central    DISTRICT.

I, Daisy LeFlore, on oath state that I am 24 years of age and a citizen by Intermarriage, of the Choctaw Nation; that I am the lawful wife of William W. LeFlore, who is a citizen, by Blood of the Choctaw Nation; that a Female child was born to me on 1st day of November, 1904; that said child has been named Anna Ruth LeFlore, and was living March 4, 1905.

                 Daisy LeFlore

Witnesses To Mark:

Subscribed and sworn to before me this 25 day of March, 1905

                 G W Adair
                       Notary Public.

### AFFIDAVIT OF ATTENDING PHYSICIAN OR MID-WIFE.

UNITED STATES OF AMERICA, Indian Territory,
   Central    DISTRICT.

I, J. W. Phillips, a Physician, on oath state that I attended on Mrs. Daisy LeFlore, wife of William W LeFlore on the 1st 22nd day of November, 1904; that there was born to her on said date a Female child; that said child was living March 4, 1905, and is said to have been named Anna Ruth LeFlore

                 J.W. Phillips, M.D.

Witnesses To Mark:

## Applications for Enrollment of Choctaw Newborn
## Act of 1905  Volume VIII

Subscribed and sworn to before me this  27  day of  March  , 1905

G W Adair
Notary Public.

---

Choc New Born 489
  Ruby Hellen[sic] Rabon  b. 9-1-03
  Otowa Thomas Rabon  b. 2-12-05

7-3129

Muskogee, Indian Territory, April 1, 1905.

James W. Rabon,
  Kinta, Indian Territory.

Dear Sir:

   Receipt is hereby acknowledged of the affidavits of Judith M. E. Rabon and Martha J. Edmonds to the birth of Otowa Thomas and Ruby Hellen[sic] Rabon, children of James W. and Judith M. E. Rabon, February 12, 1905, and September 1, 1903, and the same have been filed with our records as an application for the enrollment of said child.

Respectfully,

Chairman.

---

## AFFIDAVIT OF ATTENDING PHYSICIAN OR MIDWIFE

UNITED STATES OF AMERICA
INDIAN TERRITORY
  Western    DISTRICT

   I,  Martha Edmonds      a    midwife
on oath state that I attended on Mrs.  Judith M E Rabon   wife of   James W. Rabon
on the  1st  day of  September  , 190 3, that there was born to her on said date a  female child, that said child is now living, and is said to have been named   Ruby Helen Rabon

Martha J Edmonds

# Applications for Enrollment of Choctaw Newborn
## Act of 1905 Volume VIII

Subscribed and sworn to before me this, the 6 day of January 190 5

L D Allen Notary Public.

WITNESSETH:
Must be two witnesses who are citizens
{ Rufus Rabon
  D M Moore

We hereby certify that we are well acquainted with Martha Edmonds a midwife and know her to be reputable and of good standing in the community.

Rufus Rabon  _____

DM Moore  _____

**BIRTH AFFIDAVIT.**

## DEPARTMENT OF THE INTERIOR.
## COMMISSION TO THE FIVE CIVILIZED TRIBES.

IN RE APPLICATION FOR ENROLLMENT, as a citizen of the Choctaw Nation, of Otowa Thomas Rabon , born on the 12$^{th}$ day of February , 1905

Name of Father: James W Rabon    a citizen of the Choctaw Nation.
Name of Mother: Judith M.E. Rabon    a citizen of the Choctaw Nation.

Postoffice Kinta I.T.

**AFFIDAVIT OF MOTHER.**

UNITED STATES OF AMERICA, Indian Territory, } 
Western          DISTRICT.

I, Judith M.E. Rabon , on oath state that I am 25 years of age and a citizen by blood , of the Choctaw Nation; that I am the lawful wife of James W Rabon , who is a citizen, by Intermarriage of the Choctaw Nation; that a Male child was born to me on 12$^{th}$ day of February , 1905; that said child has been named Otowa Thomas Rabon , and was living March 4, 1905.

Judith M.E. Rabon

Witnesses To Mark:
{

## Applications for Enrollment of Choctaw Newborn
## Act of 1905   Volume VIII

Subscribed and sworn to before me this  27   day of   March       , 1905

                                      L D Allen
                                            Notary Public.

---

### AFFIDAVIT OF ATTENDING PHYSICIAN OR MID-WIFE.

UNITED STATES OF AMERICA, Indian Territory, }
    Western                  DISTRICT. }

I,   Martha J Edmonds   , a   Midwife   , on oath state that I attended on Mrs.   Judith M.E. Rabon   , wife of   James W Rabon   on the 12$^{th}$   day of   February   , 1905; that there was born to her on said date a ............... child; that said child was living March 4, 1905, and is said to have been named Otowa Thomas Rabon

                                      Martha J Edmonds

Witnesses To Mark:
{

Subscribed and sworn to before me this  27   day of   March       , 1905

                                      L D Allen
                                            Notary Public.

---

BIRTH AFFIDAVIT.
### DEPARTMENT OF THE INTERIOR.
### COMMISSION TO THE FIVE CIVILIZED TRIBES.

---

**IN RE APPLICATION FOR ENROLLMENT,** as a citizen of the   Choctaw   Nation, of Ruby Hellen[sic] Rabon   , born on the  1$^{st}$   day of   September  , 1903

Name of Father:  James W Rabon        a citizen of the   Choctaw   Nation.
Name of Mother:  Judith M.E. Rabon     a citizen of the   Choctaw   Nation.

                            Postoffice    Kinta I.T.

---

### AFFIDAVIT OF MOTHER.

UNITED STATES OF AMERICA, Indian Territory, }
    Western                  DISTRICT. }

I,   Judith M.E. Rabon   , on oath state that I am  25   years of age and a citizen by   blood   , of the   Choctaw   Nation; that I am the lawful wife of James W Rabon   , who is a citizen, by   Intermarriage   of the   Choctaw

# Applications for Enrollment of Choctaw Newborn
## Act of 1905   Volume VIII

Nation; that a   Female   child was born to me on   1st   day of   September  , 1903; that said child has been named   Ruby Hellen Rabon  , and was living March 4, 1905.

Judith M.E. Rabon

Witnesses To Mark:
{

Subscribed and sworn to before me this   27   day of   March   , 1905

L D Allen<br>Notary Public.

---

**AFFIDAVIT OF ATTENDING PHYSICIAN OR MID-WIFE.**

UNITED STATES OF AMERICA, Indian Territory, }
Western                DISTRICT.  }

I,   Martha J Edmonds  , a   Midwife  , on oath state that I attended on Mrs.   Judith M.E. Rabon  , wife of   James W Rabon   on the   1st   day of September  , 1903; that there was born to her on said date a   Female   child; that said child was living March 4, 1905, and is said to have been named Ruby Hellen Rabon

Martha J Edmonds

Witnesses To Mark:
{

Subscribed and sworn to before me this   27   day of   March   , 1905

L D Allen<br>Notary Public.

---

**NEW-BORN AFFIDAVIT.**

Number................

## ...Choctaw Enrolling Commission...

---

IN THE MATTER OF THE APPLICATION FOR ENROLLMENT, as a citizen of the Choctaw   Nation, of     Ruby Helen Rabon

born on the   1st   day of   September     190 3

Name of father   James W Rabon     a citizen of   Choctaw   Nation final enrollment No.   289

## Applications for Enrollment of Choctaw Newborn
## Act of 1905   Volume VIII

Name of mother    Judith M E Rabon          a citizen of      Choctaw
Nation final enrollment No. 9079

Postoffice     Kinta IT

**AFFIDAVIT OF MOTHER.**

UNITED STATES OF AMERICA
INDIAN TERRITORY
Western          DISTRICT

I       Judith ME Rabon              , on oath state that I am 24      years of age and a citizen by   blood    of the    Choctaw          Nation, and as such have been placed upon the final roll of the     Choctaw   Nation, by the Honorable Secretary of the Interior my final enrollment number being    9079  ; that I am the lawful wife of    James W Rabon    , who is a citizen of the    Choctaw       Nation, and as such has been placed upon the final roll of said Nation by the Honorable Secretary of the Interior, his final enrollment number being     289    and that a    female    child was born to me on the 1st    day of    September     190 3; that said child has been named   Ruby Helen Rabon    , and is now living.

J. Mary E Rabon

Witnesseth.
Must be two
Witnesses who     Rufus Rabon
are Citizens.     *(Name Illegible)*

Subscribed and sworn to before me this  6   day of   Jan     190 5

L D Allen
Notary Public.

My commission expires:  Feby 27 1907

---

Choc New Born 490
        George Mayo   b.  7-15-03

# Applications for Enrollment of Choctaw Newborn
## Act of 1905   Volume VIII

7-3978

Muskogee, Indian Territory, April 1, 1905.

J. B. Mayo,
   Olney, Indian Territory.

Dear Sir:

   Receipt is hereby acknowledged of the affidavits of Tabitha A. Mayo and Ola Glenn to the birth of George Mayo son of John B. and Tabitha Mayo, July 15, 1903, and the same have been filed with our records as an application for the enrollment of said child.

   You will be advised if further evidence is necessary in the matter of the enrollment of your child.

Respectfully,

Chairman.

## *Affidavit of Attending Physician or Midwife*

UNITED STATES OF AMERICA,
INDIAN TERRITORY,
................................ DISTRICT

   I,   Newton J Smith   a   Practicing Physician on oath state that I attended on Mrs. Tabitha A Mayo   wife of   John B Mayo on the  15$^{th}$   day of   July , 190 3, that there was born to her on said date a   living Boy child, that said child is now living, and is said to have been named   George

Newton J Smith     M. D.

Subscribed and sworn to before me this the   27   day of   February   1905

D.G. Stanford
Notary Public.
Jones County Texas

WITNESSETH:
   Must be two witnesses who are citizens and know the child.
   *(Name Illegible)*
   Pinkie Hearrell

   We hereby certify that we are well acquainted with   Newton J Smith   a   Practicing Physician   and know   him   to be reputable and of good standing in the community.

Applications for Enrollment of Choctaw Newborn
Act of 1905 Volume VIII

Must be two citizen witnesses. { *(Name Illegible)* Pinkie Hearrell

# NEW BORN AFFIDAVIT

No ............

## CHOCTAW ENROLLING COMMISSION

IN THE MATTER OF THE APPLICATION FOR ENROLLMENT as a citizen of the Choctaw Nation, of George Mayo born on the 15th day of July 1903.

Name of father John B Mayo   a citizen of   Choctaw   Nation, final enrollment No. 372
Name of mother Tabitha A Mayo   a citizen of   Choctaw   Nation, final enrollment No. 11133

Olney I.T.   Postoffice.

**AFFIDAVIT OF MOTHER**

UNITED STATES OF AMERICA
INDIAN TERRITORY
DISTRICT   Central

I   Tabitha A Mayo   , on oath state that I am   35   years of age and a citizen by   Blood   of the   Choctaw   Nation, and as such have been placed upon the final roll of the   Choctaw   Nation, by the Honorable Secretary of the Interior my final enrollment number being   11133   ; that I am the lawful wife of   John B Mayo   , who is a citizen of the   Choctaw   Nation, and as such has been placed upon the final roll of said Nation by the Honorable Secretary of the Interior, his final enrollment number being   372   and that a   mail[sic]   child was born to me on the   15   day of July 1903; that said child has been named   George Mayo   , and is now living.

WITNESSETH:
Must be two witnesses who are citizens { *(Name Illegible)* Pinkie Hearrell

Tabitha + A Mayo
her   mark

Subscribed and sworn to before me this, the   2   day of   Mar   , 1905

W A Austin
Notary Public.

My Commission Expires: Mar 2 1908

# Applications for Enrollment of Choctaw Newborn
## Act of 1905   Volume VIII

**BIRTH AFFIDAVIT.**

### DEPARTMENT OF THE INTERIOR.
### COMMISSION TO THE FIVE CIVILIZED TRIBES.

IN RE APPLICATION FOR ENROLLMENT, as a citizen of the ........................... Nation, of George Mayo, born on the 15 day of July, 1903

Name of Father: John B Mayo    a citizen of the   Choctaw   Nation.
Name of Mother: Tabitha A Mayo    a citizen of the   Choctaw   Nation.

Postoffice   Olney I.T.

### AFFIDAVIT OF MOTHER.

UNITED STATES OF AMERICA, Indian Territory, }
Central        DISTRICT.

I, Tabitha A Mayo, on oath state that I am Thirty five years of age and a citizen by Blood, of the Choctaw Nation; that I am the lawful wife of John B Mayo, who is a citizen, by intermarriage of the Choctaw Nation; that a male child was born to me on 15th day of July, 1903; that said child has been named George Mayo, and was living March 4, 1905.

                                   her
                        Tabitha A x Mayo
Witnesses To Mark:           mark
{ *(Name Illegible)*
  W E Hearrell

Subscribed and sworn to before me this 23 day of March, 1905

                      W A Austin
                      Notary Public.

### AFFIDAVIT OF ATTENDING PHYSICIAN OR MID-WIFE.

UNITED STATES OF AMERICA, Indian Territory, }
Central        DISTRICT.

I, Ola Glenn, a mid wife, on oath state that I attended on Mrs. Tabitha A Mayo, wife of John B Mayo on the 15th day of July, 1903; that there was born to her on said date a mail child; that said child was living March 4, 1905, and is said to have been named George Mayo

# Applications for Enrollment of Choctaw Newborn
## Act of 1905   Volume VIII

Ola Glenn

Witnesses To Mark:
{ *(Name Illegible)*
  W E Hearrell

Subscribed and sworn to before me this   23   day of   March   , 1905

W A Austin
Notary Public.

---

Choc New Born 491
Edith Hickman   b. 6-2-03

**BIRTH AFFIDAVIT.**

**DEPARTMENT OF THE INTERIOR.**
**COMMISSION TO THE FIVE CIVILIZED TRIBES.**

**IN RE APPLICATION FOR ENROLLMENT,** as a citizen of the   Choctaw   Nation, of Edith Hickman   , born on the   2nd   day of   June   , 1903

Name of Father: Lawrence Quinton Hickman   a citizen of the   Choctaw   Nation.
Name of Mother: Lizzie A Hickman   a citizen of the   Choctaw   Nation.

Postoffice   Spiro, Ind Ter

**AFFIDAVIT OF MOTHER.**

**UNITED STATES OF AMERICA, Indian Territory,**
Central   **DISTRICT.**

I,   Lizzie A Hickman   , on oath state that I am   28   years of age and a citizen by   blood   , of the   Choctaw   Nation; that I am the lawful wife of Lawrence Quinton Hickman   , who is a citizen, by   marriage   of the Choctaw   Nation; that a   female   child was born to me on   2nd day of June   , 1903; that said child has been named   Edith Hickman   , and was living March 4, 1905.

Lizzie A Hickman

Witnesses To Mark:
{

# Applications for Enrollment of Choctaw Newborn
## Act of 1905 Volume VIII

Subscribed and sworn to before me this 29th day of March , 1905

Wirt Franklin
Notary Public.

---

**AFFIDAVIT OF ATTENDING PHYSICIAN OR MID-WIFE.**

UNITED STATES OF AMERICA, Indian Territory,
Central DISTRICT.

I, A. P. Thompson , a physician , on oath state that I attended on Mrs. Lizzie A Hickman , wife of Lawrence Quinton Hickman on the 2nd day of June , 1903; that there was born to her on said date a female child; that said child was living March 4, 1905, and is said to have been named Edith Hickman

A.P. Thompson

Witnesses To Mark:

Subscribed and sworn to before me this 29th day of March , 1905

Wirt Franklin
Notary Public.

---

Choc New Born 492
Simon Wade b. 9-18-04

*Jim Wade father of this child on final roll as James Wade No. 7615*

*Sallie Wade mother of the child on final roll as Silan James, No. 6289*
*WF*

## Applications for Enrollment of Choctaw Newborn
## Act of 1905   Volume VIII

**COPY**

N. B. 492

Muskogee, Indian Territory, April 10, 1905.

James Wade,
    Talihina, Indian Territory.

Dear Sir:

    There is inclosed you herewith for execution application for the enrollment of your infant child, Simon Wade, born September 18, 1904.

    In the affidavits heretofore filed with the Commission the mother's name appears as Sallie Wade. She has been identified on the final rolls as Silan James, and in the inclosed application her name is written "Silan Wade (James)".

    In having these affidavits executed care should be exercised to see that all names are written in full, as they appear in the body of the affidavit, and in the event that either of the persons signing the affidavit are unable to write, signatures by mark must be attested by two witnesses. Each affidavit must be executed before a Notary Public and the notarial seal and signature of the officer must be attached to each separate affidavit.

                      Respectfully,
                        SIGNED
                      *T. B. Needles.*

SEV 12-10.                 Commissioner in Charge.

---

**BIRTH AFFIDAVIT.**

**DEPARTMENT OF THE INTERIOR.**
**COMMISSION TO THE FIVE CIVILIZED TRIBES.**

---

**IN RE APPLICATION FOR ENROLLMENT,** as a citizen of the   Choctaw   Nation, of Simon Wade   , born on the   18th   day of   September   , 1904

Name of Father: Jim Wade            a citizen of the   Choctaw   Nation.
Name of Mother: Sallie Wade         a citizen of the   Choctaw   Nation.

                    Postoffice   Talihina, Ind. Ter.

# Applications for Enrollment of Choctaw Newborn
## Act of 1905 Volume VIII

**AFFIDAVIT OF MOTHER.**

UNITED STATES OF AMERICA, Indian Territory,　}
　　Central　　　　DISTRICT.

I, Sallie Wade , on oath state that I am 19 years of age and a citizen by blood , of the Choctaw Nation; that I am the lawful wife of Jim Wade , who is a citizen, by blood of the Choctaw Nation; that a male child was born to me on 18th day of September , 1904; that said child has been named Simon Wade , and was living March 4, 1905.

　　　　　　　　　　　　　　　　　　　　　　her
　　　　　　　　　　　　　　　　　Sallie x Wade
Witnesses To Mark:　　　　　　　　　　　mark
　{ Elsie M$^c$Cartney
　　Austin James

Subscribed and sworn to before me this 28th day of March , 1905

　　　　　　　　　　　　　　　Wirt Franklin
　　　　　　　　　　　　　　　　　Notary Public.

---

**AFFIDAVIT OF ATTENDING PHYSICIAN OR MID-WIFE.**

UNITED STATES OF AMERICA, Indian Territory,　}
　　Central　　　　DISTRICT.

I, Charles H Mahar , a physician , on oath state that I attended on Mrs. Sallie Wade , wife of Jim Wade on the 18th day of September , 1904; that there was born to her on said date a male child; that said child was living March 4, 1905, and is said to have been named Simon Wade

　　　　　　　　　　　　　　　Charles H Mahar M.D.
Witnesses To Mark:
　{

Subscribed and sworn to before me this 29th day of March , 1905

　　　　　　　　　　　　　　　Wirt Franklin
　　　　　　　　　　　　　　　　　Notary Public.

## Applications for Enrollment of Choctaw Newborn
## Act of 1905 Volume VIII

Choc New Born 493
    Alvin Allen Avery  b. 9-16-04

### AFFIDAVIT OF ATTENDING PHYSICIAN OR MIDWIFE

UNITED STATES OF AMERICA
INDIAN TERRITORY
  Central     DISTRICT

    I,    C. H. Mahar    a    Practicing Physician
on oath state that I attended on Mrs. **Julia Avery** wife of   Alex Avery
on the 16 day of September , 190 4, that there was born to her on said date a   male child, that said child is now living, and is said to have been named ...........................

                                                Charles H Mahar      *M.D.*

        Subscribed and sworn to before me this, the    22    day of February    190 5

WITNESSETH:                           James Bower      Notary Public.
  Must be two witnesses { Louis Leflore
  who are citizens
               *(Name Illegible)*

    We hereby certify that we are well acquainted with    C.H. Mahar
a    Practicing Physician     and know   him    to be reputable and of good standing in the community.

                                                    Louis Leflore

                                                   *(Name Illegible)*

Applications for Enrollment of Choctaw Newborn
Act of 1905   Volume VIII

**NEW-BORN AFFIDAVIT.**

Number..................

## ...Choctaw Enrolling Commission...

---

IN THE MATTER OF THE APPLICATION FOR ENROLLMENT, as a citizen of the Choctaw Nation, of   Alvin Allen Avery

born on the  16  day of ___September___ 190 4

Name of father   Alex Avery          a citizen of    Choctaw
Nation final enrollment No. ——
            *D.C. as Hardiway*
Name of mother   Julia Avery         a citizen of    Choctaw
Nation final enrollment No. 8432

                    Postoffice    Spiro, I.T.

**AFFIDAVIT OF MOTHER.**

UNITED STATES OF AMERICA
INDIAN TERRITORY
   Central       DISTRICT

        I    Julia Avery            , on oath state that I am
   22    years of age and a citizen by  blood   of the   Choctaw   Nation,
and as such have been placed upon the final roll of the   Choctaw   Nation, by the Honorable
Secretary of the Interior my final enrollment number being    8432   ; that I am the lawful wife
of   Alex Avery     , who is a citizen of the    Choctaw    Nation, and as such has been
placed upon the final roll of said Nation by the Honorable Secretary of the Interior, his final
enrollment number being    ——   and that a    Male    child was born to me on the   16
day of  September     190 4; that said child has been named   Alvin Allen Avery   ,
and is now living.

                        Julia Avery

Witnesseth.
  Must be two   ⎫  R J *(Illegible)*
  Witnesses who ⎬
  are Citizens. ⎭  *(Name Illegible)*

    Subscribed and sworn to before me this   27   day of   Jan      190 5

                        Edward Hickman
                            Notary Public.
My commission expires:  Feb 5 1905

---

234

## Applications for Enrollment of Choctaw Newborn
### Act of 1905   Volume VIII

*Julia Avery, mother of this child on final roll as Julia Hardaway.*
*No. 8432*

BIRTH AFFIDAVIT.

### DEPARTMENT OF THE INTERIOR.
### COMMISSION TO THE FIVE CIVILIZED TRIBES.

IN RE APPLICATION FOR ENROLLMENT, as a citizen of the Choctaw Nation, of Alvin Allen Avery, born on the 16th day of Sept, 1904.

Name of Father: Alex Avery           a citizen of the United States Nation.
Name of Mother: Julia Avery          a citizen of the Choctaw Nation.

Postoffice   Spiro, Indian Territory

### AFFIDAVIT OF MOTHER.

UNITED STATES OF AMERICA, Indian Territory, }
   Central                  DISTRICT. }

I, Julia Avery, on oath state that I am 22 years of age and a citizen by blood, of the Choctaw Nation; that I am the lawful wife of Alex Avery, who is a citizen, ~~by~~ ............... of the United States Nation; that a male child was born to me on 16th day of September, 1904; that said child has been named Alvin Allen Avery, and was living March 4, 1905.

Julia Avery

Witnesses To Mark:
{

Subscribed and sworn to before me this 29th day of March, 1905.

Wirt Franklin
Notary Public.

### AFFIDAVIT OF ATTENDING PHYSICIAN OR MID-WIFE.

UNITED STATES OF AMERICA, Indian Territory, }
   Central                  DISTRICT. }

I, Charles H. Mahar, a physician, on oath state that I attended on Mrs. Julia Avery, wife of Alex Avery on the 16th day of September, 1904; that there was born to her on said date a male child; that said child was living March 4, 1905, and is said to have been named Alvin Allen Avery

## Applications for Enrollment of Choctaw Newborn
## Act of 1905  Volume VIII

Charles H Mahar, M.D.

Witnesses To Mark:

{ Subscribed and sworn to before me this 29th day of March , 1905

Wirt Franklin<br>Notary Public.

---

Choc New Born 494
    Allie May Hawkins  b. 4-15-04

**COPY**  7- N. B. 494

Muskogee, Indian Territory, April 11, 1905.

Etta M. Hawkins (Able),
    Ego, Indian Territory.

Dear Madam:

    There is inclosed you herewith for execution application for the enrollment of your infant child, ------, born April 15, 1904.

    In the affidavits heretofore filed with the Commission, you sign your name as "Ettar M. Able" at the same time stating you are the lawful wife of J. T[sic]. Hawkins. The records of the Commission show you as "Etta M. Able, wife of Marion Able."

    If you are the lawful wife of J. T. Hawkins, you will please insert your name in the blank left in the inclosed application as "Etta M. Hawkins (Able)" signing the affidavit in the same manner. You will also insert the name of the child as you desire to have her enrolled.

    In having these affidavits executed care should be exercised to see that all names are written in full, as they appear in the body of the affidavit, and in the event that either of the persons signing the affidavit are unable to write, signatures by mark must be attested by two witnesses. Each affidavit must be executed before a Notary Public and the notarial seal and signature of the officer must be attached to each separate affidavit.

Respectfully,<br>SIGNED<br>T. B. Needles.<br>Commissioner in Charge.

LM 11-21.

# Applications for Enrollment of Choctaw Newborn
## Act of 1905 Volume VIII

7 NB 494
**COPY**
Muskogee, Indian Territory, April 20, 1905.

J. H[sic]. Hawkins,
    Ego, Indian Territory.

Dear Sir:

    Receipt is hereby acknowledged of the affidavits of Etta M. Hawkins and Thomas M. Morgan to the birth of Allie May Hawkins, daughter of J. I[sic]. and Etta M. Hawkins, April 13[sic], 1904, and the same have been filed with our records as an application for the enrollment of said child.

                      Respectfully,
                      SIGNED

                        *Tams Bixby*
                        Chairman.

**BIRTH AFFIDAVIT.**

## DEPARTMENT OF THE INTERIOR.
## COMMISSION TO THE FIVE CIVILIZED TRIBES.

    **IN RE APPLICATION FOR ENROLLMENT,** as a citizen of the Choctaw Nation, of Allie May Hawkins, born on the 15th day of April, 1904.

Name of Father: J. F. Hawkins      a citizen of the U. S. Nation.
Name of Mother: Etta M. Hawkins (Able)      a citizen of the Choctaw Nation.

                      Postoffice     Ego Ind Ter

**AFFIDAVIT OF MOTHER.**

UNITED STATES OF AMERICA, Indian Territory,
    Central                 DISTRICT.

    I, Etta M. Hawkins (Ables[sic]), on oath state that I am 33 years of age and a citizen by blood, of the Choctaw Nation; that I am the lawful wife of J.F. Hawkins, who is a citizen, ~~by~~ of the United States Nation; that a female child was born to me on 15th day of April, 1904; that said child has been named Allie May Hawkins, and was living March 4, 1905.

                              Etta M Hawkins (Able)

# Applications for Enrollment of Choctaw Newborn
# Act of 1905  Volume VIII

Witnesses To Mark:
  { J C Izard
  { H Y Morgan

    Subscribed and sworn to before me this 15th day of April, 1905

                              J. T. Hoover
                                  Notary Public.

---

**AFFIDAVIT OF ATTENDING PHYSICIAN OR MID-WIFE.**

**UNITED STATES OF AMERICA, Indian Territory,**
  Central                      **DISTRICT.**

    I, Thos. M. Morgan, a Physician, on oath state that I attended on Mrs. Etta M. Hawkins (Able), wife of J F Hawkins on the 15th day of April, 1904; that there was born to her on said date a female child; that said child was living March 4, 1905, and is said to have been named Allie May Hawkins

                              Thos. M. Morgan, M.D.

Witnesses To Mark:
  { J C Izard
  { H Y Morgan

    Subscribed and sworn to before me this 15th day of April, 1905

                                  J. T. Hoover
                                  Notary Public.

---

**BIRTH AFFIDAVIT.**

                      **DEPARTMENT OF THE INTERIOR.**
              **COMMISSION TO THE FIVE CIVILIZED TRIBES.**

---

    **IN RE APPLICATION FOR ENROLLMENT,** as a citizen of the Choctaw Nation, of Allie May Hawkins, born on the 15th day of April, 1904

Name of Father: J. F. Hawkins       a citizen of the U. S. Nation.
Name of Mother: Etta M. Ables       a citizen of the Choctaw Nation.

                    Postoffice   Ego I.T.

## Applications for Enrollment of Choctaw Newborn
## Act of 1905  Volume VIII

### AFFIDAVIT OF MOTHER.

UNITED STATES OF AMERICA, Indian Territory, }
   Central                         DISTRICT. }

   I, Etta M. Ables   , on oath state that I am  33   years of age and a citizen by Blood  , of the   Choctaw   Nation; that I am the lawful wife of   J.F. Hawkins   , who is a citizen, by ................... of the   U S    Nation; that a   Female    child was born to me on   15th   day of   April   , 1904; that said child has been named   Allie May Hawkins   , and was living March 4, 1905.

Etta M Able

Witnesses To Mark:
{ J C Izard
{ J M Bethell

   Subscribed and sworn to before me this  27th   day of   March   , 1905

J. T. Hoover<br>Notary Public.

---

### AFFIDAVIT OF ATTENDING PHYSICIAN OR MID-WIFE.

UNITED STATES OF AMERICA, Indian Territory, }
................................................. DISTRICT. }

   I,   Thos. M. Morgan   , a   Physician   , on oath state that I attended on Mrs.   Etta M. Able   , wife of   J F Hawkins    on the  15th   day of   April   , 1904; that there was born to her on said date a    Female    child; that said child was living March 4, 1905, and is said to have been named  Allie May Hawkins

Thos. M. Morgan, M.D.

Witnesses To Mark:
{ J C Izard
{ J M Bethell

   Subscribed and sworn to before me this   27th   day of   March   , 1905

J. T. Hoover<br>Notary Public.

## Applications for Enrollment of Choctaw Newborn
## Act of 1905   Volume VIII

Choc New Born 495
    Willis Thomas Daniels   b. 2-13-03

---

N. B. 495
**COPY**
Muskogee, Indian Territory, April 10, 1905.

Turner Daniels,
    Stuart, Indian Territory.

Dear Sir:

    There is inclosed you herewith for execution application for the enrollment of your infant child, Willis Thomas Daniels, born February 13, 1903.

    The affidavits heretofore filed with the Commission show the child was living on February 24, 1905. It is necessary, for the child to be enrolled, that he was living on March 4, 1905. In the inclosed blank the name of the mother is written <u>Lou</u> Daniels as it appears on the records of the Commission.

    In having these affidavits executed care should be exercised to see that all names are written in full, as they appear in the body of the affidavit, and in the event that either of the persons signing the affidavit are unable to write, signatures by mark must be attested by two witnesses. Each affidavit must be executed before a Notary Public and the notarial seal and signature of the officer must be attached to each separate affidavit.

                          Respectfully,
                          SIGNED
                          *T. B. Needles.*
SEV 11-10.                  Commissioner in Charge.

---

7- N B 495.
**COPY**
Muskogee, Indian Territory, April 26, 1905.

Turner Daniels,
    Stuart, Indian Territory.

Dear Sir:

    Receipt is hereby acknowledged of the affidavits of Lou Daniels and N. D. Abernathy to the birth of Willis Thomas Daniels, son of Turner and Lou Daniels, February 13, 1903, and the same have been filed with our records in the matter of the enrollment of said child.

## Applications for Enrollment of Choctaw Newborn
## Act of 1905   Volume VIII

Respectfully,
SIGNED

*Tams Bixby*
Chairman.

---

**BIRTH AFFIDAVIT.**

## DEPARTMENT OF THE INTERIOR,
By Blood Roll #7771      COMMISSION TO THE FIVE CIVILIZED TRIBES.
By Inter   "   " 262

*IN RE Application for Enrollment,* as a citizen of the     Choctaw     Nation, of   Willis Thomas Daniels , born on the   13   day of  February   , 1903

Name of Father:  Turner Daniels          a citizen of the   Choctaw     Nation.
Name of Mother:  Lue Daniels             a citizen of the   Choctaw     Nation.

Post-Office:     Stuart, I.T.

---

**AFFIDAVIT OF MOTHER.**

UNITED STATES OF AMERICA,
   INDIAN TERRITORY.
   Central           District.

I,  Lue Daniels        , on oath state that I am   33   years of age and a citizen by marriage    , of the   Choctaw   Nation; that I am the lawful wife of  Turner Daniels   , who is a citizen, by   Blood    of the  Choctaw  Nation; that a    male    child was born to me on    13"    day of  February    , 1903 , that said child has been named  Willis Thomas Daniels    , and is now living.

Lue Daniels

**WITNESSES TO MARK:**
   Robert Newton
   Kate Newton

Subscribed and sworn to before me this  FEB 24 1905   , 1905.

JH Elliott

My com exp July 8 1908              **NOTARY PUBLIC.**

---

241

## Applications for Enrollment of Choctaw Newborn
## Act of 1905 Volume VIII

**AFFIDAVIT OF ATTENDING PHYSICIAN OR MID-WIFE.**

UNITED STATES OF AMERICA,
INDIAN TERRITORY.
Central District.

I, Nancy Abernathy , a Midwife , on oath state that I attended on Mrs. Lue Daniels , wife of Turner Daniels on the 13" day of February , 1903 ; that there was born to her on said date a boy child; that said child is now living and is said to have been named Willis Thomas Daniels

Mrs Nancy Abernathy

**WITNESSES TO MARK:**

Subscribed and sworn to before me this 23 day of January , 1905.

My commission expires Mar. 15, 1905

Jas. L. Lewis
*NOTARY PUBLIC.*
Milton, I.T.

**BIRTH AFFIDAVIT.**

### DEPARTMENT OF THE INTERIOR.
### COMMISSION TO THE FIVE CIVILIZED TRIBES.

**IN RE APPLICATION FOR ENROLLMENT,** as a citizen of the Choctaw Nation, of Willis Thomas Daniels , born on the 13 day of February , 1903

Name of Father: Turner Daniels    a citizen of the Choctaw Nation.
Name of Mother: Lou Daniels    a citizen of the Choctaw Nation.

Postoffice Stuart I.T.

**AFFIDAVIT OF MOTHER.**

UNITED STATES OF AMERICA, Indian Territory,
Central DISTRICT.

I, Lou Daniels , on oath state that I am 33 years of age and a citizen by intermarriage , of the Choctaw Nation; that I am the lawful wife of Turner Daniels , who is a citizen, by blood of the Choctaw Nation; that a male child was born to me on 13 day of February , 1903; that said child has been named Willis Thomas Daniels , and was living March 4, 1905.

Lou Daniels

## Applications for Enrollment of Choctaw Newborn
## Act of 1905   Volume VIII

Witnesses To Mark:

{

    Subscribed and sworn to before me this   **APR 17 1905** day of    , 1905

                                       J H Elliott

My com exp July 8" 1908                                 Notary Public.

---

### AFFIDAVIT OF ATTENDING PHYSICIAN OR MID-WIFE.

UNITED STATES OF AMERICA, Indian Territory, }
   Central                 DISTRICT.

    I,   N D Abernathy   , a   midwife   , on oath state that I attended on Mrs.   Lou Daniels   , wife of   Turner Daniels   on the 13  day of  February , 1903; that there was born to her on said date a   male   child; that said child was living March 4, 1905, and is said to have been named Willis Thomas Daniels

                                  Mrs N D Abernathy

Witnesses To Mark:

{

    Subscribed and sworn to before me this 20   day of   April   , 1905

                                Jas. L. Lewis

My commission expires Mar. 11, 1909                *NOTARY PUBLIC.*

                                Milton, I.T.

---

Choc New Born 496
        Gertrude Harris  b. 7-24-04
        Mamie Harris  b. 2-5-03

## Applications for Enrollment of Choctaw Newborn
## Act of 1905   Volume VIII

BIRTH AFFIDAVIT.

### DEPARTMENT OF THE INTERIOR.
### COMMISSION TO THE FIVE CIVILIZED TRIBES.

IN RE APPLICATION FOR ENROLLMENT, as a citizen of the Choctaw Nation, of Mamie Harris, born on the 5th day of February, 1903

Name of Father: Luther M. Harris    a citizen of the United States ~~Nation~~.
Name of Mother: Annie Folsom Harris    a citizen of the Choctaw Nation.

Postoffice   Spiro, Ind. Ter.

#### AFFIDAVIT OF MOTHER.

UNITED STATES OF AMERICA, Indian Territory, }
Central         DISTRICT.

I, Annie Folsom Harris, on oath state that I am 24 years of age and a citizen by blood, of the Choctaw Nation; that I am the lawful wife of Luther M Harris, who is a citizen, ~~by~~ ............ of the United States ~~Nation~~; that a female child was born to me on 5th day of February, 1903; that said child has been named Mamie Harris, and was living March 4, 1905.

Annie Folsom Harris

Witnesses To Mark:
{

Subscribed and sworn to before me this 29th day of March, 1905

Wirt Franklin
Notary Public.

#### AFFIDAVIT OF ATTENDING PHYSICIAN OR MID-WIFE.

UNITED STATES OF AMERICA, Indian Territory, }
Central         DISTRICT.

I, A. P. Thompson, a physician, on oath state that I attended on Mrs. Annie Folsom Harris, wife of Luther M Harris on the 5th day of February, 1903; that there was born to her on said date a female child; that said child was living March 4, 1905, and is said to have been named Mamie Harris

A.P. Thompson

Witnesses To Mark:
{

# Applications for Enrollment of Choctaw Newborn
## Act of 1905  Volume VIII

Subscribed and sworn to before me this 29th day of  March  , 1905

Wirt Franklin<br>Notary Public.

---

**BIRTH AFFIDAVIT.**

## DEPARTMENT OF THE INTERIOR.
## COMMISSION TO THE FIVE CIVILIZED TRIBES.

---

**IN RE APPLICATION FOR ENROLLMENT**, as a citizen of the  Choctaw  Nation, of Gertrude Harris  , born on the 24th day of July  , 1904

Name of Father: Luther M. Harris        a citizen of the United States ~~Nation~~.
Name of Mother: Annie Folsom Harris     a citizen of the  Choctaw   Nation.

Postoffice   Spiro, Ind. Ter.

---

### AFFIDAVIT OF MOTHER.

UNITED STATES OF AMERICA, Indian Territory, ⎫
  Central            DISTRICT.              ⎭

I,  Annie Folsom Harris  , on oath state that I am  24  years of age and a citizen by  blood  , of the  Choctaw  Nation; that I am the lawful wife of Luther M Harris  , who is a citizen, ~~by~~ .............. of the  United States ~~Nation~~; that a  female  child was born to me on  24th day of July  , 1904; that said child has been named  Gertrude Harris  , and was living March 4, 1905.

Annie Folsom Harris

Witnesses To Mark:
{

Subscribed and sworn to before me this 29th day of  March  , 1905

Wirt Franklin<br>Notary Public.

---

### AFFIDAVIT OF ATTENDING PHYSICIAN OR MID-WIFE.

UNITED STATES OF AMERICA, Indian Territory, ⎫
  Central            DISTRICT.              ⎭

I,  A. P. Thompson  , a  physician  , on oath state that I attended on Mrs.  Annie Folsom Harris  , wife of  Luther M Harris   on the 24th day of

# Applications for Enrollment of Choctaw Newborn
## Act of 1905   Volume VIII

July      , 1904; that there was born to her on said date a     female     child; that said child was living March 4, 1905, and is said to have been named  Gertrude Harris

A.P. Thompson

Witnesses To Mark:

{ Subscribed and sworn to before me this 29th  day of    March       , 1905

Wirt Franklin<br>Notary Public.

---

Choc New Born 497
    Claude McLaughlin  b. 8-15-03

**BIRTH AFFIDAVIT.**

## DEPARTMENT OF THE INTERIOR.
## COMMISSION TO THE FIVE CIVILIZED TRIBES.

**IN RE APPLICATION FOR ENROLLMENT,** as a citizen of the     Choctaw     Nation, of  Claude M$^c$Laughlin     , born on the  15  day of  August  , 1903

Name of Father: George W. M$^c$Laughlin     a citizen of the  Choctaw   Nation.
Name of Mother: Lillie M$^c$Laughlin       a citizen of the  Choctaw   Nation.

Postoffice    Ardmore, Ind Ter

---

**AFFIDAVIT OF MOTHER.**

**UNITED STATES OF AMERICA, Indian Territory,**
    Southern         **DISTRICT.**

    I,   Lillie M$^c$Laughlin      , on oath state that I am   26    years of age and a citizen by ——— , of the   United States   Nation; that I am the lawful wife of   George W. M$^c$Laughlin     , who is a citizen, by Blood   of the     Choctaw      Nation; that a    male    child was born to me on   15  day of  August      , 1903; that said child has been named   Claude M$^c$Laughlin      , and was living March 4, 1905.

Lillie M$^c$Laughlin

Witnesses To Mark:
   { Angeline Porter

## Applications for Enrollment of Choctaw Newborn
## Act of 1905  Volume VIII

Subscribed and sworn to before me this 8th. day of   April   , 1905

J.R. Ratley
Notary Public.

---

**AFFIDAVIT OF ATTENDING PHYSICIAN OR MID-WIFE.**

**UNITED STATES OF AMERICA, Indian Territory,**
**Southern                  DISTRICT.**

I,  W$^m$ T. Boyie   , a  physician   , on oath state that I attended on Mrs. Lillie M$^c$Laughlin   , wife of   George W. M$^c$Laughlin   on the 15 day of August   , 190;3 that there was born to her on said date a    male    child; that said child was living March 4, 1905, and is said to have been named Claude M$^c$Laughlin

W$^m$ T. Boyie

Witnesses To Mark:
{ M. S. Wolverton
{ A. A. Wolverton

Subscribed and sworn to before me this 10th. day of   April    , 1905

M.S. Wolverton
Notary Public.

---

Choctaw N.B. 497.

**COPY**

Muskogee, Indian Territory, April 14, 1905.

George W. McLaughlin,
    Ardmore, Indian Territory.

Dear Sir:

Receipt is hereby acknowledged of the affidavits of Lillie McLaughlin and Wm. T. Boyie to the birth of laude McLaughlin, son of George W. and Lillie McLaughlin, August 15, 1903; also the marriage license and certificate between G.W. McLaughlin and Lily Porter, and the same have been filed with our records in the matter of the enrollment of said child.

Respectfully,

SIGNED

*Tams Bixby*
Commissioner in Charge.

# Applications for Enrollment of Choctaw Newborn
## Act of 1905   Volume VIII

N.B. 497

**COPY**

Muskogee, Indian Territory, April 3, 1905.

George W. McLaughlin,
    Ardmore, Indian Territory.

Dear Sir:

    There is inclosed you herewith for execution application for the enrollment of your infant child, Claude McLaughlin, born August 15, 1903.

    In the affidavits heretofore filed with the Commission the name of the father appeared as G. W. McLaughlin. I the inclosed application it is George W. McLaughlin as it appears on the approved Choctaw roll.

    In having these affidavits executed care should be exercised to see that all names are written in full, as they appear in the body of the affidavit, and in the event that either of the persons signing the affidavit are unable to write, signatures by mark must be attested by two witnesses. Each affidavit must be executed before a Notary Public and the notarial seal and signature of the officer must be attached to each separate affidavit.

    You are advised, however, that before the application for said child can be finally disposed of it will be necessary that you furnish the Commission with the original or a certified copy of the marriage license and certificate of yourself and wife, Lillie McLaughlin.

    Please give this matter your immediate attention.

Respectfully,

SIGNED

*Tams Bixby*
Chairman.

LM 3-5

---

7-NB-497

Muskogee, Indian Territory, September 5, 1905.

George W. McLaughlin,
    Ardmore, Indian Territory.

Dear Sir:

    Receipt is hereby acknowledged of your letter of the 28th ultimo in which you request the return of the marriage license between yourself and your wife, Lillie

## Applications for Enrollment of Choctaw Newborn
## Act of 1905   Volume VIII

McLaughlin, which was filed in this office with the application for the enrollment of your infant child, Claude McLaughlin.

In reply thereto, you are advised that the marriage license cannot at this time be returned to you as it is necessary to be retained as a part of the record in the matter of the enrollment case of your said child.

It is noted that said marriage license was issued by the Clerk of the United States Court for the Southern District of the Indian Territory at Ardmore, Indian Territory, and it is suggested that you may be able to obtain a certified copy of the same from him.

                                    Respectfully,

                                    Acting Commissioner.

---

<u>Choc New Born 498</u>
    Mollie Julius   b.  11-12-02

                                                      7-3724.

                    Muskogee, Indian Territory, January 6, 1905.

Solomon Julius,
    Bennington, Indian Territory.

Dear Sir:

Referring to the application for enrollment as a citizen of the Choctaw Nation of Mollie Julius, infant daughter of Solomon and Serena Julius, born November 12, 1902; you are advised that the Commission is without authority to enroll this child as a citizen by blood of the Choctaw Nation, it appearing that said child was born ,November 12, 1902, subsequent to the ratification by the citizens of the Choctaw and Chickasaw Nations on September 25, 1902, of an act of Congress approved July 1, 1902 (32 Stats., 641).

Section twenty-eight thereof provides as follows:

"The names of all persons living on the date of the final ratification of this agreement entitled to be enrolled as provided in section 27 hereof shall be placed upon the rolls made by said Commission, and no child born thereafter to a citizen or freedman and no person intermarried thereafter to a citizen shall be entitled to

## Applications for Enrollment of Choctaw Newborn
## Act of 1905   Volume VIII

enrollment or to participate in the distribution of the tribal property of the Choctaws and Chickasaws."

Respectfully,

Acting Chairman.

---

**COPY**

Choctaw N.B. 498.

Muskogee, Indian Territory, April 19, 1905.

Solomon Julius,
    Bennington, Indian Territory.

Dear Sir:

Receipt is hereby acknowledged of the affidavits of Serena Julius and Eliza Julius to the birth of Mollie Julius, daughter of Solomon and Serena Julius, November 12, 1902, and the same have been filed with our records in the matter of the enrollment of said child.

Respectfully,

SIGNED

*Tams Bixby*
Chairman.

---

**COPY**

N. B. 498

Muskogee, Indian Territory, April 10, 1905.

Solomon Julius,
    Bennington, Indian Territory.

Dear Sir:

There is inclosed you herewith for execution application for the enrollment of your infant child, Mollie Julius, born November 12, 1902.

The affidavits heretofore filed with the Commission show the child was living on November 19, 1902. It is necessary, for the child to be enrolled, that she was living on March 4, 1905. You will please insert the mother's age in the place left blank for that purpose.

## Applications for Enrollment of Choctaw Newborn
## Act of 1905   Volume VIII

In having these affidavits executed care should be exercised to see that all names are written in full, as they appear in the body of the affidavit, and in the event that either of the persons signing the affidavit are unable to write, signatures by mark must be attested by two witnesses. Each affidavit must be executed before a Notary Public and the notarial seal and signature of the officer must be attached to each separate affidavit.

Respectfully,
SIGNED

*T. B. Needles.*

SEV 9-10.   Commissioner in Charge.

BIRTH AFFIDAVIT.

## DEPARTMENT OF THE INTERIOR,
COMMISSION TO THE FIVE CIVILIZED TRIBES.

IN RE APPLICATION FOR ENROLLMENT, as a citizen of the Choctaw Nation, of Mollie Julius , born on the 12 day of November , 190 2

Name of Father: Solomon Julius    a citizen of the Choctaw Nation.
Name of Mother: Serena Julius    a citizen of the Choctaw Nation.

Post-Office :    Bennington I.T.

**AFFIDAVIT OF MOTHER.**

UNITED STATES OF AMERICA,
INDIAN TERRITORY,
Central    District.

I, Solomon Julius , on oath state that I am 48 years of age and a citizen by blood , of the Choctaw Nation; that I am the lawful ~~wife~~ *husband* of Serena Julius , who is a citizen, by blood of the Choctaw Nation; that a female child was born to ~~me us~~ on the 12 day of November , 190 2, that said child has been named Mollie Julius , and is now living.

　　　　　　　　　　　　　　　　　　　his
　　　　　　　　　　　　　　　　Solomon x Julius
WITNESSES TO MARK:　　　　　　　　　mark
　　{ R. M. Nalson
　　　W<sup>m</sup> C Bunn

Subscribed and sworn to before me this 19 day of November , 1902

D.N. Linebaugh
*NOTARY PUBLIC.*

# Applications for Enrollment of Choctaw Newborn
## Act of 1905 Volume VIII

**BIRTH AFFIDAVIT.**

### DEPARTMENT OF THE INTERIOR.
### COMMISSION TO THE FIVE CIVILIZED TRIBES.

IN RE APPLICATION FOR ENROLLMENT, as a citizen of the Choctaw Nation, of Mollie Julius, born on the 12 day of November, 1902

Name of Father: Solomon Julius    a citizen of the Choctaw Nation.
Name of Mother: Serena Julius    a citizen of the Choctaw Nation.

Postoffice Bennington I.T.

#### AFFIDAVIT OF MOTHER.

UNITED STATES OF AMERICA, Indian Territory, }
Central     DISTRICT.

I, Serena Julius, on oath state that I am 50 years of age and a citizen by blood, of the Choctaw Nation; that I am the lawful wife of Solomon Julius, who is a citizen, by blood of the Choctaw Nation; that a female child was born to me on 12 day of November, 1902; that said child has been named Mollie Julius, and was living March 4, 1905.

            her
       Serena Julius
Witnesses To Mark:    mark
  { *(Name Illegible)*
  { Eli Julius

Subscribed and sworn to before me this 15 day of April, 1905

       Thomas H Boyless
       Notary Public.

#### AFFIDAVIT OF ATTENDING PHYSICIAN OR MID-WIFE.

UNITED STATES OF AMERICA, Indian Territory, }
Central     DISTRICT.

I, Eliza Julius, a midwife, on oath state that I attended on Mrs. Serena Julius, wife of Solomon Julius on the 12 day of November, 1902; that there was born to her on said date a female child; that said child was living March 4, 1905, and is said to have been named Mollie Julius

       Eliza Julius

## Applications for Enrollment of Choctaw Newborn
## Act of 1905    Volume VIII

Witnesses To Mark:
{

    Subscribed and sworn to before me this  15   day of   April         , 1905

                                      Thomas H Boyless
                                      Notary Public.

---

7-NB-498

                        Muskogee, Indian Territory, November 9, 1906.

Chief Clerk,
        Chickasaw Land Office,
                Ardmore, Indian Territory.

Dear Sir:

    It appearing that Mollie Julius whose name appears at No. 479 upon the roll of new born citizens of the Choctaw Nation under the Act of Congress approved March 3, 1905, of Congress approved March 3, 1905, died in September 1903, your office is directed to take no further action looking to the issuance of citizenship certificate or the making of allotments to such citizen.

                                  Respectfully,

                                                        Commissioner.

---

7-NB-498

                        Muskogee, Indian Territory, November 9, 1906.

Chief Clerk,
        Choctaw Land Office,
                Atoka, Indian Territory.

Dear Sir:

    It appearing that Mollie Julius whose name appears at No. 479 upon the roll of new born citizens of the Choctaw Nation under the Act of Congress approved March 3, 1905, of Congress approved March 3, 1905, died in September 1903, your office is directed to take no further action looking to the issuance of citizenship certificate or the making of allotments to such citizen.

                                  Respectfully,

                                                        Commissioner.

# Applications for Enrollment of Choctaw Newborn
## Act of 1905   Volume VIII

7-NB-498

Muskogee, Indian Territory, November ?, 1906.

Fred V. Kinkade,
    Ardmore, Indian Territory.

Dear Sir:

    Receipt is hereby acknowledged of your two letters of October 30, 1905, in which you refer to an attempt made by Serena Julius to sell the claim of her child Mollie Julius whose name appears upon the approved roll of new born Choctaws at No. 479, and state that you have evidence that this child died in September 1902 and that you will furnish this office such evidence if so desired.

    In reply to your letter you are advised that the evidence heretofore filed with this office shows that Mollie Julius, child of Solomon and Serena Julius died in September 1903.

                  Respectfully,

                                  Commissioner.

Subject:
Date of Death of
Mollie Julius, Number
479 on roll of
New Born Choctaws
Act of March 3, 1905.

Muskogee, Indian Territory, September 10, 1907.

The Honorable,
    The Secretary of the Interior.

Sir:

    I have the honor to transmit herewith the record in the matter of the date of the death of Mollie Julius whose name appears upon the approved roll of new born citizens of the Choctaw Nation under the act of Congress approved March 3, 1905, at Number 479.

    On September 27, 1906, Serena Julius and Eliza Julius made affidavits to the death of Mollie Julius on September 20, 1903, and the testimony of Serena Julius, mother

## Applications for Enrollment of Choctaw Newborn
## Act of 1905   Volume VIII

of the child, was also taken at the Chickasaw Land Office, from which it appears that Mollie Julius died on September 20, 1903, the date named in the affidavits.

No selection of allotment has been made for Mollie Julius.

In view of the recommendation of the Acting Commissioner of Indian Affairs of April 13, 1907, in the Cherokee case of Mose Riley, et al. which was approved by the Secretary of the Interior on June 5, 1907, I have the honor to recommend that upon the copies of the final roll of new born citizens of the Choctaw Nation under the act of Congress approved March 3, 1905, in the Department and the Indian Office there be placed opposite the name of Mollie Julius at Number 479 the notation "Died prior to March 4, 1905; not entitled to allotment" and also upon the original letter transmitting the schedule containing the name of Mollie Julius for Departmental action.

It is also recommended that this office be authorized to make like notation upon the copies of the roll and letters of transmittal in its possession.

Respectfully,

Acting Commissioner.

Through the Commissioner
of Indian Affairs.

7 N B 498.

(COPY)                                          G.A.W.

I.T.
76107-1907

File 053
-------------P

DEPARTMENT OF THE INTERIOR,
OFFICE OF INDIAN AFFAIRS,
WASHINGTON.         October 8, 1907.

Subject:
In re death of Mollie
Julius, No. 479 new
born Choctaws.

Commissioner to the Five Civilized Tribes,
    Muskogee, Indian Territory.

Sir:

Referring to the Acting Commissioner's report of September 10, 1907, relative to the death of Mollie Julius, whose name appears on the approved roll of new born citizens of the Choctaw Nation at No. 479, there is enclosed a copy of Office letter of September

## Applications for Enrollment of Choctaw Newborn
## Act of 1905   Volume VIII

24, 1907, to the Department, concurring in your recommendation that there be endorsed on the roll of new born citizens of the Choctaw Nation, opposite the name of Mollie Julius, the notation, "Died prior to March 4, 1905; not entitled to enrollment:

On September 25 the Department approved the recommendation of the Office, and the roll in the possession of the Office has been so endorsed.

In accordance with the authority granted by the Department, you are requested to so endorse the roll in your possession.

Very respectfully,

(SIGNED)   C.F. Larrabee
RJH--SD.                                              Acting Commissioner.

---

Choc New Born 499
    Sister Cooper   b. 11-11-02

Choctaw 2525.

Muskogee, Indian Territory, April 3, 1905.

James T. Cooper,
    Whitefield, Indian Territory.

Dear Sir:

Receipt is hereby acknowledged of your affidavit and the affidavit of F. A. Fannin to the birth of Sister Cooper, daughter of James T. and Tory Cooper, November 11, 1902, and the same have been filed with our records as an application for the enrollment of said child. application for the enrollment of said chi d.

Respectfully,

Chairman.

## Applications for Enrollment of Choctaw Newborn
## Act of 1905   Volume VIII

N. B. 499

**COPY**

Muskogee, Indian Territory, April 10, 1905.

James Cooper,
    Whitefield, Indian Territory.

Dear Sir:

It appears from The affidavits heretofore filed with the Commission that the mother of the applicant, Sister Cooper, is dead. It is therefore necessary that you secure the affidavits of two persons who have actual knowledge of the fact that the child was born, date of her birth, that she was living on March 4, 1905 and that Tory Cooper was her mother.

Please give this matter your immediate attention.

Respectfully,

SIGNED

*T. B. Needles.*
Commissioner in Charge.

---

7-NB-499

Muskogee, Indian Territory, April 18, 1906.

James Cooper,
    Mill Creek, Indian Territory.

Dear Sir:

Your letter of April 7, 1906, addressed to the United States Indian Agent has been by him referred to this office for consideration and appropriate action. Therein you state that you made application for enrollment of a new born child April 1905, but have heard nothing further relative to its enrollment.

In reply to your letter you are advised that on July 22, 1905, the enrollment of Sister Cooper, child of James and Tory Cooper as a new born citizen of the Choctaw Nation, was approved by the Secretary of the Interior.

If this is not the child referred to and you will give the name of your child, the matter of your inquiry will receive further consideration.

## Applications for Enrollment of Choctaw Newborn
## Act of 1905   Volume VIII

Respectfully,

Acting Commissioner.

NB 499

Muskogee, Indian Territory, May 1, 1905.

James T. Cooper,
    Whitefield, Indian Territory.

Dear Sir:

    Receipt is hereby acknowledged of the joint affidavit of Annie Forrest and Alice Forrest to the birth of Sister Cooper, daughter of James T. and Tory Cooper, November 11, 1902, and the same have been filed with our records as an application for the enrollment of said child.

Respectfully,

Chairman.

**WILSON A. SHONEY,** COMMISSIONER

OFFICE OF

## CHOCTAW ENROLLING COMMISSION

Stigler, I.T.

Central District
    Indian Territory

    I, F. A. Fannin state on oath that I attended on Mrs. Tory Cooper, wife of James Cooper at the time of her death, 11 day of April, 1904.

F.A. Fannin M.D.

Subscribed to before me
This 3 day of Jan. 1904

James Bower
    N.P.

## Applications for Enrollment of Choctaw Newborn
## Act of 1905   Volume VIII

### AFFIDAVIT OF ATTENDING PHYSICIAN OR MIDWIFE

UNITED STATES OF AMERICA
INDIAN TERRITORY
  Central    DISTRICT

I,   F.A. Fannin    a    Practicing Physician on oath state that I attended on Mrs.  Tory Cooper  wife of  James Cooper on the  11  day of  Nov  , 190 2, that there was born to her on said date a  female child, that said child is now living, and is said to have been named  Sister Cooper

                              F.A. Fannin M.D.

Subscribed and sworn to before me this, the  3  day of   Jan    190 5

WITNESSETH:                    James Bower    Notary Public.
Must be two witnesses { Annie Forrest
who are citizens
                       Alice Forrest

We hereby certify that we are well acquainted with _____
a _____ and know _____ to be reputable and of good standing in the community.

    J S Stigler

    William Jones

### NEW-BORN AFFIDAVIT.

        Number..............

### ...Choctaw Enrolling Commission...

IN THE MATTER OF THE APPLICATION FOR ENROLLMENT, as a citizen of the Choctaw    Nation, of    Sister Cooper

born on the  11  day of __November__ 190 2

Name of father  James Cooper        a citizen of    Choctaw
Nation final enrollment No.  7329
Name of mother  Tory Cooper        a citizen of    Choctaw
Nation final enrollment No.  7330

                              Postoffice    Whitefield IT

## Applications for Enrollment of Choctaw Newborn
## Act of 1905 Volume VIII

### AFFIDAVIT OF MOTHER.

UNITED STATES OF AMERICA
INDIAN TERRITORY
   Central      DISTRICT

I    James Cooper   *for his wife*   , on oath state that I am 29 years of age and a citizen by blood of the Choctaw Nation, and as such have been placed upon the final roll of the Choctaw Nation, by the Honorable Secretary of the Interior my final enrollment number being 7330 ; that I am the lawful wife of   James Cooper   , who is a citizen of the   Choctaw   Nation, and as such has been placed upon the final roll of said Nation by the Honorable Secretary of the Interior, his final enrollment number being   7329   and that a   Female   child was born to me on the   11   day of   November   190 2; that said child has been named   Sister Cooper , and is now living.

                                                        Tory Cooper
Witnesseth.                                       By James Cooper

Must be two Witnesses who are Citizens.   }   W<sup>m</sup> Martin
   Frank Wallace

Subscribed and sworn to before me this   3   day of   Jan    190 5

                                                  James Bower
                                                      Notary Public.

My commission expires:
   Sept 23-1907

---

United States of America, Indian Territory.
Western District.

I,   Annie Forrest   and   Alice Forrest   state on oath that we are   43   and   23   years of age respectively, and residents of the above named district. That we were present at the home of Mrs. Tory Cooper   on the   11   day of   Nov   190 2 . That we know that on said date there was born to the said Mrs.   Tory Cooper   on said date a   Female   child. That said child was living on the 4th day of March 1905, and is said to have been named   Sister Cooper

     Whitefield I.T.                    Annie Forrest
                                     Alice Forrest

Subscribed and sworn to before me this   27   day of April, 1905.

                                             John H Oliver
                                           Notary Public.

## Applications for Enrollment of Choctaw Newborn
## Act of 1905   Volume VIII

**BIRTH AFFIDAVIT.**

### DEPARTMENT OF THE INTERIOR.
### COMMISSION TO THE FIVE CIVILIZED TRIBES.

**IN RE APPLICATION FOR ENROLLMENT,** as a citizen of the Choctaw Nation, of Sister Cooper, born on the 11$^{th}$ day of November, 1902

Name of Father: James T. Cooper     a citizen of the Choctaw Nation.
Name of Mother: Torry[sic] Cooper     a citizen of the Choctaw Nation.

Postoffice     Whitefield Ind Terr

**AFFIDAVIT OF MOTHER.**

UNITED STATES OF AMERICA, Indian Territory,
Central     DISTRICT.

I, James T Cooper, on oath state that I am 29 y[sic] years of age and a citizen by Blood, of the Choctaw Nation; that I am the lawful ~~wife~~ *husband* of Father Torry Cooper, who is a citizen, by Blood of the Choctaw Nation; that a Female child was born to ~~me~~ *Torry Cooper* on 11$^{th}$ day of Nov, 1902, that said child has been named Sister, and is now living. *And further state the mother of the child Torry Cooper is dead*

Witnesses To Mark:     James T Cooper
    F.A. Fannin
    S.E. Mitchell

Subscribed and sworn to before me this 27$^{th}$ day of March, 1905.

Henry F Cooper
Notary Public.

**AFFIDAVIT OF ATTENDING PHYSICIAN OR MID-WIFE.**

UNITED STATES OF AMERICA, Indian Territory,
Central     DISTRICT.

I, Frank A Fannin, a Physician, on oath state that I attended on Mrs. Torry Cooper, wife of James T Cooper on the 11$^{th}$ day of November, 1902; that there was born to her on said date a Female child; that said child is now living and is said to have been named Sister

F.A. Fannin M.D.

# Applications for Enrollment of Choctaw Newborn
## Act of 1905  Volume VIII

Witnesses To Mark:
{ S.E. Mitchell
{ J.T. Forrester

Subscribed and sworn to before me this 27 day of March, 1905.

Henry F Cooper
Notary Public.

---

Choc New Born 500
Grace May Fitzer b. 8-8-03

**BIRTH AFFIDAVIT.**

### DEPARTMENT OF THE INTERIOR.
### COMMISSION TO THE FIVE CIVILIZED TRIBES.

**IN RE APPLICATION FOR ENROLLMENT,** as a citizen of the Choctaw Nation, of Gracie May Fitzer, born on the 8$^{th}$ day of Aug, 1903

Name of Father: William W. Fitzer    a citizen of the U.S. Nation.
Name of Mother: Lourinda Fitzer    a citizen of the Choctaw Nation.

Postoffice Quinton, Ind. Ter.

**AFFIDAVIT OF MOTHER.**

**UNITED STATES OF AMERICA, Indian Territory,**
Western **DISTRICT.**

I, Lourinda Fitzer, on oath state that I am 22 years of age and a citizen by Blood, of the Choctaw Nation; that I am the lawful wife of William W. Fitzer, who is a citizen, ~~by~~ ............ of the U.S. Nation; that a Female child was born to me on 8$^{th}$ day of August, 1903; that said child has been named Gracie May Fitzer, and was living March 4, 1905.

Lourinda Fitzer

Witnesses To Mark:
{
{

## Applications for Enrollment of Choctaw Newborn
## Act of 1905 Volume VIII

Subscribed and sworn to before me this 27" day of March , 1905

My com expires          L. C. Tirey
Jan 17-1907          Notary Public.

---

**AFFIDAVIT OF ATTENDING PHYSICIAN OR MID-WIFE.**

UNITED STATES OF AMERICA, Indian Territory,
    Western        DISTRICT.

I, E Johnson , a Physician , on oath state that I attended on Mrs. Lourinda Fitzer , wife of William W. Fitzer on the 8$^{th}$ day of Aug, 1903; that there was born to her on said date a Female child; that said child was living March 4, 1905, and is said to have been named Gracie May Fitzer

E Johnson - M.D.

Witnesses To Mark:

Subscribed and sworn to before me this 30$^{th}$ day of Mch , 1905

L.C. Tirey
Notary Public.

---

**NEW-BORN AFFIDAVIT.**

Number..................

## ...Choctaw Enrolling Commission...

---

IN THE MATTER OF THE APPLICATION FOR ENROLLMENT, as a citizen of the Choctaw Nation, of Gracy May Fitzer

born on the 8$^{th}$ day of ___August___ 190 3

Name of father    W.W. Fitzer          a citizen of    white
Nation final enrollment No. ——
Name of mother    Lourinda Fitzer       a citizen of    Choctaw
Nation final enrollment No. 7359

                               Postoffice    Quinton I.T.

# Applications for Enrollment of Choctaw Newborn
## Act of 1905  Volume VIII

### AFFIDAVIT OF MOTHER.

UNITED STATES OF AMERICA
INDIAN TERRITORY
Western   DISTRICT

I   Lourinda Fitzer   , on oath state that I am 22   years of age and a citizen by   blood   of the   Choctaw   Nation, and as such have been placed upon the final roll of the   Choctaw   Nation, by the Honorable Secretary of the Interior my final enrollment number being   7359 ; that I am the lawful wife of   W. W. Fitzer   , who is a citizen of the   white   Nation, and as such has been placed upon the final roll of said Nation by the Honorable Secretary of the Interior, his final enrollment number being ——— and that a   female   child was born to me on the   8th   day of   August   190 3; that said child has been named   Gracy May Fitzer   , and is now living.

Lourinda Fitzer

Witnesseth.

Must be two Witnesses who are Citizens.   Tobias Brashears
George W Sims

Subscribed and sworn to before me this   6   day of   Jan   190 5

L.C. Tirey
Notary Public.

My commission expires:   Jan 17-1907

---

## AFFIDAVIT OF ATTENDING PHYSICIAN OR MIDWIFE

UNITED STATES OF AMERICA
INDIAN TERRITORY
Western   DISTRICT

I,   E Johnson   a   practicing physician on oath state that I attended on Mrs.   Lourinda Fitzer   wife of   W W Fitzer   on the   8th   day of   August   , 190 3, that there was born to her on said date a   female   child, that said child is now living, and is said to have been named   Gracy May Fitzer

E Johnson M.D.

Subscribed and sworn to before me this, the   6"   day of   Jan   190 5

L.C. Tirey   Notary Public.

WITNESSETH:
Must be two witnesses who are citizens   Tobias Brashears
George W Sims

## Applications for Enrollment of Choctaw Newborn
## Act of 1905   Volume VIII

We hereby certify that we are well acquainted with     E Johnson a     practicing physician     and know     him     to be reputable and of good standing in the community.

    Tobias Brashears                     _____

    George W Sims                      _____

---

Choctaw 2536.

Muskogee, Indian Territory, April 3, 1905.

William W. Fitzer,
    Quinton, Indian Territory.

Dear Sir:

    Receipt is hereby acknowledged of the affidavits of Lourinda Fitzer and E. Johnson to the birth of Gracie May Fitzer, daughter of William W. and Lourinda Fitzer, August 6, 1903, and the same have been filed with our records as an application for the enrollment of said child.

                                   Respectfully,

                                                   Chairman.

---

7-NB-500

Muskogee, Indian Territory, June 7, 1905.

Lourinda Fitzer,
    Quinton, Indian Territory.

Dear Sir:

    Receipt is hereby acknowledged of your letter of May 20, 1905, asking if your child Gracie May Fitzer has been approved so you can file on her allotment and if certain land described therein can be reserved for her.

    In reply to your letter you are advised that the name of your daughter Gracie May Fitzer has been placed upon a schedule of citizens by blood of the Choctaw Nation which is being prepared for forwarding to the Secretary of the Interior, but pending the approval of her enrollment by him no reservation of land or selection of allotment can be made for said child.

                              Respectfully,
                                              Commissioner in Charge.

## Applications for Enrollment of Choctaw Newborn
## Act of 1905   Volume VIII

Choc New Born 501
    Elick Hallmark   b. 2-14-04

---

7 N.B. 501.

Muskogee, Indian Territory, May 4, 1905.

John J. Hallmark,
    Lula, Indian Territory.

Dear Sir:

    Receipt is hereby acknowledged of the joint affidavit of R. S. Baker and Ike Morton to the birth of your child, Alick[sic] Hallmark, February 14, 1904, and the same have been filed with our records in the matter of the enrollment of said child.

        Respectfully,

                Chairman.

---

**COPY**

N. B. 501

Muskogee, Indian Territory, April 10, 1905.

John J. Hallmark,
    Lula, Indian Territory.

Dear Sir:

    There is inclosed you herewith for execution application for the enrollment of your infant child, Elick Hallmark, born February 14, 1904.

    In having these affidavits executed care should be exercised to see that all names are written in full, as they appear in the body of the affidavit, and in the event that either of the persons signing the affidavit are unable to write, signatures by mark must be attested by two witnesses. Each affidavit must be executed before a Notary Public and the notarial seal and signature of the officer must be attached to each separate affidavit.

        Respectfully,

        SIGNED

        *T. B. Needles.*

SEV 4-10.                Commissioner in Charge.

## Applications for Enrollment of Choctaw Newborn
## Act of 1905  Volume VIII

Choctaw 3278.

Muskogee, Indian Territory, April 3, 1905.

John J. Hallmark,
    Lula, Indian Territory.

Dear Sir:

    Receipt is hereby acknowledged of the affidavits of Sarah Hallmark and Mary Atkinson to the birth of Alick Hallmark, son of John J. and Sarah Hallmark, February 14, 1904, and the same have been filed with our records as an application for the enrollment of said child.

                      Respectfully,

                                          Chairman.

**COPY**

7 NB 501

Muskogee, Indian Territory, April 25, 1905.

J. J. Hallmark,
    Lula, Indian Territory.

Dear Sir:

    Receipt is hereby acknowledged of your letter of April 15, 1905, relative to the application for the enrollment of Eleck Hallmark, in which you state that the midwife in attendance at the birth of said child has moved away, and you are therefore unable to fill out the affidavit.

    In reply to your letter you are informed that if you cannot secure the affidavit of the physician or midwife in attendance, it will be necessary that you furnish the affidavits of two disinterested persons who know of the birth of this child, that he is the child of your wife, Sarah Hallmark, and that he was living on March 4, 1905.

                      Respectfully,

                            SIGNED

                          *Tams Bixby*
                             Chairman.

## Applications for Enrollment of Choctaw Newborn
## Act of 1905 Volume VIII

Tupelo, I.T.  5/1ˢ/1905
Central District

on this the 1ˢᵗ day of May 1905 personally appeared before me a Notary Public of the above named district, that R. S. Baker and Ike Morton to me personally well knows, does make affidavits that they know John J Hallmark and Sarah Hallmark his wife and that there was born to them a male child on the 14ᵗʰ day of February 1904 and that the sid[sic] child's name is Elick Hallmark, and that he is now living.

Witness  R. S. Baker
         Ike Morton

Subscribed and sworn to before me this sworred[sic] to before me this 1 day of May - 1905.

J. H. Clark
Notary Public.

---

**BIRTH AFFIDAVIT.**

### DEPARTMENT OF THE INTERIOR.
### COMMISSION TO THE FIVE CIVILIZED TRIBES.

---

**IN RE APPLICATION FOR ENROLLMENT**, as a citizen of the    Chacktaw[sic]    Nation, of   Elick Hallmark    , born on the   14   day of   Feb  , 1904

Name of Father: John J. Hallmark          a citizen of the  Chacktaw  Nation.
Name of Mother: Sarah Hallmark           a citizen of the  Chacktaw  Nation.

Postoffice   Lula I T

---

**AFFIDAVIT OF MOTHER.**

**UNITED STATES OF AMERICA, Indian Territory,** ⎫
      Sentrall[sic]         **DISTRICT.** ⎭

I, Sarah Hallmark     , on oath state that I am   34   years of age and a citizen by   blood  , of the   Chacktaw Nation; that I am the lawful wife of   John J Hallmark  , who is a citizen, by  marriage   of the    Chacktaw   Nation; that a male   child was born to me on   14   day of   Feb   , 1904; that said child has been named   Elick Hallmark   , and was living March 4, 1905.

                                  her
                          Sarah x Hallmark
Witnesses To Mark:                mark
  ⎰ Anna Morton
  ⎱ *(Name Illegible)*

## Applications for Enrollment of Choctaw Newborn
## Act of 1905   Volume VIII

Subscribed and sworn to before me this   30  day of     March     , 1905

          J. H. Clark
           Notary Public.

---

**AFFIDAVIT OF ATTENDING PHYSICIAN OR MID-WIFE.**

UNITED STATES OF AMERICA, Indian Territory, }
 Sentrall      DISTRICT.  }

  I,   Mary Atkinson        , a ................................, on oath state that I attended on Mrs.   Sarah Hallmark    , wife of   John J Hallmark    on the  14  day of  Feb  , 1904; that there was born to her on said date a     male     child; that said child was living March 4, 1905, and is said to have been named Elick Hallmark

Witnesses To Mark:
 { J. L. Sheckells
  Ed King

Subscribed and sworn to before me this   30  day of     March     , 1905

          J. H. Clark
           Notary Public.

---

Choc New Born 502
  Charles S. Stanley   b.  11-20-04

              Chocktaw-591.

      Muskogee, Indian Territory, April 1, 1905.

William M. Stanley,
  Valliant, Indian Territory.

Dear Sir:

  Receipt is hereby acknowledged of the affidavits of Salena Stanley and D. O. Spencer to the birth of Charles S. Stanley, son of William M. and Salena Stanley, November 20, 1904, and the same have been filed with our records as an application for the enrollment of said child.

# Applications for Enrollment of Choctaw Newborn
## Act of 1905   Volume VIII

Respectfully,

Chairman.

---

Choctaw 591.

Muskogee, Indian Territory, April 11, 1905.

William M. Stanley,
    Parsons, Indian Territory.

Dear Sir:

    Receipt is hereby acknowledged of your letter of April 4, asking if the application for the enrollment of your child, Charles S. Stanley, has been received.

    In reply to your letter you are informed that the affidavits heretofore forwarded to the birth of your son, Charles S. Stanley, have been filed with our records as an application for the enrollment of said child and if further evidence is necessary to enable the Commission to determine his right to enrollment you will be duly notified.

Respectfully,

Commissioner in Charge.

---

## AFFIDAVIT OF ATTENDING PHYSICIAN OR MIDWIFE

UNITED STATES OF AMERICA
INDIAN TERRITORY
Central     DISTRICT

    I,   D.O. Spencer      a      Physician on oath state that I attended on Mrs. Salena Stanley   wife of William M Stanley on the 20$^{th}$ day of November , 190 4, that there was born to her on said date a   male child, that said child is now living, and is said to have been named   Charles Spencer Stanley

D. O. Spencer     M.D.

WITNESSETH:
Must be two witnesses who are citizens and know the child.   { R.F. Wilson
John W Fowler

Subscribed and sworn to before me this, the ................... day of ................................ 190......

................................ Notary Public.

## Applications for Enrollment of Choctaw Newborn
## Act of 1905   Volume VIII

We hereby certify that we are well acquainted with   D.O. Spencer a   Physician   and know   him   to be reputable and of good standing in the community.

> R.F. Wilson
> John W Fowler

**NEW-BORN AFFIDAVIT.**

Number..............

...Choctaw Enrolling Commission...

IN THE MATTER OF THE APPLICATION FOR ENROLLMENT, as a citizen of the Choctaw   Nation, of   Charles Spencer Stanley

born on the 20$^{th}$   day of __November__   190 4

Name of father   William M. Stanley   a citizen of   Choctaw Nation final enrollment No.  627
Name of mother   Salena Stanley   a citizen of   Choctaw Nation final enrollment No.  1350

Postoffice   Valliant, I.T.

**AFFIDAVIT OF MOTHER.**

UNITED STATES OF AMERICA
INDIAN TERRITORY
Central   DISTRICT

I   Salena Stanley   , on oath state that I am 34   years of age and a citizen by   blood   of the   Choctaw   Nation, and as such have been placed upon the final roll of the   Choctaw   Nation, by the Honorable Secretary of the Interior my final enrollment number being   1350 ; that I am the lawful wife of   William M Stanley   , who is a citizen of the   Choctaw   Nation, and as such has been placed upon the final roll of said Nation by the Honorable Secretary of the Interior, his final enrollment number being   627   and that a   Male   child was born to me on the 20$^{th}$   day of   November   190 4; that said child has been named  Charles Spencer Stanley   , and is now living.

Salena Stanley

Witnesseth.

Must be two Witnesses who are Citizens.   } R.F. Wilson
John W Fowler

# Applications for Enrollment of Choctaw Newborn
## Act of 1905   Volume VIII

Subscribed and sworn to before me this   23   day of   Feb   190 5

W.A. Shoney
Notary Public.

My commission expires:

---

**BIRTH AFFIDAVIT.**

## DEPARTMENT OF THE INTERIOR.
## COMMISSION TO THE FIVE CIVILIZED TRIBES.

---

IN RE APPLICATION FOR ENROLLMENT, as a citizen of the   Choctaw   Nation, of Charles S. Stanley   , born on the 20$^{th}$   day of November   , 1904

Name of Father: William M. Stanley         a citizen of the   Choctaw   Nation.
Name of Mother: Salena Stanley              a citizen of the   Choctaw   Nation.

Postoffice   Valliant I.T.

---

**AFFIDAVIT OF MOTHER.**

UNITED STATES OF AMERICA, Indian Territory,
    Central           DISTRICT.

I,   Salena Stanley   , on oath state that I am   35   years of age and a citizen by   Blood   , of the   Choctaw   Nation that I am the lawful wife of   William M. Stanley   , who is a citizen, by Marriage   of the   Choctaw   Nation; that a male   child was born to me on   20$^{th}$   day of   November   , 1904; that said child has been named   Charles S. Stanley   , and was living March 4, 1905.

Salena Stanley

Witnesses To Mark:

Subscribed and sworn to before me this   27$^{th}$   day of   March   , 1905

E.J. Gardner
Notary Public.

## Applications for Enrollment of Choctaw Newborn
## Act of 1905   Volume VIII

### AFFIDAVIT OF ATTENDING PHYSICIAN OR MID-WIFE.

UNITED STATES OF AMERICA, Indian Territory,  
Central                                    DISTRICT.

    I,   D. O. Spencer   , a   Physician   , on oath state that I attended on Mrs.   Salena Stanley   , wife of   William M Stanley   on the   20th   day of   November  , 1904; that there was born to her on said date a   male   child; that said child was living March 4, 1905, and is said to have been named Charles S. Stanley

                                      D. O. Spencer M.D.

Witnesses To Mark:

{

    Subscribed and sworn to before me this   27th   day of   March   , 1905

                                      E.J. Gardner  
                                        Notary Public.

---

Choc New Born 503  
      Louise Dibrell   b. 11-19-04

                        **COPY**                              7 N B 503

                      Muskogee, Indian Territory, April 12, 1905.

Charles E. Dibrell,  
    Duncan, Indian Territory.

Dear Sir:

    Receipt is hereby acknowledged of your letter of March 29, 1905, requesting that the age of your wife Allie Dibrell twenty-three years be inserted and in compliance with your request the age of Allie Dibrell has been inserted in her affidavit recently filed in the matter of her application for the enrollment of your child Louise Dibrell.

                        Respectfully,  
                        SIGNED  
                        *T. B. Needles.*  
                        Commissioner in Charge.

## Applications for Enrollment of Choctaw Newborn
## Act of 1905 Volume VIII

**COPY**  7 N B 503

Muskogee, Indian Territory, April 12, 1905.

*(The above letter given again.)*

---

March 29, 1905.

Commission to the Five Civilized Tribes,
    Muskogee, Ind. Ter.

Gentlemen:

    A few days ago I sent you an application for the enrollment of my infant child, Louise Dibrell, but in the affidavit of my wife I failed to insert her age. Allie Dibrell's age is twenty three years and you are hereby authorized to insert it in her affidavit.

Very Truly,

(signed) Chas E Dibrell

---

**BIRTH AFFIDAVIT.**

### DEPARTMENT OF THE INTERIOR.
### COMMISSION TO THE FIVE CIVILIZED TRIBES.

---

    **IN RE APPLICATION FOR ENROLLMENT**, as a citizen of the Choctaw Nation, of Louise Dibrell, born on the 19 day of Nov, 1904

Name of Father: Charles E Dibrell     a citizen of the Choctaw Nation.
Name of Mother: Allie Dibrell     a citizen of the Choctaw Nation.

Postoffice    Duncan, Ind. Ter.

---

**AFFIDAVIT OF MOTHER.**

UNITED STATES OF AMERICA, Indian Territory, }
    Southern      DISTRICT. }

    I, Allie Dibrell, on oath state that I am 23 years of age and a citizen by intermarriage, of the Choctaw Nation; that I am the lawful wife of Charles E Dibrell, who is a citizen, by blood of the Choctaw Nation; that a female child was born to me on 19 day of Nov, 1904; that said child has been named Louise Dibrell, and was living March 4, 1905.

## Applications for Enrollment of Choctaw Newborn
## Act of 1905   Volume VIII

Allie Dibrell

Witnesses To Mark:
{

    Subscribed and sworn to before me this   27   day of      march        , 1905

E.H. Bond<br>Notary Public.

---

**AFFIDAVIT OF ATTENDING PHYSICIAN OR MID-WIFE.**

UNITED STATES OF AMERICA, Indian Territory, }
   So                     DISTRICT.}

    I,   H.A. Conger            , a    Physician      , on oath state that I attended on Mrs.   Allie Dibrell     , wife of   Charles E Dibrell    on the   19   day of   Nov   , 1904; that there was born to her on said date a     female     child; that said child was living March 4, 1905, and is said to have been named   Louise Dibrell

H.A. Conger M.D.

Witnesses To Mark:
{

    Subscribed and sworn to before me this   27   day of      march        , 1905

E.H. Bond<br>Notary Public.

---

<u>Choc New Born 504</u>
    Julia Carr   b. 3-2-05

# Applications for Enrollment of Choctaw Newborn
## Act of 1905   Volume VIII

Choctaw 3153

Muskogee, Indian Territory, April 1, 1905.

Dennis Carr,
    Albany, Indian Territory.

Dear Sir:

    Receipt is hereby acknowledged of the affidavits of Jane Carr and N. L. Capshaw to the birth of Julia Carr, daughter of Dennis and Jane Carr March 3, 1905, and the same have been filed with our records as an application for the enrollment of said child.

    Respectfully,

    Chairman.

---

**BIRTH AFFIDAVIT.**

### DEPARTMENT OF THE INTERIOR.
### COMMISSION TO THE FIVE CIVILIZED TRIBES.

**IN RE APPLICATION FOR ENROLLMENT,** as a citizen of the Choctaw Nation, of Julia Carr, born on the $2^{nd}$ day of March, 1905

Name of Father: Denis[sic] Carr    a citizen of the Choctaw Nation.
Name of Mother: Jane Carr    a citizen of the Choctaw Nation.

    Postoffice   Albany, I.T.

---

**AFFIDAVIT OF MOTHER.**

UNITED STATES OF AMERICA, Indian Territory,
    Central    DISTRICT.

    I, Jane Carr, on oath state that I am 33 years of age and a citizen by blood, of the Choctaw Nation; that I am the lawful wife of Dennis Carr, who is a citizen, by blood of the Choctaw Nation; that a female child was born to me on second day of March, 1905; that said child has been named Julia Carr, and was living March 4, 1905.

                her
            Jane x Carr
Witnesses To Mark:    mark
    D.L. Cain
    Bellie Mills

# Applications for Enrollment of Choctaw Newborn
## Act of 1905   Volume VIII

Subscribed and sworn to before me this   27th day of   March   , 1905

D.L. Cain
Notary Public.

---

**AFFIDAVIT OF ATTENDING PHYSICIAN OR MID-WIFE.**

UNITED STATES OF AMERICA, Indian Territory, }
................................................ DISTRICT. }

I, N.L. Capshaw   , a   midwife   , on oath state that I attended on Mrs.   Jane Carr   , wife of   Dennis Carr   on the   second day of   March , 1905; that there was born to her on said date a   female   child; that said child was living March 4, 1905, and is said to have been named   Julia Carr

N.L. Capshaw

Witnesses To Mark:
{

Subscribed and sworn to before me this   27th day of   March   , 1905

D.L. Cain
Notary Public.

---

Choc New Born 505
    Ruben Airington   b. 2-23-05

Choctaw 1463.

Muskogee, Indian Territory, April 3, 1905.

Arthur Airington,
    Graham, Indian Territory.

Dear Sir:

    Receipt is hereby acknowledged of the affidavits of Francis Going Airington and J. E. Booth to the birth of Ruben Airington, son of Arthur and Francis Going Airington, February 23, 1905, and the same have been filed with our records as an application for the enrollment of said child.

# Applications for Enrollment of Choctaw Newborn
## Act of 1905   Volume VIII

Respectfully,

Chairman.

---

**BIRTH AFFIDAVIT.**

DEPARTMENT OF THE INTERIOR.
## COMMISSION TO THE FIVE CIVILIZED TRIBES.

---

**IN RE APPLICATION FOR ENROLLMENT,** as a citizen of the   Choctaw   Nation, of Ruben Airington   , born on the 23   day of   Feb  , 1905

Name of Father:  Arthur G Airington   a citizen of the   Choctaw   Nation.
Name of Mother: Francis Going Airington   a citizen of the   Choctaw   Nation.

Postoffice   Graham, I.T.

---

**AFFIDAVIT OF MOTHER.**

UNITED STATES OF AMERICA, Indian Territory, }
    Southern        DISTRICT.                }

I,   Francis Going Airington   , on oath state that I am   17 years of age and a citizen by   Blood   , of the   Choctaw   Nation; that I am the lawful wife of Arthur G Airington   , who is a citizen, by   Blood   of the   Choctaw   Nation; that a   male   child was born to me on   23   day of   Feb  , 1905, that said child has been named   Ruben Airington   , and is now living.

                        her
              Francis x Going Airington
Witnesses To Mark:      mark
{ M. D. Butler
{ A.G. Airington

Subscribed and sworn to before me this 21   day of   March   , 1905.

M.D. Butler
Notary Public.

## Applications for Enrollment of Choctaw Newborn
## Act of 1905 Volume VIII

### AFFIDAVIT OF ATTENDING PHYSICIAN OR MID-WIFE.

UNITED STATES OF AMERICA, Indian Territory, }
Southern                DISTRICT. }

    I, J. E. Booth , a M. D. , on oath state that I attended on Mrs. Francis G Airington , wife of A G Airington on the 23 day of Feb , 1905; that there was born to her on said date a male child; that said child is now living and is said to have been named Ruben Airington

J. E. Booth M.D.

Witnesses To Mark:
{

    Subscribed and sworn to before me this 21 day of March , 1905.

M.D. Butler<br>Notary Public.

---

Choc New Born 506
    Absolum Wallen b. 2-26-05

7-2463

Muskogee, Indian Territory, April 1, 1905.

Thompson Wallen,
    McCurtain, Indian Territory.

Dear Sis:

    Receipt is hereby acknowledged of the affidavits of Sarah Wallen and Sinnie Wallen to the birth of Absolum Wallen, son of Thompson and Sarah Wallen, February 26, 1905, and the same have been filed with our records as an application for the enrollment of said child.

Respectfully,

Chairman.

## Applications for Enrollment of Choctaw Newborn
## Act of 1905 Volume VIII

BIRTH AFFIDAVIT.

## DEPARTMENT OF THE INTERIOR.
## COMMISSION TO THE FIVE CIVILIZED TRIBES.

IN RE APPLICATION FOR ENROLLMENT, as a citizen of the Choctaw Nation, of Absolum Wallen, born on the 26 day of February, 1905

Name of Father: Thompson Wallen     a citizen of the Choctaw Nation.
Name of Mother: Sarah Wallen     a citizen of the Choctaw Nation.

Postoffice M<sup>c</sup>Curtain, Ind. Ter.

### AFFIDAVIT OF MOTHER.

UNITED STATES OF AMERICA, Indian Territory, }
    Central     DISTRICT.

I, Sarah Wallen, on oath state that I am 44 years of age and a citizen by marriage, of the Choctaw Nation; that I am the lawful wife of Thompson Wallen, who is a citizen, by blood of the Choctaw Nation; that a male child was born to me on 26 day of February, 1905; that said child has been named Absolum Wallen, and was living March 4, 1905.

                               her
                         Sarah x Wallen
Witnesses To Mark:            mark
    { Sarah Folsom
    { Sim Wallen

Subscribed and sworn to before me this 29 day of March, 1905

My Com Exp 2/2/08           Frank E Parke
                               Notary Public.

### AFFIDAVIT OF ATTENDING PHYSICIAN OR MID-WIFE.

UNITED STATES OF AMERICA, Indian Territory, }
    Central     DISTRICT.

I, Sinnie Wallen, a midwife, on oath state that I attended on Mrs. Sarah Wallen, wife of Thompson Wallen on the 26 day of February, 1905; that there was born to her on said date a male child; that said child was living March 4, 1905, and is said to have been named ~~Solomon~~ Wallen

                            her     *Absolom*
                        Sinnie x Wallen
                            mark

# Applications for Enrollment of Choctaw Newborn
## Act of 1905 Volume VIII

Witnesses To Mark:
 { Saul Folsom
 { Sim Wallen

    Subscribed and sworn to before me this 29 day of March , 1905

My Com Exp 2/2/08                   Frank E Parke
                                            Notary Public.

---

I do certify that I erroneously wrote "Solomon" and erased same supplying "Absolum" the correct name.

                                    Frank E. Parke
                                        N.P.

---

Choc New Born 507
    Troy Yoder b. 11-11-04

                                                       7-183

                    Muskogee, Indian Territory, March 7, 1905.

Maide Yoder (Powers),
    Whitebead, Indian Territory.

Dear Madam:

    Receipt is hereby acknowledged of your affidavit and the affidavit of A. J. Robinson to the birth of Troy Yoder, infant son of James and Maide Yoder May[sic] 11, 1904, and the same have been filed with our records as an application for the enrollment of said child.

                         Respectfully,

                                       Commissioner in Charge.

## Applications for Enrollment of Choctaw Newborn
## Act of 1905   Volume VIII

**COPY**

7 N B 507

Muskogee, Indian Territory, April 15, 1905.

James Yoder,
    Whitebead, Indian Territory.

Dear Sir:

    There is inclosed you herewith for execution application for the enrollment of your infant child, Troy Yoder, born November 11, 1904.

    The affidavits heretofore filed with the Commission show the child was living on March 2, 1905. It is necessary, for the child to be enrolled, that he was living on March 4, 1905.

    In having these affidavits executed care should be exercised to see that all names are written in full, as they appear in the body of the affidavit, and in the event that either of the persons signing the affidavit are unable to write, signatures by mark must be attested by two witnesses. Each affidavit must be executed before a Notary Public and the notarial seal and signature of the officer must be attached to each separate affidavit.

    Respectfully,

SIGNED

*Tams Bixby*
Chairman.

LM 15-145

---

7 N. B. 507.

Muskogee, Indian Territory, May 4, 1905.

James Yoder,
    Whitebead, Indian Territory.

Dear Sir:

    Receipt is hereby acknowledged of the affidavits of Maide Yoder (Powers) and A. J. Robinson to the birth of Troy Yoder, son of James and Maide Yoder, November 1, 1904m[sic] and the same have been filed with our records in the matter of the enrollment of said child.

    Respectfully,

Chairman.

## Applications for Enrollment of Choctaw Newborn
## Act of 1905   Volume VIII

7-N.B. 507.

Muskogee, Indian Territory, May 25, 1905.

Mrs. Maidie[sic] P. Yoder,
    White Bead, Indian Territory.

Dear Sir[sic]:

    Receipt is hereby acknowledged of your letter of May 20, asking if you can have an allotment set aside for your child who is not yet approved.

    In reply to your letter you are advised that it is presumed you refer to your child, Troy Yoder, and you are advised that no selection of allotment or reservation of land can be permitted for children for whom application is made under the provisions of the act of Congress approved March 3, 1905, until their enrollment has been approved by the Secretary of the Interior.

Respectfully,

Chairman.

---

**BIRTH AFFIDAVIT.**

    ***IN RE-APPLICATION FOR ENROLLMENT***, as a citizen of the   Choctaw   Nation, of Troy Yoder, born on the 11th   day of November , 1904

Name of Father: James Yoder        a citizen of the United States   ~~Nation~~.
Name of Mother: Maide Yoder (nee Powers)    a citizen of the   Choctaw   Nation.

Postoffice   White Bead, I.T.

---

**AFFIDAVIT OF MOTHER.**

UNITED STATES OF AMERICA, INDIAN TERRITORY,
    Southern   District.

    I,  Maide Yoder (nee Maide Powers)  , on oath state that I am  19  years of age and a citizen by  Blood  , of the  Choctaw  Nation; that I am the lawful wife of  James Yoder , who is a citizen, by ................. of the  United States  Nation; that a  male child was born to me on  Eleventh  day of  November  , 1904 , that said child has been named  Troy Yoder  , and is now living.

Maide Yoder
(nee Maide Powers)

# Applications for Enrollment of Choctaw Newborn
## Act of 1905   Volume VIII

Witnesses To Mark:

Subscribed and sworn to before me this  2$^{nd}$   day of   March   , 1905.

                                        Marion Henderson
                                              Notary Public.

---

### AFFIDAVIT OF ATTENDING PHYSICIAN OR MID-WIFE.

UNITED STATES OF AMERICA, INDIAN TERRITORY,
   Southern                District.

I,   A J Robinson   , a   Physician   , on oath state that I attended on Mrs.  Maide Yoder (nee Powers)   , wife of   James Yoder   on the   eleventh   day of   November   , 190 4; that there was born to her on said date a   male   child; that said child is now living and is said to have been named   Troy Yoder

                                        A J Robinson M.D.

Witnesses To Mark:

Subscribed and sworn to before me this   25   day of   February   , 1905.

                                        Marion Henderson
                                          Notary Public.

---

**BIRTH AFFIDAVIT.**

### DEPARTMENT OF THE INTERIOR.
### COMMISSION TO THE FIVE CIVILIZED TRIBES.

---

**IN RE APPLICATION FOR ENROLLMENT,** as a citizen of the   Choctaw   Nation, of   Troy Yoder   , born on the   11$^{th}$   day of   November   , 1904

Name of Father:   James Yoder         a citizen of the   Choctaw   Nation.
Name of Mother:  Maide Yoder (Powers)   a citizen of the   Choctaw   Nation.

                            Postoffice     Whitebead I.T.

# Applications for Enrollment of Choctaw Newborn
## Act of 1905   Volume VIII

### AFFIDAVIT OF MOTHER.

UNITED STATES OF AMERICA, Indian Territory, }
  Southern Judicial    DISTRICT.

    I, Maide Yoder (Powers, on oath state that I am 19 years of age and a citizen by blood, of the Choctaw Nation; that I am the lawful wife of James Yoder, who is a citizen, by —— of the United States Nation; that a male child was born to me on 11" day of November, 1904; that said child has been named Troy Yoder, and was living March 4, 1905.

                            Maide Yoder - Powers

Witnesses To Mark:
{

    Subscribed and sworn to before me this 28 day of April, 1905

                            Marion Henderson
                            Notary Public.

### AFFIDAVIT OF ATTENDING PHYSICIAN OR MID-WIFE.

UNITED STATES OF AMERICA, Indian Territory, }
  Southern Judicial    DISTRICT.

    I, A.J. Robinson, a physician, on oath state that I attended on Mrs. Maide Yoder (Powers), wife of James Yoder on the 11" day of November, 1904; that there was born to her on said date a male child; that said child was living March 4, 1905, and is said to have been named Troy Yoder

                            A J Robinson M.D.

Witnesses To Mark:
{

    Subscribed and sworn to before me this 22$^{nd}$ day of April, 1905

                            Ora Patchell
                            Notary Public.

# Applications for Enrollment of Choctaw Newborn
## Act of 1905 Volume VIII

Choc New Born 508
    John E. Wise, Jr  b. 4-29-03
    Lela Wise  b. 9-15-04

---

7-183

Muskogee, Indian Territory, March 21, 1905.

Bond & Melton,
    Attorneys at Law,
        Chickasha, Indian Territory.

Gentlemen:

    Receipt is hereby acknowledged of your letter of March 16, 1905, enclosing the affidavits of Vesta Wise (Powers) and Ella Jump to the birth of John E. Wise Jr., child of John E. and Vesta Wise, April 29, 1903; and the affidavits of Vesta Wise and A. J. Robinson to the birth of Lela Wise, daughter of John E. and Vesta Wise, September 15, 1904, and the same have been filed with our records as an application for the enrollment of said children.

    You ask that these applications be filed at once as you desire to have land set aside for the children named therein, and in reply you are advised that the Commission cannot permit reservations of allotments for children born subsequent to September 25, 1902, until their enrollment has been approved by the Secretary of the Interior.

                            Respectfully,

                                    Chairman.

---

*(The above letter given again.)*

---

## Applications for Enrollment of Choctaw Newborn
## Act of 1905   Volume VIII

9[sic]   7 N B 508

**COPY**

Muskogee, Indian Territory, April 15, 1905.

John E. Wise,
  Whitebead, Indian Territory.

Dear Sir:

There is inclosed you herewith for execution application for the enrollment of your infant children, John E. Wise, Jr., and Lela Wise, born April 29, 1903 and September 15, 1904, respectively.

The affidavits heretofore filed with the Commission show the children were living on February 27, 1905. It is necessary, for them to be enrolled, that they were living on March 4, 1905.

In having these affidavits executed care should be exercised to see that all names are written in full, as they appear in the body of the affidavit, and in the event that either of the persons signing the affidavit are unable to write, signatures by mark must be attested by two witnesses. Each affidavit must be executed before a Notary Public and the notarial seal and signature of the officer must be attached to each separate affidavit.

Respectfully,

SIGNED *Tams Bixby*

LM 15-150.                                                                                           Chairman.

---

7 N.B. 508.

Muskogee, Indian Territory, May 4, 1905.

John E. Wise,
  Whitebead, Indian Territory.

Dear Sir:

Receipt is hereby acknowledged of the affidavits of Vesta Wise (Powers) and A. J. Robinson to the birth of John E. Wise, Jr., and Lela Wise, children of John E. and Vesta Wise, April 2, 1903 and September 15, 1904, respectively, and the same have been filed with our records in the matter of the enrollment of said children.

Respectfully,

Chairman.

# Applications for Enrollment of Choctaw Newborn
## Act of 1905   Volume VIII

BIRTH AFFIDAVIT.

## DEPARTMENT OF THE INTERIOR.
## COMMISSION TO THE FIVE CIVILIZED TRIBES.

IN RE APPLICATION FOR ENROLLMENT, as a citizen of the Choctaw Nation, of Lela Wise, born on the 15" day of September, 1904

Name of Father: John Wise    a citizen of the United States Nation.
Name of Mother: Vesta Wise (Powers)    a citizen of the Choctaw Nation.

Postoffice   Whitebead I.T.

### AFFIDAVIT OF MOTHER.

UNITED STATES OF AMERICA, Indian Territory, } Southern DISTRICT.

I, Vesta Wise (Powers), on oath state that I am 17 years of age and a citizen by blood, of the Choctaw Nation; that I am the lawful wife of John Wise, who is a citizen, ~~by~~ —— of the United States Nation; that a female child was born to me on 15" day of September, 1904; that said child has been named Lela Wise, and was living March 4, 1905.

Vesta Wise (Powers)

Witnesses To Mark:
{

Subscribed and sworn to before me this 28 day of April, 1905

Marion Henderson
Notary Public.

### AFFIDAVIT OF ATTENDING PHYSICIAN OR MID-WIFE.

UNITED STATES OF AMERICA, Indian Territory, } Southern DISTRICT.

I, A J Robinson, a Physician, on oath state that I attended on Mrs. Vesta Wise (Powers), wife of John Wise on the 15" day of September, 1904; that there was born to her on said date a female child; that said child was living March 4, 1905, and is said to have been named Lela Wise

A.J. Robinson M.D.

## Applications for Enrollment of Choctaw Newborn
## Act of 1905   Volume VIII

Witnesses To Mark:

{

Subscribed and sworn to before me this 28 day of   April   , 1905

Marion Henderson
Notary Public.

---

BIRTH AFFIDAVIT.

IN RE-APPLICATION FOR ENROLLMENT, as a citizen of the   Choctaw   Nation, of Lela Wise , born on the 15$^{th}$   day of September , 190 4

Name of Father:   John Wise                a citizen of the  United States   ~~Nation.~~
Name of Mother:  Vesta Wise (nee Powers)   a citizen of the   Choctaw   Nation.

Postoffice   White Bead I.T.

---

AFFIDAVIT OF MOTHER.

UNITED STATES OF AMERICA, INDIAN TERRITORY, }
Southern                    District. }

I,  Vesta Wise (nee Powers)  , on oath state that I am  17  years of age and a citizen by  Blood  , of the  Choctaw  Nation; that I am the lawful wife of  John Wise , who is a citizen, by ................ of the  United States  Nation; that a  Female  child was born to me on  fifteenth  day of  September  , 1904 , that said child has been named  Lela Wise  , and is now living.

Vesta Wise

Witnesses To Mark:

{

Subscribed and sworn to before me this  27$^{th}$  day of  February  , 1905.

O.W. Patchell
Notary Public.

---

AFFIDAVIT OF ATTENDING PHYSICIAN OR MID-WIFE.

UNITED STATES OF AMERICA, INDIAN TERRITORY, }
Southern                    District. }

I,  A J Robinson  , a  Physician  , on oath state that I attended on Mrs.  Vesta Wise (nee Powers)  , wife of  John Wise  on the fifteenth  day of September  , 190 4; that there was born to her on said date a  Female  child; that said child is now living and is said to have been named  Lela Wise

# Applications for Enrollment of Choctaw Newborn
## Act of 1905 Volume VIII

A J Robinson M.D.

Witnesses To Mark:
{

Subscribed and sworn to before me this 25th day of February, 1905.

Marion Henderson
Notary Public.

---

BIRTH AFFIDAVIT.

## DEPARTMENT OF THE INTERIOR.
## COMMISSION TO THE FIVE CIVILIZED TRIBES.

IN RE APPLICATION FOR ENROLLMENT, as a citizen of the Choctaw Nation, of John E Wise Jr, born on the 29" day of April, 1903

Name of Father: John E. Wise          a citizen of the United States Nation.
Name of Mother: Vesta Wise (Powers)   a citizen of the Choctaw Nation.

Postoffice   Whitebead I.T.

---

### AFFIDAVIT OF MOTHER.

UNITED STATES OF AMERICA, Indian Territory, }
    Southern             DISTRICT.

I, Vesta Wise (Powers), on oath state that I am 17 years of age and a citizen by blood, of the Choctaw Nation; that I am the lawful wife of John Wise, who is a citizen, ~~by~~ —— of the United States Nation; that a male child was born to me on 29" day of April, 1903; that said child has been named John E. Wise Jr, and was living March 4, 1905.

Vesta Wise (Powers)

Witnesses To Mark:
{

Subscribed and sworn to before me this 28 day of April, 1905

Marion Henderson
Notary Public.

## Applications for Enrollment of Choctaw Newborn
## Act of 1905   Volume VIII

### AFFIDAVIT OF ATTENDING PHYSICIAN OR MID-WIFE.

UNITED STATES OF AMERICA, Indian Territory,  
Southern DISTRICT.

I, A J Robinson, a Physician, on oath state that I attended on Mrs. Vesta Wise (Powers), wife of John Wise on the 29" day of April, 1903; that there was born to her on said date a male child; that said child was living March 4, 1905, and is said to have been named John E Wise Jr

A.J. Robinson M.D.

Witnesses To Mark:

Subscribed and sworn to before me this 28 day of April, 1905

Marion Henderson  
Notary Public.

### BIRTH AFFIDAVIT.

**IN RE-APPLICATION FOR ENROLLMENT**, as a citizen of the Choctaw Nation, of John E Wise Jr, born on the $29^{th}$ day of April, 190 3

Name of Father: John E. Wise         a citizen of the United States Nation.  
Name of Mother: Vesta Wise (nee Powers)   a citizen of the Choctaw Nation.

Postoffice   Whitebead I.T.

### AFFIDAVIT OF MOTHER.

UNITED STATES OF AMERICA, INDIAN TERRITORY,  
Southern Judicial District.

I, Vesta Wise nee Powers, on oath state that I am 17 years of age and a citizen by blood, of the Choctaw Nation; that I am the lawful wife of John Wise, who is a citizen, by .................... of the United States Nation; that a male child was born to me on $29^{th}$ day of April, 1903, that said child has been named John E Wise Jr, and is now living.

Vesta Wise

Witnesses To Mark:

Subscribed and sworn to before me this $27^{th}$ day of February, 1905.

O.W. Patchell  
Notary Public.

# Applications for Enrollment of Choctaw Newborn
## Act of 1905   Volume VIII

AFFIDAVIT OF ATTENDING PHYSICIAN OR MID-WIFE.

UNITED STATES OF AMERICA, INDIAN TERRITORY,
Southern Judicial District.

I, Ellen Jump , a midwife , on oath state that I attended on Mrs. Vesta Wise , wife of John Wise on the 29$^{th}$ day of April , 190 3; that there was born to her on said date a male child; that said child is now living and is said to have been named John E. Wise Jr

Ellen Jump

Witnesses To Mark:

Subscribed and sworn to before me this 27$^{th}$ day of April , 1905.

O.W. Patchell
Notary Public.

---

Choc New Born 509
    Opal McGahey  b. 7-17-03

Choctaw 4403

Muskogee, Indian Territory, April 3, 1905.

Arthur D. McGahey,
    Cliff, Indian Territory.

Dar Sir:

Receipt is hereby acknowledged of the affidavits of Annie McGahey and E. F. Lewis to the birth of Opal McGahey, daughter of Arthur D. and Annie McGahey, July 17, 1903, and the same have been filed with our records as an application for the enrollment of said child.

Respectfully,

Chairman.

## Applications for Enrollment of Choctaw Newborn
## Act of 1905   Volume VIII

7 N. B. 509

**COPY**

Muskogee, Indian Territory, April 10, 1905.

Arthur McGahey,
    Cliff, Indian Territory.

Dear Sir:

    You are hereby advised that before the application for the enrollment of your infant child, Opal McGahey, can be finally disposed of, it will be necessary that you furnish either the original or a certified copy of the license and certificate of your marriage to Annie McGahey, forwarding same to the Commission at the earliest practicable date.

                              Respectfully,

                    SIGNED        *T. B. Needles.*

LM                                   Commissioner in Charge.

---

7-NB-509.

**COPY**

Muskogee, Indian Territory, April 25, 1905.

Annie McGahey,
    Cliff, Indian Territory.

Dear Madam:

    Receipt is hereby acknowledged of your letter of April 20th, transmitting marriage license and certificate between Arthur McGahey and Annie Lowles, which you offer in support of the application for the enrollment of your child, Opal McGahey, and the same have been filed with the records in this case.

                              Respectfully,

                    SIGNED

                                *Tams Bixby*
                                Chairman.

## Applications for Enrollment of Choctaw Newborn
## Act of 1905  Volume VIII

**BIRTH AFFIDAVIT.**

### DEPARTMENT OF THE INTERIOR.
### COMMISSION TO THE FIVE CIVILIZED TRIBES.

IN RE APPLICATION FOR ENROLLMENT, as a citizen of the    Choctaw    Nation, of Opal M$^c$Gahey   , born on the 17$^{th}$   day of   July  , 1903

Name of Father:  Authur[sic] D. M$^c$Gahey    a citizen of the    Choctaw    Nation.
Name of Mother:  Annie M$^c$Gahey        a citizen of the   ———    Nation.

Postoffice   Cliff, I.T.

**AFFIDAVIT OF MOTHER.**

UNITED STATES OF AMERICA, Indian Territory,
Southern         DISTRICT.

I,  Annie M$^c$Gahey  , on oath state that I am  19  years of age and a citizen by  intermarriage  , of the  Choctaw  Nation; that I am the lawful wife of Author[sic] D. M$^c$Gahey  , who is a citizen, by blood  of the  Choctaw Nation; that a  female  child was born to me on  17$^{th}$  day of  July  , 1903; that said child has been named  Opal M$^c$Gahey  , and was living March 4, 1905.

Annie McGahey

Witnesses To Mark:
{

Subscribed and sworn to before me this  29$^{th}$  day of  March  , 1905

D R Johnston
Notary Public.

**AFFIDAVIT OF ATTENDING PHYSICIAN OR MID-WIFE.**

UNITED STATES OF AMERICA, Indian Territory,
Southern         DISTRICT.

I,   E F Lewis    , a   Physician   , on oath state that I attended on Mrs.  Annie M$^c$Gahey  , wife of   Author[sic] D. M$^c$Gahey   on the 17$^{th}$  day of July  , 1903; that there was born to her on said date a   female   child; that said child was living March 4, 1905, and is said to have been named Opal M$^c$Gahey

E.F. Lewis M.D.

Witnesses To Mark:
{

## Applications for Enrollment of Choctaw Newborn
## Act of 1905   Volume VIII

Subscribed and sworn to before me this   29$^{th}$   day of    March    , 1905

D R Johnston<br>
Notary Public.

---

**FILED**

SEPT 12 1902 8AM

*C. M. CAMPBELL, Clerk.*
Southern Dist. Ind. Ter.

---

**Certificate of Record of Marriage**

United States of America, ⎫
   Indian Territory,      ⎬ sct.
      Southern District. ⎭

I, C. M. CAMPBELL, Clerk of the United States Court, in the Territory and District aforesaid DO HEREBY CERTIFY, that the License for and Certificate of Marriage of

MR       Arthur M$^c$Gahey              and

M        Annie Lawler[sic]

were filed in my office in said Territory and District the    12$^{th}$    day of    Sept    A.D., 190 2   and duly recorded in Book   F   of Marriage Record, Page   496

WITNESS my hand and Seal of said Court, at Ardmore,<br>
this   12"   day of   September   A.D. 190 2<br><br>
C. M. Campbell<br>
CLERK.

Return this License to the United States Clerk at Ardmore, that it may be recorded, when it will be mailed to the proper address.

Ardmoreite Steam Print.

**Applications for Enrollment of Choctaw Newborn**
**Act of 1905   Volume VIII**

## MARRIAGE LICENSE

**N°.**

UNITED STATES OF AMERICA,
INDIAN TERRITORY,   ss:   To Any Person Authorized by Law to Solemnize Marriage, Greeting:
SOUTHERN DISTRICT.

You are hereby commanded to solemnize the Rite and publish the Banns of Matrimony between Mr.   Arthur McGahee[sic]   of   Madill   in the Indian Territory, aged 21 years, and M   Annie Lawlis   of   Cliff   in the Indian Territory, aged 17 years, according to law; and do you officially sign and return this License to the parties therein named.

Witness my hand and official Seal, this   10th   day of   Sept.   A. D. 190 2

C.M. Campbell
Clerk of the United States Court.

### Certificate of Marriage.

UNITED STATES OF AMERICA,
INDIAN TERRITORY,   ss:
SOUTHERN DISTRICT.         I,   A. V. Harris   do hereby certify that on the   10th   day of   September   , A. D. 190 2 , I did duly according to law, as commanded in the foregoing License, solemnize the Rite and publish the Banns of Matrimony between the parties therein named.

Witness my hand this   10   day of   September   A. D. 190 2

My credentials are recorded in the office of the Clerk of the United States Court, Indian Territory, Southern District, at Ardmore, Book   B   , Page 21

(NOTE-The person officiating should fill in the spaces for book and page and sign here.)   
A.V. Harris
a   Elder, M.P.C.

---

NOTE (a)-The License and Certificate of Marriage must be returned to the office of the Clerk of the United States Court in the Indian Territory, at Ardmore, within sixty days from the date thereof, or the party to whom the License was issued will be liable in the amount of One Hundred Dollars ($100).

NOTE (b)-No person is authorized to perform the Marriage Ceremony in the Southern District unless the proper credentials have first been recorded in the Clerk's office.

## Applications for Enrollment of Choctaw Newborn
## Act of 1905   Volume VIII

Choc New Born 510
    Clyde Hill   b. 11-26-04

Choctaw 2577.

Muskogee, Indian Territory, April 3, 1905.

Rufus Hill,
    Heavener, Indian Territory.

Dear Sir:

    Receipt is hereby acknowledged of the affidavits of Josephine Hill and M. A. Stewart to the birth of Clyde Hill, Daughter[sic] of Rufus and Josephine Hill, November 26, 1904, and the same have been filed with our records as an application for the enrollment of said child.

        Respectfully,

                Chairman.

**BIRTH AFFIDAVIT.**
### DEPARTMENT OF THE INTERIOR.
### COMMISSION TO THE FIVE CIVILIZED TRIBES.

    **IN RE APPLICATION FOR ENROLLMENT,** as a citizen of the   Choctaw   Nation, of   Clyde Hill   , born on the 26th   day of   November   , 1904

Name of Father: Rufus Hill        a citizen of the United States ~~Nation~~.
Name of Mother: Josephine Hill        a citizen of the   Choctaw   Nation.

        Postoffice    Heavener, Ind. Ter.

**AFFIDAVIT OF MOTHER.**

**UNITED STATES OF AMERICA, Indian Territory,**
    Central          **DISTRICT.**

    I,   Josephine Hill   , on oath state that I am   21   years of age and a citizen by   blood   , of the   Choctaw   Nation; that I am the lawful wife of   Rufus Hill   , who is a citizen, ~~by~~ ............ of the   United States   Nation; that a   female   child was born to me on   26th   day of   November   , 1904; that said child has been named   Clyde Hill   , and was living March 4, 1905.

                Josephine Hill

## Applications for Enrollment of Choctaw Newborn
## Act of 1905   Volume VIII

Witnesses To Mark:

{

Subscribed and sworn to before me this  27th  day of  March  , 1905

Wirt Franklin
Notary Public.

---

**AFFIDAVIT OF ATTENDING PHYSICIAN OR MID-WIFE.**

UNITED STATES OF AMERICA, Indian Territory,
Central          DISTRICT.

I,  M. A. Stewart  , a  Physician  , on oath state that I attended on Mrs. Josephine Hill  , wife of  Rufus Hill  on the 26$^{th}$  day of  November , 1904; that there was born to her on said date a  female  child; that said child was living March 4, 1905, and is said to have been named  Clyde Hill

M.A. Stewart

Witnesses To Mark:

{

Subscribed and sworn to before me this  29  day of  March  , 1905

NS Castelow
Notary Public.

My Com Expr 20-1907

---

### *Affidavit of Attending Physician or Midwife*

UNITED STATES OF AMERICA,
INDIAN TERRITORY,
Central    DISTRICT

I,  M.A. Stewart   a   Practicing Physician on oath state that I attended on Mrs. Josephine Hill (nee Wilson)  wife of  Rufus Hill on the  26  day of  November  , 190 4, that there was born to her on said date a  Female child, that said child is now living, and is said to have been named  Clyde Hill

M.A. Stewart    M. D.

Subscribed and sworn to before me this the    16  day of  February    1905

James Bower
Notary Public.

298

Applications for Enrollment of Choctaw Newborn
Act of 1905   Volume VIII

WITNESSETH:
Must be two witnesses who are citizens and know the child. { John Folsom
David Ward

We hereby certify that we are well acquainted with M. A. Stewart a Practicing Physician and know him to be reputable and of good standing in the community.

Must be two citizen witnesses. { John Folsom
David Ward

# NEW BORN AFFIDAVIT

No _____

## CHOCTAW ENROLLING COMMISSION

IN THE MATTER OF THE APPLICATION FOR ENROLLMENT as a citizen of the Choctaw Nation, of **Clyde Hill** born on the 26 day of **November** 190 4

Name of father **Rufus Hill** a citizen of **non** Nation, final enrollment No. ——— *(nee Wilson)*

Name of mother **Josephine Hill** ^ a citizen of **Choctaw** Nation, final enrollment No. **6892**

Heavener I.T. Postoffice.

**AFFIDAVIT OF MOTHER**

UNITED STATES OF AMERICA
INDIAN TERRITORY
DISTRICT   Central

I Josephine Hill (nee Wilson), on oath state that I am 21 years of age and a citizen by blood of the Choctaw Nation, and as such have been placed upon the final roll of the Choctaw Nation, by the Honorable Secretary of the Interior my final enrollment number being 6892 ; that I am the lawful wife of Rufus Hill , who is a citizen of the non Nation, and as such has been placed upon the final roll of said Nation by the Honorable Secretary of the Interior, his final enrollment number being —— and that a Female child was born to me on the 26 day of Nov 190 4; that said child has been named Clyde Hill , and is now living.

# Applications for Enrollment of Choctaw Newborn
## Act of 1905 Volume VIII

Josephine Hill

WITNESSETH:
Must be two witnesses { John Folsom
who are citizens { David Ward

Subscribed and sworn to before me this, the 16 day of February, 1905

James Bower
Notary Public.

My Commission Expires:
Sept 23-1907

---

Choc New Born 511
Lillie R. Kinney  b. 7-9-04

## AFFIDAVIT OF ATTENDING PHYSICIAN OR MIDWIFE

UNITED STATES OF AMERICA
INDIAN TERRITORY
Central    DISTRICT

I, Ida Wright  a  midwife on oath state that I attended on Mrs. Dodie Kinney nee Gardner  wife of  Elijah H Kinney on the 9th day of  July , 1904, that there was born to her on said date a  female  child, that said child is now living, and is said to have been named  Lillian R. Kinney

Ida Wright    ~~M.D.~~

WITNESSETH:
Must be two witnesses { William W Swink
who are citizens and
know the child. { H L Lawler

Subscribed and sworn to before me this, the 24th day of Feb 1905

W. A. Shoney    Notary Public.

We hereby certify that we are well acquainted with  Ida Wright a  midwife  and know  her  to be reputable and of good standing in the community.

{ William W Swink
{ H L Lawler

## Applications for Enrollment of Choctaw Newborn
## Act of 1905   Volume VIII

**NEW-BORN AFFIDAVIT.**

Number...............

### ...Choctaw Enrolling Commission...

IN THE MATTER OF THE APPLICATION FOR ENROLLMENT, as a citizen of the Choctaw Nation, of Lillie R. Kinney

born on the 9th day of July 190 4

Name of father   Elijah H Kinney        a citizen of   Choctaw
Nation final enrollment No. ———
Name of mother   Dodie Gardner         a citizen of   Choctaw
Nation final enrollment No.  15070

Postoffice   Valliant IT

**AFFIDAVIT OF MOTHER.**

UNITED STATES OF AMERICA
INDIAN TERRITORY
Central     DISTRICT

I   Dodie Kinney nee Gardner   , on oath state that I am 17 years of age and a citizen by blood of the Choctaw Nation, and as such have been placed upon the final roll of the Choctaw Nation, by the Honorable Secretary of the Interior my final enrollment number being  15070 ; that I am the lawful wife of   Elijah H Kinney   , who is a citizen of the ———Nation, and as such has been placed upon the final roll of said Nation by the Honorable Secretary of the Interior, his final enrollment number being  ——— and that a   female   child was born to me on the  9th day of   July   190 4; that said child has been named   Lillie R Kinney   , and is now living.

Dodie Kinney

Witnesseth.
Must be two ⎫  William W Swink
Witnesses who ⎬
are Citizens. ⎭  H L Lawler

Subscribed and sworn to before me this  24th  day of  Feb   190 5

W. A. Shoney
Notary Public.

My commission expires:  Jan 10, 1909

## Applications for Enrollment of Choctaw Newborn
## Act of 1905  Volume VIII

BIRTH AFFIDAVIT.

### DEPARTMENT OF THE INTERIOR.
### COMMISSION TO THE FIVE CIVILIZED TRIBES.

IN RE APPLICATION FOR ENROLLMENT, as a citizen of the Choctaw Nation, of Lillie R. Kinney, born on the 9$^{th}$ day of July, 1904

Name of Father: Elijah H. Kinney    a citizen of the United States Nation.
Name of Mother: Dodie Kinney (nee Gardner)    a citizen of the Choctaw Nation.

Postoffice    Vallaint[sic] Ind Terr

### AFFIDAVIT OF MOTHER.

UNITED STATES OF AMERICA, Indian Territory, }
Central         DISTRICT.

I, Dodie Kinney (nee Gardner), on oath state that I am 17 years of age and a citizen by Blood, of the Choctaw Nation; that I am the lawful wife of Elijah H Kinney, who is a citizen, by —— of the United States ~~Nation~~; that a female child was born to me on 9$^{th}$ day of July, 1904; that said child has been named Lillie R. Kinney, and was living March 4, 1905.

Dodie Kinney nee Gardner

Witnesses To Mark:
{

Subscribed and sworn to before me this 28$^{th}$ day of March, 1905.

E.J. Gardner
Notary Public.

### AFFIDAVIT OF ATTENDING PHYSICIAN OR MID-WIFE.

UNITED STATES OF AMERICA, Indian Territory, }
Central         DISTRICT.

I, Ida Wright, a Midwife, on oath state that I attended on Mrs. Dodie Kinney, wife of Elijah H Kinney on the 9$^{th}$ day of July, 1904; that there was born to her on said date a female child; that said child was living March 4, 1905, and is said to have been named Lillie R Kinney

Ida Wright

Witnesses To Mark:
{

## Applications for Enrollment of Choctaw Newborn
## Act of 1905   Volume VIII

Subscribed and sworn to before me this 28$^{th}$ day of March, 1905

E.J. Gardner
Notary Public.

---

Choc New Born 512
    Ella King   b. 3-21-04

Choctaw 5553.

Muskogee, Indian Territory, April 3, 1905.

Sam T. Roberts,
    Talihina, Indian Territory.

Dear Sir:

    Receipt is hereby acknowledged of your letter without date, enclosing the affidavits of Emma King and Lizzie Bohannon to the birth of Ella King, daughter or Robert and Emma King, March 21, 1904, and the same have been filed with our records as an application for the enrollment of said child.

Respectfully,

Chairman.

---

BIRTH AFFIDAVIT.

## DEPARTMENT OF THE INTERIOR,
### COMMISSION TO THE FIVE CIVILIZED TRIBES.

    *IN RE Application for Enrollment,* as a citizen of the Choctaw Nation, of Ella King, born on the 21 day of March, 1904

*Enrolled as Choctaws*

Name of Father: Robert King      a citizen of the Chickasaw Nation.
    *by Intermarriage*  *Enrolled as Choctaws*
Name of Mother: Emma King      a citizen of the Chickasaw Nation.

Post-Office: Talihina I.T.

# Applications for Enrollment of Choctaw Newborn
## Act of 1905   Volume VIII

### AFFIDAVIT OF MOTHER.

UNITED STATES OF AMERICA, }
    INDIAN TERRITORY.
    Central    District.

I, Emma King , on oath state that I am 32 years of age and a citizen by Intermarriage , of the Choctaw - Chickasaw Nation; that I am the lawful wife of Robert King , who is a citizen, by Blood of the Chickasaw - Enrolled as Choctaw Nation; that a female child was born to me on 21 day of March , 190 4, that said child has been named Ella King , and is now living.

                                            her
                                       Emma x King
**WITNESSES TO MARK:**                         mark
{ Chas Thompson
{ D. Thomas

Subscribed and sworn to before me this 23 day of March , 1905.

                                      Sam T. Roberts Jr.
                                          NOTARY PUBLIC.

### AFFIDAVIT OF ATTENDING PHYSICIAN OR MID-WIFE.

UNITED STATES OF AMERICA, }
    INDIAN TERRITORY.
    Central    District.

I, Lizzie Bohannon , a midwife , on oath state that I attended on Mrs. Emma King , wife of Robert King on the 21 day of March , 1904; that there was born to her on said date a female child; that said child is now living and is said to have been named Ella King

                                            her
                                      Lizzie x Bohannon
**WITNESSES TO MARK:**                         mark
{ Chas Thompson
{ D. Thomas

Subscribed and sworn to before me this 23 day of March , 1905.

                                      Sam T. Roberts Jr.
                                          NOTARY PUBLIC.

## Applications for Enrollment of Choctaw Newborn
## Act of 1905   Volume VIII

Choc New Born 513
    Bettie E. James   b. 4-13-03
    Etta M. James   b. 12-23-04

7-NB-513

                              Muskogee, Indian Territory, July 20, 1905.

Rogers James,
    Chickasha, Indian Territory.

Dear Sir:

    Receipt is hereby acknowledged of your letter of July 10, 1905, asking if your minor children Bettie Edith and Etta Mabel James have been approved by the Secretary of the Interior.

    In reply to your letter you are advised that the names of your children Bettie E. and Etta M. James have been placed upon a schedule of citizens by blood of the Choctaw Nation which has been forwarded the Secretary of the Interior and you will be notified when their enrollment is approved.

                      Respectfully,

                                              Commissioner.

**BIRTH AFFIDAVIT.**
### DEPARTMENT OF THE INTERIOR.
### COMMISSION TO THE FIVE CIVILIZED TRIBES.

    **IN RE APPLICATION FOR ENROLLMENT,** as a citizen of the     Choctaw     Nation, of Bettie E. James     , born on the 13   day of April   , 1903

Name of Father: Rogers James          a citizen of the   Choctaw    Nation.
Name of Mother: Gertha M James       a citizen of the   Choctaw    Nation.

                        Postoffice    Chickasha, I.T.

**AFFIDAVIT OF MOTHER.**

**UNITED STATES OF AMERICA, Indian Territory,**
      Southern          **DISTRICT.**

    I,    Gertha M James     , on oath state that I am   24    years of age and a citizen by    Intermarriage     , of the    Choctaw    Nation; that I am the lawful wife of

# Applications for Enrollment of Choctaw Newborn
## Act of 1905   Volume VIII

Rogers James , who is a citizen, by Blood of the Choctaw Nation; that a Female child was born to me on 13th day of April , 1903; that said child has been named Bettie E James , and was living March 4, 1905.

Gertha M. James

Witnesses To Mark:
{

Subscribed and sworn to before me this 21 day of March , 1905

R M Cochran
Notary Public.

---

### AFFIDAVIT OF ATTENDING PHYSICIAN OR MID-WIFE.

UNITED STATES OF AMERICA, Indian Territory,
................................................ DISTRICT.

I, A C Thompson , a Physician , on oath state that I attended on Mrs. Gertha M James , wife of Rogers James on the 13 day of April , 1903; that there was born to her on said date a Female child; that said child was living March 4, 1905, and is said to have been named Bettie E James

A.C. Thompson

Witnesses To Mark:
{

Subscribed and sworn to before me this 24 day of March , 1905

R M Cochran
Notary Public.

---

BIRTH AFFIDAVIT.

### DEPARTMENT OF THE INTERIOR.
## COMMISSION TO THE FIVE CIVILIZED TRIBES.

---

IN RE APPLICATION FOR ENROLLMENT, as a citizen of the Choctaw Nation, of Etta M. James , born on the 23 day of December , 1904

Name of Father: Rogers James        a citizen of the Choctaw Nation.
Name of Mother: Gertha M James      a citizen of the Choctaw Nation.

Postoffice   Chickasha, I.T.

# Applications for Enrollment of Choctaw Newborn
## Act of 1905   Volume VIII

**AFFIDAVIT OF MOTHER.**

UNITED STATES OF AMERICA, Indian Territory,
Southern DISTRICT.

I, Gertha M James, on oath state that I am 24 years of age and a citizen by Intermarriage, of the Choctaw Nation; that I am the lawful wife of Rogers James, who is a citizen, by Blood of the Choctaw Nation; that a Female child was born to me on 23$^d$ day of December, 1904; that said child has been named Etta M James, and was living March 4, 1905.

Gertha M. James

Witnesses To Mark:

Subscribed and sworn to before me this 21 day of Mch, 1905

R M Cochran
Notary Public.

---

**AFFIDAVIT OF ATTENDING PHYSICIAN OR MID-WIFE.**

UNITED STATES OF AMERICA, Indian Territory,
Southern DISTRICT.

I, Mary Ann Thompson, a Midwife, on oath state that I attended on Mrs. Gertha M James, wife of Rogers James on the 23$^d$ day of Dec, 1904; that there was born to her on said date a Female child; that said child was living March 4, 1905, and is said to have been named Etta M James

Mary Ann Thompson

Witnesses To Mark:

Subscribed and sworn to before me this 21 day of Mch, 1905

R M Cochran
Notary Public.

## Applications for Enrollment of Choctaw Newborn
## Act of 1905 Volume VIII

Choc New Born 514
    Charlie W. Grant   b. 2-9-05
    Tom S. Grant   b. 8-7-03

**BIRTH AFFIDAVIT.**

### DEPARTMENT OF THE INTERIOR.
### COMMISSION TO THE FIVE CIVILIZED TRIBES.

**IN RE APPLICATION FOR ENROLLMENT,** as a citizen of the Choctaw Nation, of Charlie W. Grant, born on the 9th day of Feb, 1905

Name of Father: Tom Grant     a citizen of the Choctaw Nation.
Name of Mother: Mardie Grant     a citizen of the Choctaw Nation.

        Postoffice   Arbuckle, I.T.

### AFFIDAVIT OF MOTHER.

UNITED STATES OF AMERICA, Indian Territory,
  Southern      DISTRICT.

    I, Mardie Grant, on oath state that I am 24 years of age and a citizen by Intermarriage, of the Choctaw Nation; that I am the lawful wife of Tom Grant, who is a citizen, by blood of the Choctaw Nation; that a male child was born to me on 9th day of Feb, 1905; that said child has been named Charlie W. Grant, and was living March 4, 1905.

                Mardie Grant

Witnesses To Mark:
  { J. T. Harden
    Taylor Polk

    Subscribed and sworn to before me this 25 day of March, 1905

                W.M. Lewis
                    Notary Public.

## Applications for Enrollment of Choctaw Newborn
## Act of 1905   Volume VIII

### AFFIDAVIT OF ATTENDING PHYSICIAN OR MID-WIFE.

UNITED STATES OF AMERICA, Indian Territory, }
  Southern            DISTRICT.

I, George J. Wilson, a Physician, on oath state that I attended on Mrs. Mardie Grant, wife of Tom Grant on the 9th day of Feb, 1905; that there was born to her on said date a male child; that said child was living March 4, 1905, and is said to have been named Charlie W Grant

G.J. Wilson, M.D.

Witnesses To Mark:
{

Subscribed and sworn to before me this 25 day of March, 1905

W.M. Lewis
Notary Public.

---

BIRTH AFFIDAVIT.

### DEPARTMENT OF THE INTERIOR.
### COMMISSION TO THE FIVE CIVILIZED TRIBES.

IN RE APPLICATION FOR ENROLLMENT, as a citizen of the Choctaw Nation, of Tom S. Grant, born on the 7th day of August, 1903

Name of Father: Tom Grant            a citizen of the Choctaw Nation.
Name of Mother: Mardie Grant         a citizen of the Choctaw Nation.

Postoffice    Arbuckle, I.T.

---

### AFFIDAVIT OF MOTHER.

UNITED STATES OF AMERICA, Indian Territory, }
  Southern            DISTRICT.

I, Mardie Grant, on oath state that I am 24 years of age and a citizen by Intermarriage, of the Choctaw Nation; that I am the lawful wife of Tom Grant, who is a citizen, by blood of the Choctaw Nation; that a male child was born to me on 7th day of August, 1903; that said child has been named Tom S. Grant, and was living March 4, 1905.

Mardie Grant

## Applications for Enrollment of Choctaw Newborn
## Act of 1905  Volume VIII

Witnesses To Mark:
{ J. T. Harden
  Taylor Polk

Subscribed and sworn to before me this 25$^{th}$ day of   March   , 1905

W.M. Lewis
Notary Public.

**AFFIDAVIT OF ATTENDING PHYSICIAN OR MID-WIFE.**

UNITED STATES OF AMERICA, Indian Territory, }
Southern            DISTRICT.

I,   George J. Wilson   , a   Physician   , on oath state that I attended on Mrs.   Mardie Grant   , wife of  Tom Grant   on the 7$^{th}$ day of  August  , 1903; that there was born to her on said date a   male   child; that said child was living March 4, 1905, and is said to have been named Tom S. Grant

G.J. Wilson, M.D.

Witnesses To Mark:
{

Subscribed and sworn to before me this  25 day of   March   , 1905

W.M. Lewis
Notary Public.

---

<u>Choc New Born 515</u>
    Rowan Jackson  b. 11-20-03

# Applications for Enrollment of Choctaw Newborn
## Act of 1905   Volume VIII

Choctaw 3939.

Muskogee, Indian Territory, April 1, 1905.

James T. Jackson,
    Caddo, Indian Territory.

Dear Sir:

    Receipt is hereby acknowledged of the affidavits of Lena Jackson and LeRoy Long to the birth of Rowan Jackson, son of James T. Jackson and Lena Jackson, November 29, 1903, and the same have been filed with our records as an application for the enrollment of said child.

                  Respectfully,

                                  Chairman.

---

**BIRTH AFFIDAVIT.**

## DEPARTMENT OF THE INTERIOR.
## COMMISSION TO THE FIVE CIVILIZED TRIBES.

---

IN RE APPLICATION FOR ENROLLMENT, as a citizen of the    Choctaw    Nation, of Rowan Jackson    , born on the 29   day of   November   , 1903

Name of Father: James T. Jackson         a citizen of the  Choctaw   Nation.
Name of Mother: Lena Jackson           a citizen of the  Choctaw   Nation.

                    Postoffice    Caddo, Ind Ter

---

**AFFIDAVIT OF MOTHER.**

UNITED STATES OF AMERICA, Indian Territory,
    Central                   DISTRICT.

    I,   Lena Jackson   , on oath state that I am   26   years of age and a citizen by Blood   , of the   Choctaw   Nation; that I am the lawful wife of   James T. Jackson   , who is a citizen, by Intermarriage   of the   Choctaw   Nation; that a   Male   child was born to me on   the 29   day of   November   , 1903; that said child has been named   Rowan Jackson   , and was living March 4, 1905.

                            Lena Jackson

Witnesses To Mark:

## Applications for Enrollment of Choctaw Newborn
## Act of 1905   Volume VIII

Subscribed and sworn to before me this 24" day of March, 1905

B.F. Maddox
Notary Public.

My commission expires
Feb 24 1909

---

**AFFIDAVIT OF ATTENDING PHYSICIAN OR MID-WIFE.**

UNITED STATES OF AMERICA, Indian Territory,
Central                DISTRICT.

I, Leroy Long, a Practicing Phasition[sic], on oath state that I attended on Mrs. Lena Jackson, wife of James T. Jackson on the 29 day of November, 1903; that there was born to her on said date a Male child; that said child was living March 4, 1905, and is said to have been named Rowan Jackson

LeRoy Long

Witnesses To Mark:

Subscribed and sworn to before me this 25th day of March, 1905

Brooks Fort
Notary Public.

Com Ex 3/6/07

---

# NEW BORN AFFIDAVIT

No

## CHOCTAW ENROLLING COMMISSION

IN THE MATTER OF THE APPLICATION FOR ENROLLMENT as a citizen of the Choctaw Nation, of    Rowan Jackson    born on the 29th day of November   190 3

Name of father   James T Jackson    a citizen of   Choctaw   Nation, final enrollment No.   7-D-784
Name of mother   Lena Jackson    a citizen of   Choctaw   Nation, final enrollment No.   11062

Caddo I.T.                    Postoffice.

## Applications for Enrollment of Choctaw Newborn
## Act of 1905   Volume VIII

**AFFIDAVIT OF MOTHER**

UNITED STATES OF AMERICA  
INDIAN TERRITORY  
DISTRICT    Central

I    Lena Jackson    , on oath state that I am   25    years of age and a citizen by   Blood    of the    Choctaw    Nation, and as such have been placed upon the final roll of the   Choctaw    Nation, by the Honorable Secretary of the Interior my final enrollment number being   11062   ; that I am the lawful wife of   James T. Jackson   , who is a citizen of the    Choctaw    Nation, and as such has been placed upon the final roll of said Nation by the Honorable Secretary of the Interior, his final enrollment number being  7D-784    and that a    male    child was born to me on the    $29^{th}$   day of   November   190 3; that said child has been named    Rowan Jackson    , and is now living.

WITNESSETH:                                                                Lena Jackson  
Must be two witnesses  { Henry Byington  
who are citizens         R H Byington

Subscribed and sworn to before me this, the   $6^{th}$   day of   February   , 190 5

A E Folsom  
Notary Public.

My Commission Expires:  
9" Jan 1909

## *Affidavit of Attending Physician or Midwife*

UNITED STATES OF AMERICA,  
INDIAN TERRITORY,  
Central    DISTRICT

I,    Leroy Long    a    Practicing Physician on oath state that I attended on Mrs.   Lena Jackson    wife of   James T. Jackson on the    $29^{th}$   day of  November   , 190 3, that there was born to her on said date a    male child, that said child is now living, and is said to have been named   Rowan Jackson

LeRoy Long           M. D.

Subscribed and sworn to before me this the   $9^{th}$   day of   February    1905

Brooks Fort  
Notary Public.

# Applications for Enrollment of Choctaw Newborn
## Act of 1905  Volume VIII

WITNESSETH:
Must be two witnesses who are citizens and know the child. { Henry Byington
R H Byington

We hereby certify that we are well acquainted with Leroy Long a Physician and know him to be reputable and of good standing in the community.

Must be two citizen witnesses. { Henry Byington
R H Byington

---

Choc New Born 516
  Horace Clay McClure  b. 10-29-02

7-3591.

Muskogee, Indian Territory, December 12, 1902.

Napoleon B. McClure,
  Bennington, Indian Territory.

Dear Sir:

Receipt is hereby acknowledged of the application for enrollment as a citizen of the Choctaw Nation of Harris Clay McClure, infant son of Napoleon B. and May Dell McClure, born October 29, 1902.

You are advised that the Commission is without authority to enroll this child as a citizen of the Choctaw Nation it appearing that said child was born was born October 1[sic], 1902, subsequent to the ratification by the citizens of the Choctaw and Chickasaw Nations on September 25, 1902, of an act of Congress approved July 1, 1902 (32 Stats., 641).

Section twenty-eight thereof provides as follows:

"The names of all persons living on the date of the final ratification of this agreement entitled to be enrolled as provided in section 27 hereof shall be placed upon the rolls made by said Commission; and no child born thereafter to a citizen or freedman and no person intermarried thereafter to a citizen shall be entitled to enrollment or to participate in the distribution of the tribal property of the Choctaws and Chickasaws."

## Applications for Enrollment of Choctaw Newborn
## Act of 1905 Volume VIII

Respectfully,

Acting Chairman.

Choctaw 3591.

Muskogee, Indian Territory, April 3, 1905.

Napoleon B. McClure,
    Bennington, Indian Territory.

Dear Sir:

    Receipt is hereby acknowledged of the affidavits of Maydell[sic] McClure and Georgia Ann Talley to the birth of Horace Clay McClure, son of Napoleon B. and Maydell McClure, October 29, 1902, and the same have been filed with our records as an application for the enrollment of said child.

    Receipt is also acknowledged of the affidavits of Maydell McClure and D. M. Stark to the birth of Anna May McClure, daughter of Napoleon B. and Maydell McClure, March 5, 1905, and you are advised that the Commission is only authorized by the Act of Congress approved May 3, 1905, for a period of sixty days from the date of said Act, to receive applications for the enrollment of children born to enrolled citizens by blood of the Choctaw and Chickasaw Nations between September 25, 1902 and March 4, 1905. You will therefore see that the Commission is without authority to enroll your child, Anna May McClure.

Respectfully,

Chairman.

**BIRTH AFFIDAVIT.**

## DEPARTMENT OF THE INTERIOR,
### COMMISSION TO THE FIVE CIVILIZED TRIBES.

    IN RE APPLICATION FOR ENROLLMENT, as a citizen of the Choctaw Nation, of Harris Clay McClure, born on the 29$^{th}$ day of October, 1902

Name of Father: Napoleon B McClure      a citizen of the Choctaw Nation.
*by marriage*
Name of Mother: Maydell McClure      a citizen of the Choctaw Nation.

Post-Office:      Benington[sic] Ind Ter

# Applications for Enrollment of Choctaw Newborn
## Act of 1905   Volume VIII

**AFFIDAVIT OF MOTHER.**

UNITED STATES OF AMERICA,  
   INDIAN TERRITORY,  
   Central         District.

I,  Maydell McClure  , on oath state that I am  23  years of age and a citizen by  Marriage  , of the  Choctaw  Nation; that I am the lawful wife of  Napoleon B McClure  , who is a citizen, by  blood  of the Choctaw Nation; that a  male  child was born to me on the  29th  day of  October  , 190 2, that said child has been named  Harris Clay  , and is now living.

                              Maydell McClure

**WITNESSES TO MARK:**
{ A. S. George
{ J. M. George

Subscribed and sworn to before me this  26th  day of  November  , 1905.

                              H. B. Hardy
                              NOTARY PUBLIC.

---

**AFFIDAVIT OF ATTENDING PHYSICIAN OR MID-WIFE.**

UNITED STATES OF AMERICA,  
   INDIAN TERRITORY,  
   Central         District.

I,  George Ann Tally  , a  nurse  , on oath state that I attended on Mrs.  Maydell McClure  , wife of  Napoleon B McClure  on the  29th  day of  October  , 190 2; that there was born to her on said date a  male  child; that said child is now living and is said to have been named  Harris Clay

                            his[sic]
                   George Ann x Tally
**WITNESSES TO MARK:**                      mark
{ A.S. George
{ J M George

Subscribed and sworn to before me this  26th  day of  November  , 1905.

                              H. B. Hardy
                              NOTARY PUBLIC.

## Applications for Enrollment of Choctaw Newborn
## Act of 1905   Volume VIII

I H B Hardy Notary Public in and for the Central District at Caney Indian Territory hereby certify that in writing the name McClure in the forgoing affidavits of Mrs. Madell McClure and Mrs. George Ann Tally the nurse I omitted the Second letter "C" which I corrected by writing it in after Mrs McClure signed her name noting that she had so spelled it and that in all places when McClure is spelled McLure in both joint affidavits the difference in the spelling is for the same identical persons and that the *(illegible)* in the spelling of the name Mrs George Ann Tally was made and the name Tally written thereon before signing and swearing her and before the witnesses J M George and A S George signed their names

Witness my hand and seal this 26<sup>th</sup> day of Nov 192[sic]

HB Hardy
Notary Public

**BIRTH AFFIDAVIT.**

## DEPARTMENT OF THE INTERIOR,
### COMMISSION TO THE FIVE CIVILIZED TRIBES.

IN RE APPLICATION FOR ENROLLMENT, as a citizen of the   Choctaw   Nation, of   Harris Clay McClure   , born on the   29<sup>th</sup>   day of   October   , 1902

Name of Father:  Napoleon B McClure         a citizen of the   Choctaw   Nation.
                                             *intermarriage*
Name of Mother:  Maydell McClure             a citizen of the   Choctaw   Nation.

Post-Office :    Bennington Ind Ter

**AFFIDAVIT OF MOTHER.**

UNITED STATES OF AMERICA,
INDIAN TERRITORY,
Central         District.

I,   Maydell McClure   , on oath state that I am   26   years of age and a citizen by Marriage   , of the   Choctaw   Nation; that I am the lawful wife of   Napoleon B McClure   , who is a citizen, by  blood  of the   Choctaw   Nation; that a   male   child was born to me on the   29<sup>th</sup>   day of   October   , 190 2, that said child has been named   Harris Clay McClure   , and is now living.

Maydell McClure

**WITNESSES TO MARK:**

# Applications for Enrollment of Choctaw Newborn
## Act of 1905  Volume VIII

Subscribed and sworn to before me this 29$^{th}$  day of  March , 1905.

C.C. McClard
NOTARY PUBLIC.

### AFFIDAVIT OF ATTENDING PHYSICIAN OR MID-WIFE.

UNITED STATES OF AMERICA,
INDIAN TERRITORY,
Central   District.

I,  George Ann Tally , a  midwife , on oath state that I attended on Mrs.  Maydell McClure , wife of  Napoleon B McClure  on the  29$^{th}$  day of October , 190 2; that there was born to her on said date a  male  child; that said child is now living and is said to have been named  Harris Clay McClure

her
George Ann x Tally
mark

WITNESSES TO MARK:
B.M. Stark
W.W. Stark

Subscribed and sworn to before me this 29$^{-h}$  day of  March , 1905.

C.C. McClard
NOTARY PUBLIC.

---

Choc New Born 517
Thelma Holman  b. 9-16-03

BIRTH AFFIDAVIT.

### DEPARTMENT OF THE INTERIOR.
### COMMISSION TO THE FIVE CIVILIZED TRIBES.

IN RE APPLICATION FOR ENROLLMENT, as a citizen of the  Choctaw  Nation, of Thelma Holman , born on the  16$^{th}$  day of  Sept , 1903

Name of Father:  Charles R Holman   a citizen of the  Choctaw  Nation.
Name of Mother:  Sarah Holman   a citizen of the  Choctaw  Nation.

Postoffice  Garvin, Ind. Ter.

# Applications for Enrollment of Choctaw Newborn
## Act of 1905   Volume VIII

**AFFIDAVIT OF MOTHER.**

UNITED STATES OF AMERICA, Indian Territory,  }
    Central             DISTRICT. }

    I, Sarah Holman, on oath state that I am 25 years of age and a citizen by Blood, of the Choctaw Nation; that I am the lawful wife of Charles R Holman, who is a citizen, by Intermarriage of the Choctaw Nation; that a Female child was born to me on 16$^{th}$ day of Sept, 1903; that said child has been named Thelma Holman, and was living March 4, 1905.

                            Sarah Holman

Witnesses To Mark:
{

    Subscribed and sworn to before me this 24$^{th}$ day of March, 1905

My commission expires Sept 8, 1908        T.G. Carr
                                          Notary Public.

---

**AFFIDAVIT OF ATTENDING PHYSICIAN OR MID-WIFE.**

UNITED STATES OF AMERICA, Indian Territory,  }
    Central             DISTRICT. }

    I, B.L. Denison, a Physician, on oath state that I attended on Mrs. Sarah Holman, wife of Charles R Holman on the 16 day of Sept., 1903; that there was born to her on said date a Female child; that said child was living March 4, 1905, and is said to have been named Thelma Holman

                            B. L. Denison M.D.

Witnesses To Mark:
{

    Subscribed and sworn to before me this 24$^{th}$ day of March, 1905

My commission expires Sept 8, 1908        T.G. Carr
                                          Notary Public.

## Applications for Enrollment of Choctaw Newborn
## Act of 1905   Volume VIII

Choc New Born 518
    Tandy Darneal   b. 3-8-03

Choctaw-2670.

Muskogee, Indian Territory, April 1, 1905.

James Darneal,
    Oak Lodge, Indian Territory.

Dear Sir:

    Receipt is hereby acknowledged of the affidavits of Sallie Darneal and Mrs. M. J. Milkett to the birth of Tandy Darneal, son of James and Sallie Darneal, March 8, 1903, and the same have been filed with our records as an application for the enrollment of said child.

        Respectfully,

                Chairman.

### *Affidavit of Attending Physician or Midwife*

UNITED STATES OF AMERICA,
    INDIAN TERRITORY,
Central      DISTRICT

    I, Nancy J. Milkett a Midwife on oath state that I attended on Mrs. Sallie Darneal wife of James Darneal on the 8 day of March , 190 3, that there was born to her on said date a male child, that said child is now living, and is said to have been named Tandy Darneal

                her
        Nancy x J. Milkett     ~~M. D.~~
                mark

Subscribed and sworn to before me this the 3 day of March 190......

        James Bower
          Notary Public.

WITNESSETH:
    Must be two witnesses who are citizens and know the child.
{ Louis Leflore
{ Leonidas E Merryman

    We hereby certify that we are well acquainted with Nancy J Milkett a Midwife and know her to be reputable and of good standing in the community.

Applications for Enrollment of Choctaw Newborn
Act of 1905  Volume VIII

Must be two citizen witnesses. { Louis Leflore
Leonidas E Merryman

## NEW BORN AFFIDAVIT

No _____

### CHOCTAW ENROLLING COMMISSION

IN THE MATTER OF THE APPLICATION FOR ENROLLMENT as a citizen of the Choctaw Nation, of  Tandy Darneal  born on the 8 day of  March  190 3

Name of father  James Darneal  a citizen of  Choctaw  Nation, final enrollment No. 7751
Name of mother  Sallie Darneal  a citizen of  Choctaw  Nation, final enrollment No. 7752

Oak Lodge I.T.  Postoffice.

**AFFIDAVIT OF MOTHER**

UNITED STATES OF AMERICA }
INDIAN TERRITORY
DISTRICT   Central

I  Sallie Darneal  , on oath state that I am  46  years of age and a citizen by  blood  of the  Choctaw  Nation, and as such have been placed upon the final roll of the  Choctaw  Nation, by the Honorable Secretary of the Interior my final enrollment number being  7752 ; that I am the lawful wife of  James Darneal;  , who is a citizen of the  Choctaw  Nation, and as such has been placed upon the final roll of said Nation by the Honorable Secretary of the Interior, his final enrollment number being  7751  and that a  male  child was born to me on the  8  day of  March 190 3; that said child has been named  Tandy Darneal , and is now living.

her<br>Sallie x Darneal<br>mark

WITNESSETH:
Must be two witnesses who are citizens { Louis Leflore
Leonidas E Merryman

# Applications for Enrollment of Choctaw Newborn
## Act of 1905 Volume VIII

Subscribed and sworn to before me this, the 4 day of March , 190 5

James Bower
Notary Public.

My Commission Expires:
Sept 23 1907

**BIRTH AFFIDAVIT.**

## DEPARTMENT OF THE INTERIOR.
## COMMISSION TO THE FIVE CIVILIZED TRIBES.

IN RE APPLICATION FOR ENROLLMENT, as a citizen of the Choctaw Nation, of Tandy Darneal , born on the 8 day of March , 1903

Name of Father: James Darneal     a citizen of the Choctaw Nation.
Name of Mother: Sallie Darneal     a citizen of the Choctaw Nation.

Postoffice    Oak Lodge, Ind Ter

**AFFIDAVIT OF MOTHER.**

UNITED STATES OF AMERICA, Indian Territory, }
Central            DISTRICT.

I, Sallie Darneal , on oath state that I am 47 years of age and a citizen by Blood , of the Choctaw Nation; that I am the lawful wife of James Darneal , who is a citizen, by Blood of the Choctaw Nation; that a Male child was born to me on 8th day of March , 1903; that said child has been named Tandy Darneal , and was living March 4, 1905.

                                    her
                        Sallie x Darneal
Witnesses To Mark:        mark
{ Edwin L *(Illegible)*
{ W.E. Harrell

Subscribed and sworn to before me this 27 day of March , 1905

MY COMMISSION EXPIRES AUG. 6, 1908      W.E. Harrell
                                     Notary Public.

Applications for Enrollment of Choctaw Newborn
Act of 1905   Volume VIII

**AFFIDAVIT OF ATTENDING PHYSICIAN OR MID-WIFE.**

UNITED STATES OF AMERICA, Indian Territory, }
Central       DISTRICT.

I, Mrs M J Millkett , a Midwife , on oath state that I attended on Mrs. Sallie Darneal , wife of James Darneal on the 8 day of March , 1903; that there was born to her on said date a male child; that said child was living March 4, 1905, and is said to have been named Tandy Darneal

Mrs M J Millkett

Witnesses To Mark:
{

Subscribed and sworn to before me this 27 day of March , 1905

MY COMMISSION EXPIRES AUG. 6, 1908          W.E. Harrell
                                            Notary Public.

# NEW BORN AFFIDAVIT

No

## CHOCTAW ENROLLING COMMISSION

IN THE MATTER OF THE APPLICATION FOR ENROLLMENT as a citizen of the Choctaw Nation, of    Tandy Darneal    born on the  8  day of  March   190 3

Name of father  James Darneal    a citizen of  Choctaw  Nation, final enrollment No. 7751
Name of mother  Sallie Darneal   a citizen of  Choctaw  Nation, final enrollment No. 7752

Oak Lodge I.T.    Postoffice.

**AFFIDAVIT OF MOTHER**

UNITED STATES OF AMERICA }
   INDIAN TERRITORY       }
DISTRICT   Central        }

I  Sallie Darneal   , on oath state that I am  46  years of age and a citizen by  blood  of the  Choctaw  Nation, and as such have been placed upon

## Applications for Enrollment of Choctaw Newborn
## Act of 1905   Volume VIII

the final roll of the   Choctaw    Nation, by the Honorable Secretary of the Interior my final enrollment number being   7752   ; that I am the lawful wife of   James Darneal   , who is a citizen of the   Choctaw    Nation, and as such has been placed upon the final roll of said Nation by the Honorable Secretary of the Interior, his final enrollment number being   7751   and that a   male   child was born to me on the   8   day of   March 190 3; that said child has been named   Tandy Darneal   , and is now living.

                                                                      her

WITNESSETH:                                  Sallie  x  Darneal

Must be two witnesses { Louis Leflore                   mark
who are citizens           Leonidas E Merryman

    Subscribed and sworn to before me this, the   4   day of    March   , 190 5

                                      James Bowen
                                                  Notary Public.

My Commission Expires:
    Sep 23 1907.

---

Choc New Born 519
       Nora Harris  b. 4-8-03

                                                         Choctaw 2865.

                    Muskogee, Indian Territory, April 1, 1905.

Battice Harris,
    Kinta, Indian Territory.

Dear Sir:

    Receipt is hereby acknowledged of the affidavits of Emily Harris and Mary Lewis to the birth of Nora Harris, daughter of Battice and Emily Harris, April 8, 1903, and the same have been filed with our records as an application for the enrollment of said child.

                                Respectfully,
                                                        Chairman.

## Applications for Enrollment of Choctaw Newborn
## Act of 1905   Volume VIII

**COPY**

Choctaw N.B. 519.

Muskogee, Indian Territory, April 17, 1905.

Emily Harris,
    Kinta, Indian Territory.

Dear Madam:

    Receipt is hereby acknowledged of our letter of April 13, in which you ask if you can file for your child, Nora Harris, before her enrollment is approved by the Secretary of the Interior.

    In reply to your letter you are informed that no selection of allotment can be permitted for children for whom application is made under the provisions of the act of Congress approved March 3, 1905, until their enrollment has been approved by the Secretary of the Interior.

Respectfully,

SIGNED

*Tams Bixby*
Chairman.

---

## AFFIDAVIT OF ATTENDING PHYSICIAN OR MIDWIFE

UNITED STATES OF AMERICA
INDIAN TERRITORY
    Western    DISTRICT

*known as Sexton*

    I,    Mary Lewis    a    midwife on oath state that I attended on Mrs.    Emily Harris    wife of    Battiest Harris on the    8th    day of    April    , 190 3 , that there was born to her on said date a    female child, that said child is now living, and is said to have been named    Nora Harris

                                                            her

*Attest to Mark Calvin Lewis*    Mary x Lewis, known as Sexton
                                                  mark

Subscribed and sworn to before me this, the    6th    day of    Jan    190 5

WITNESSETH:                                      L.C. Tirey    Notary Public.
Must be two witnesses { Wesley Mc Coy
who are citizens            Lewis Carner

## Applications for Enrollment of Choctaw Newborn
## Act of 1905   Volume VIII

We hereby certify that we are well acquainted with    Mary Lewis   a    midwife    and know    her    to be reputable and of good standing in the community.

Wesley McCoy                              _____

Lewis Carner                              _____

**NEW-BORN AFFIDAVIT.**

Number..............

### ...Choctaw Enrolling Commission...

IN THE MATTER OF THE APPLICATION FOR ENROLLMENT, as a citizen of the Choctaw    Nation, of    Nora Harris

born on the   8th   day of   April   190 3

Name of father    Battiest Harris           ~~a citizen~~ *citizen* of    freedman
Nation final enrollment No.   1722
Name of mother    Emily Harris           a citizen of    Choctaw
Nation final enrollment No.   8422

                                   Postoffice    Kinta I.T.

**AFFIDAVIT OF MOTHER.**

UNITED STATES OF AMERICA
INDIAN TERRITORY
   Western     DISTRICT

I    Emily Harris          , on oath state that I am   29   years of age and a citizen by   blood   of the   Choctaw   Nation, and as such have been placed upon the final roll of the   Choctaw   Nation, by the Honorable Secretary of the Interior my final enrollment number being   8422  ; that I am the lawful wife of   Battiest Harris   , who is a *freedman* citizen of the   Choctaw   Nation, and as such has been placed upon the final roll of said Nation by the Honorable Secretary of the Interior, his final enrollment number being   1722   and that a   female   child was born to me on the   8th   day of   April   190 3; that said child has been named   Nora Harris , and is now living.

                                   Emily Harris

Witnesseth.
   Must be two  ⎱   Wesley McCoy
   Witnesses who ⎰
   are Citizens.      Calvin Lewis

## Applications for Enrollment of Choctaw Newborn
## Act of 1905   Volume VIII

Subscribed and sworn to before me this   6"   day of   Jan   190 5

L. C. Tirey
Notary Public.

My commission expires:   Jan 17-1907

---

**BIRTH AFFIDAVIT.**

### DEPARTMENT OF THE INTERIOR.
### COMMISSION TO THE FIVE CIVILIZED TRIBES.

---

IN RE APPLICATION FOR ENROLLMENT, as a citizen of the   Choctaw   Nation, of Nora Harris   , born on the   8   day of   April   , 1903

Name of Father: Battice Harris              a citizen of the   Freedman   Nation.
Name of Mother: Emily Harris                a citizen of the   Choctaw   Nation.

Postoffice   Kinta I.T.

---

**AFFIDAVIT OF MOTHER.**

UNITED STATES OF AMERICA, Indian Territory,
Western            DISTRICT.

I,   Emily Harris   , on oath state that I am   thirty   years of age and a citizen by   Blood   , of the   Choctaw   Nation; that I am the lawful wife of   Battice Harris   , who is a citizen, by Freedman   of the   Choctaw   Nation; that a female   child was born to me on   8   day of   April   , 1903; that said child has been named   Nora Harris   , and was living March 4, 1905.

Emily Harris

Witnesses To Mark:

Subscribed and sworn to before me this   27  day of   March   , 1905

L. D. Allen
Notary Public.

# Applications for Enrollment of Choctaw Newborn
## Act of 1905   Volume VIII

**AFFIDAVIT OF ATTENDING PHYSICIAN OR MID-WIFE.**

UNITED STATES OF AMERICA, Indian Territory, }
  Western           DISTRICT. }

I, Mary Lewis , a ———— , on oath state that I attended on Mrs. Emily Harris , wife of Battice Harris on the 8 day of April , 1903; that there was born to her on said date a female child; that said child was living March 4, 1905, and is said to have been named Nora Harris

                             her
                         Mary x Lewis
Witnesses To Mark:           mark
  { F E Watkins
    C M Kimbro

Subscribed and sworn to before me this   3/27   day of   March   , 1905

                       L. D. Allen
                             Notary Public.

# Index

**ABERNATHY**
- Mrs N D .................................... 243
- N D ................................. 240,243
- Nancy ..................................... 242

**ABLE**
- Etta M .................... 236,237,238,239
- Ettar M .................................... 236
- Marion ..................................... 236

**ABLES**
- Eta M ...................................... 239
- Etta M ................................ 237,238

**ADAIR**
- G W ............................. 219,220,221

**ADAMS**
- J A ................................ 212,213,217
- J A, MD ............................. 213,218

**AGENT**
- Annie G ................................... 8,9
- Henry Clay ............................... 8,9
- Vey V ..................................... 8,9

**AIRINGTON**
- Arthur ..................................... 277
- Arthur G .................................. 278
- Francis G ................................. 279
- Francis Going ...................... 277,278
- A G ..................................... 278,279
- Ruben .......................... 277,278,279

**ALLEN**
- G W ........................................... 7
- L D .......... 222,223,224,225,327,328

**ANDERSON**
- Bill ..................................... 154,155
- Grubbs ............................... 154,155
- Houston 194,195,196,197,199,200,201
- Houston D ........................... 194,195
- Jane ... 194,195,196,197,198,200,201
- Joseph ...................................... 75
- Lela ... 194,195,196,197,199,200,201
- Leo Bennett .... 194,195,196,197,199
- Levina ..................................... 197
- Margarett ........................... 155,156
- Margarette ............................... 154
- Mary .................................. 118,119
- Noel ................................... 118,119
- Noel May .......................... 118,119

**ANGELL**
- W H ..................... 77,89,92,93,94,95

**ATKINSON**
- Mary ................................. 267,269

**AUSTIN**
- D J .......................................... 126
- W A .............................. 227,228,229

**AVERY**
- Alex .................................. 233,234,235
- Alvin Allen ................... 233,234,235
- Julia ................................ 233,234,235

**BACON**
- Melvina .................................... 197

**BAKER**
- R S ................................... 266,268
- W M ........................................ 166

**BARNES**
- Robert H ................................. 148
- Robert J ................. 135,136,145,149

**BATTICE**
- Nicholas .......... 136,137,138,139,140
- Rason ............. 136,137,138,139,140
- Sallie ....................................... 138
- Sallie A ................. 136,137,139,140

**BATTIEST**
- Nicholas
  135,137,139,141,142,143,144,145,
  146,147,148,149,150
- Ranson ............ 142,143,144,145,147
- Rason 135,137,141,147,148,149,150
- Rayson ..................................... 146
- Resin ...................................... 140
- Sallie ....................................... 137
- Sallie A
  135,136,141,142,143,144,145,146,
  147,148,149,150

**BEAMS**
- Belle C .............................. 133,134
- Benjamin Edward ................ 133,134
- Benjimin Edward ...................... 133
- A G .................................... 133,134

**BELL**
- Davis U ................................... 195
- Davis W ............................. 198,201

**BENCH**
- Sam ..................................... 42,43

**BENTLEY**
- Dr J C ....................................... 17
- J C ............................................ 14

# Index

J C, MD .................................16,18
John C ...........................................16
BETHELL
   J M...............................................239
BIRD
   Billie...................................205,207
   Billy................202,203,204,206,207
   Edna................203,204,205,206,207
   L B.... 201,202,203,204,205,206,207
BIXBY
   Tams
     5,87,96,102,103,111,113,114,122,
     126,157,209,237,241,247,248,250,267
     ,282,287,293,325
BLAYLOCK
   T A ................................................210
   T A, MD .......................................210
   Thomas A .....................................209
   Thos A ..........................................211
   Thos A, MD .................................211
BOBO
   Lacey P ................ 191,197,199,200
BOGLE
   Ada B.....................................127,128
   David H .................................127,128
   Henry Carl ...................................127
BOHANNON
   Lizzie.....................................303,304
BOHNEER
   J J....................................................19,20
BOHRUE
   A ......................................19,20,21,22
BOND
   E H .................................................275
   Florence................................179,183
   Henry J ....................................44,45
BOND & MELTON .........................286
BOOTH
   J E .........................................277,279
   J E, MD .......................................279
BOWER
   James
     48,57,106,107,108,167,233,258,259,
     260,298,300,320,322,324
BOYIE
   Wm T.............................................247
BOYLESS

Thomas H ...........................252,253
BRASHEARS
   Tobias...................................264,265
BROCK
   Henry............................................ 7
BRONAUGH
   M ...................................................144
   V .............................................144,147
BROOKS
   Pearl............................212,215,216
BULLARD
   Andrew C .........................98,99,101
BULLY
   Amanda ..............................38,39,137
   Amanda A....................................37,38
   Anderson ...........................37,38,39
   James Anderson.......................37,39
   John .............................................37,38
BUNN
   Wm C .........................................251
BURKE
   J M................................................137
BURNS
   Houston ......................................198
   Jane.. 194,195,196,197,198,199,200,
   201
   Leo Bennett ...............................198
   Wm J ....................................193,194
BUTLER
   M D .......................................278,279
BYINGTON
   David ...............................38,39,137
   Emma ..........................156,157,158
   Gilber............................................156
   Gilbert..........................156,157,158
   Henry
     140,141,142,143,144,145,146,149,
     150,313,314
   Joel ....................... 149,156,157,158
   Lorena141,142,143,146,148,149,150
   R H .......................................313,314
BYRD
   W O ......... 135,136,137,138,148,149
CAIN
   D L .......................................276,277
CALDWELL
   May Ann........................................12

## Index

Mary Ann ........................... 10,11,12
Willey ................................ 12
Willie ............................... 10,11
Wilson ............................. 10,11,12
CALFER
   L119
CAMP
   John B ................................ 163,164
   Levander ............................ 163,164
   Lillie May ...................... 162,163,164
CAMPBELL
   C M ........................................ 295,296
   J B ......................................... 65
CAMPELUBE
   Columbus ............................. 175,176
CAPSHAW
   N L ......................................... 276,277
CARNER
   Lewis ..................................... 325,326
CARNES
   Ellis ...................................... 84
   Serane ................................... 81,85
   Serena .................................. 82,83
   Solomon ............................. 144,147
CARNEY
   Agnes ................................... 175,176
   Louisiana ............................. 175,176
   Nolis ..................................... 175
   Norris ................................... 175
CARR
   Denis .................................... 276
   Dennis .................................. 276,277
   Jane ...................................... 276,277
   Julia ..................................... 275,276,277
   T G ....................................... 319
CARSON
   M D ..................................... 177,178,179
CASTEEL
   Jno ....................................... 76
CASTELOW
   N S ....................................... 298
CHATMAN
   Nancie ................................. 42,43
   Nancy .................................. 41
CHILDS
   J S ......................................... 32
   J S, MD ................................ 32

CHRISTAN
   Minerva M ........................ 14
CHRISTIE
   Amanda ............................. 37,39
   Jesse L ............................... 12,13
CHRISTY
   Jesse .................................. 11
   Joshua ............................... 59,63
CHUBBEE
   Laymon ........................... 145,147,148
   Moses ............................... 139
CLARK
   J H .................................... 268,269
   John .................................. 27
COBBLE
   J D .................................... 31
COBLER
   Mrs E A ............................ 30,31
COCHRAN
   R M .................................. 306,307
COLBERT
   Aaron ............................... 80,81,82,83,84
   Aron .................................. 85
   Sam ................................... 79,80,81,82,83,84,85
   Serena ............................. 80,82,83,84
   Sims .................................. 98,100
COLEMAN
   R B ................................... 155,156
COLLIN
   Mertha ............................. 195,198,201
CONGER
   H A ................................... 275
   H A, MD ........................... 275
CONNOWAY
   Dr P K ............................... 177
   P E .................................... 176
   P K, MD ............................ 177
   Philip K ............................ 179
CONTELOW
   N S ................................... 50
COON
   Alva D .............................. 74,75
   Alvin ................................ 74,75
   A D .................................. 74,75,76
   Rhoda .............................. 74,75,76
   Vernon Alvin .................. 73,74
   Vernon Alvin Coon ........ 75

# Index

COOPER
  Henry F .................................. 261,262
  James ..................... 257,258,259,260
  James T ........................ 256,258,261
  Sister ........ 256,257,258,259,260,261
  Torry ............................................ 261
  Tory ................ 256,257,258,259,260
COTTON
  Haidee ..................... 180,181,182,183
  Heidee ........................................ 179
  Pink ................ 179,180,181,182,183
  Waneta Jeane ............................. 179
  Waneta Jeanne 179,180,181,182,183
CROSS
  John H ......................... 152,153,154
  M E ............................................... 154
CROWDER
  Alice ..................................... 41,42,43
CURRY
  Gus A .......................................... 103
  Guy A .......................................... 101
CURTIS
  W L ............................................. 9,10
DABNEY
  J A ..................... 44,46,70,71,73
  J A, MD .......................... 44,46,71
DANIELS
  Lou ........................... 240,242,243
  Lue ................................... 241,242
  Turner .................... 240,241,242,243
  Willie Thomas ........................... 241
  Willis Thomas ............. 240,242,243
DARLING
  W A ............................................... 35
DARNEAL
  James .............. 320,321,322,323,324
  Sallie ............... 320,321,322,323,324
  Tandy .............. 320,321,322,323,324
DAVIS
  Nathan ......................... 87,88,90,91
  Oscar ........................................... 193
DEEN
  J A ....................................... 181,182
DENISON
  B L ............................................... 319
  B L, MD ..................................... 319
DIBRELL
  Allie ............................. 273,274,275
  Charles E ...................... 273,274,275
  Chas E ........................................ 274
  Louise ......................... 273,274,275
DICKEY
  Dr R P .................................. 131,132
  R P ...................... 128,129,131,133
  R P, MD .................................... 129
DONNELLY
  W C .................................... 125,126
DOWNARD
  W H ............................................. 32
DOWNING
  S H ........................................ 42,43
DREW
  Sallie A
    135,136,139,143,145,147,148,149,
    150
DUNCAN
  T H ........................................ 85,86
DUNLAP
  Mattie F ..................................... 191
DWIGHT
  M T .............................................. 43
EDMONDS
  Martha ................................ 221,222
  Martha J ....................... 221,223,224
ELLIOTT
  Gertrude A
    110,111,112,113,114,115,116,117
  Gertrude I ............................ 114,115
  Gertrude Irene
     ....... 110,111,112,113,115,116,117
  J H ...................................... 241,243
  T 110
  T W ..................................... 110,112
  Turner W
     ....... 111,112,113,114,115,116,117
FANNIE
  E J ............................................... 125
FANNIN
  E J ................................. 126,215,216
  F A ..................... 256,258,259,261
  F A, MD ..................... 258,259,261
  Frank A ....................................... 261
FARMER
  N S ............................................... 78

## Index

**FENNELL**
  Thomas ............................................. 14
**FITZER**
  Grace May ..................................... 262
  Gracie May ..................... 262,263,265
  Gracy May ............................ 263,264
  Lourinda ................ 262,263,264,265
  W W ....................................... 263,264
  William W ..................... 262,263,265
**FLINCHUM**
  C C .......... 119,121,122,124,125,126
  Columbus ............... 120,121,122,123
  Columbus C .................................. 122
  Eller Cecie ........................... 119,125
  Eller Cessie .... 119,120,121,122,123, 124
  James A ......................................... 121
  Julia A .......................................... 121
  Mrs J A ......................................... 120
  Sissie .............................................. 120
  Susie ............... 119,121,122,123,125
  Susie A .................................. 121,122
  Susy ............................................... 124
**FOLSOM**
  A E ................................ 88,90,91,313
  John ........................... 57,58,299,300
  Sarah .............................................. 280
  Saul ................................................ 281
**FONDREN**
  G B ....................................203,205,207
  G B, MD ........................................ 207
**FORREST**
  Alice ............................. 258,259,260
  Annie ........................... 258,259,260
**FORRESTER**
  J T ................................................. 262
**FORT**
  Brooks ................................... 312,313
**FOWLER**
  H L .................................... 3,12,13
  John W ...................... 12,13,270,271
**FRANKLIN**
  Wirt...49,58,59,98,100,105,109,110, 119,175,176,187,188,230,232,235,236 ,244,245,246,298
**FRASHER**
  Geo Q ............................................. 186

**FRAZIER**
  Johnson ..................................... 16,17
**FROST**
  S W ................................................ 179
**FULSOM**
  Nettie .............................................. 18
**FULTON**
  Dr J S ......................................... 88,91
  J F .................................................... 94
  J S ............. 76,78,88,89,91,92,93,95
  J S, MD ............................... 76,88,91
**GARDNER**
  Dodie .......................... 300,301,302
  E J ....................... 272,273,302,303
**GARLAND**
  Josiah ....................................... 62,63
  Ward, Jr .................................. 62,63
**GARY**
  J L ............................................. 96,97
  Jesse .......................... 87,88,90,91
**GAYNER**
  Wm ...................................................8
**GEORGE**
  J M ......................................... 316,317
  A S ......................................... 316,317
**GIBSON**
  Wilson ................................... 156,158
**GILL**
  Dr John J .................................... 115
  Jno J ..................................... 115,117
  Jno J, MD ............................. 115,117
  John H ........................................ 111
**GILLUM**
  Ben F .......................... 172,173,174
**GIPSON**
  Jencey ........................................... 188
  Jincey ........................................... 189
**GLENN**
  Ola ....................................... 226,228
**GOINS**
  Elizabeth ................... 152,153,154
**GOODE**
  Jas C ....................................... 42,43
**GOODENOUGH**
  A D ....................................... 184,185
**GRANT**
  Charlie W ............................ 308,309

333

| | |
|---|---|
| Mardie ........................ 308,309,310 | Emily ............. 324,325,326,327,328 |
| Tom ............................ 308,309,310 | Gertrude ...................... 243,245,246 |
| Tom S ......................... 308,309,310 | Luther M ............................ 244,245 |
| **GRAYSON** | Mamie ................................. 243,244 |
| Sinie ........................................ 119 | Nora ............... 324,325,326,327,328 |
| **GREGORY** | A V ............................................ 296 |
| Edwin S .................................. 67,68 | W S ............................................ 194 |
| **GRILLETTE** | **HARRISON** |
| Emma ....................................... 189 | W H ........................................ 51,52 |
| **GRILLIETTE** | **HAWKINS** |
| Emma ....................................... 192 | Allie May ............... 236,237,238,239 |
| **GRIMSLEY** | Etta M ...................... 236,237,238 |
| J O ........................................ 36,37 | J F .......................... 237,238,239 |
| **GRISHAM** | J H ............................................ 237 |
| G L ................................... 30,31,33 | J I ............................................. 237 |
| M C ............................................ 33 | J T ............................................ 236 |
| **GROSS** | **HAYES** |
| Alford ........................................ 14 | Edward ..................................... 158 |
| Mary ........................................... 14 | **HEARRELL** |
| **GUTHRIE** | Pinkie .................................. 226,227 |
| Gertie B .................................. 33,34 | W E .................................... 228,229 |
| Rebecca .................................. 33,34 | **HEISTEIN** |
| William W .............................. 33,34 | Milton .................... 213,214,217,218 |
| **HALLMARK** | **HEKABE** |
| Alick ................................... 266,267 | Lettie ........................................... 11 |
| Elick .................... 266,267,268,269 | **HENDERSON** |
| J J ........................................... 267 | Ida .................................... 44,45,46 |
| John J .................. 266,267,268,269 | Lillie B ................................... 44,45 |
| Sarah ........................ 267,268,269 | Lilly B ................................ 43,44,46 |
| **HAMMOND** | Marion ..... 284,285,288,289,290,291 |
| Delia ................................... 127,128 | Samuel M ................................ 45,46 |
| E S .............................................. 128 | Samuel N .................................... 44 |
| **HARDAWAY** | **HENLEY** |
| Julia .......................................... 235 | B Frank .................. 176,177,178,179 |
| **HARDEN** | Edna A ........................... 176,177,178 |
| J T ...................................... 308,310 | Edna E .................................. 178,179 |
| **HARDIWAY** | Thelma .................. 176,177,178,179 |
| Julia .......................................... 234 | **HICKBY** |
| **HARDY** | Lidia ............................................ 12 |
| H B ..................................... 316,317 | **HICKMAN** |
| **HARRELL** | E L ............................................ 114 |
| H B ................................... 16,17,18 | Edith ......................................... 229 |
| W E ....................... 115,322,323 | Edward .................................... 234 |
| **HARRIS** | Lawrence Quinton ..................... 229 |
| Annie Folsom ...................... 244,245 | Lizzie A ..................................... 229 |
| Battice ........................ 324,327,328 | **HILL** |
| Battiest ............................. 325,326 | Clyde .............................. 297,298,299 |

# Index

Cornelius D..........50,51,52,53,54,55
Esther J........................51,53,54,55
Esther Julia ...................50,52,53,55
Izora..........................50,51,52,53,54
Josephine...............297,298,299,300
Rufus ...........................297,298,299
**HIPP**
  Viola..........................................210
**HOLLOWAY**
  John...........................................193
**HOLMAN**
  Charles R..............................318,319
  Sarah....................................318,319
  Thelma..................................318,319
**HOMER**
  S J..........................................28,29
**HOOE**
  Archie F..........18,19,20,21,22,23,24
  Edna May .................18,19,20,23,24
  Mattie ............18,19,20,21,22,23,24
  Robert Israel ...........................20,21
  Robert Isreal ..................18,21,22,23
**HOOVER**
  J T.......................................238,239
**HORTON**
  L D ...............41,43,79,80,83,84,147
**HUDSON**
  Dr V W ........................................ 9
  V W ............................................ 8
  V W, MD..................................... 9
**HYSO**
  F S..........................................211
**IZARD**
  J C........................................238,239
**JACKSON**
  Cassey.......................................173
  Cassie ..................................171,174
  James T............................311,312,313
  Lena..................................311,312,313
  Lizzie................................180,183
  Rowan..................310,311,312,313
**JACOB**
  H B ............................................11
**JAMES**
  Austin .......................................232
  Bettie E................................305,306
  Bettie Edith...............................305

Etta M...........................305,306,307
Etta Mabel ...............................305
Gertha M ......................305,306,307
Lena......................................80,83
Rogers..........................305,306,307
Silan......................................230,231
**JARREL**
  H C ........................................184
**JEFFERSON**
  Lizzie.......................................189
**JOHNSON**
  E263,264,265
  E, MD..................................263,264
**JOHNSTON**
  D P.....................................134,135
  D R.....................................294,295
**JONES**
  C C ................................61,62,63,64
  Charles P ...........................34,35,36
  Lewie Haral ............................34,35
  Lonie Harral ...........................34,36
  Marthey E.....................183,184,185
  Ollie May......................183,184,185
  Perry.............................183,184,185
  Vara E......................................35,36
  Vera E......................................34,35
  W E......................................51,52,54
  W E, MD..................................51,54
  William.....................................259
  William E ..................................53
**JULIUS**
  Eli.............................................252
  Eliza..........................250,252,254
  Mollie
    249,250,251,252,253,254,255,256
  Serena............249,250,251,252,254
  Solomon ........249,250,251,252,254
**JUMP**
  Ella............................................286
  Ellen..........................................292
**JUSTICE**
  Bettie M....................48,49,106,107
**KARL**
  Viola......................................67,68
**KEARNEY**
  W M..........................................128
  W M, MD..................................128

KENNEDY
  D S .................. 44,45,46,47,71,72,73
KENNEMER
  F E ........................................210,211
KIMBRO
  C M ..............................................328
KINCH
  William ..........................................59
  Wm ................................................63
KING
  Ed ................................................269
  Ella ........................................303,304
  Emma ....................................303,304
  Robert ....................................303,304
KINKADE
  Fred V .........................................254
KINNEY
  Dodie ....................................300,301,302
  Elijah H ................................300,301,302
  Lillian R .....................................300
  Lillie R ..................................300,301,302
KINSLOW
  L B ................................................59
KIRKSEY
  Bettie ........................................57,58
  Bettie M .. 104,105,106,107,108,109,
  110
  John ..............................106,107,108
  John A ....................104,105,109,110
  John Clifton ...........104,105,107,108
  Pearl ................104,106,108,109,110
LARRABEE
  C F ..............................................256
LARTY
  D M ............................................117
LAWLER
  Annie ..........................................295
  H L .......................................300,301
LAWLIS
  Annie ..........................................296
LAYLOCK
  T A ..............................................208
LEE
  Robert E .................192,193,198,201
LEFLORE
  Mack H ................................193,194
LEFLORE

Ann Ruth .....................................218
Anna Ruth ..............................218,220
Daisy ......................................218,219,220
Jennings Bryan ....................218,219
Louis .....................................233,320,321,324
W W ............................................218
William W ..............................218,219,220
LESTER
  W F .....................................67,69,70
  William F ......................................69
LEWIS
  Calvin ....................................325,326
  Cephus ........................................101
  E F .............................133,134,292,294
  E F, MD .................................134,294
  Jas L ....................................242,243
  Mary .....................324,325,326,328
  Susan ........95,96,97,98,99,100,101
  W M ....................................308,309,310
LINEBAUGH
  D N ..............................................251
LOCKE
  Victor M, JP .........................187,188
LOGAN
  C E ................................................74
  C E, MD ........................................76
  Dr C E ...........................................76
LONG
  LeRoy ..........................................311
  Leroy ...................................312,313,314
  LeRoy, MD .................................313
LOVING
  Amanda ........................................59
  Eva B ...................................16,17,18
LOWLES
  Annie ..........................................293
LYNN
  Alcie L ..................................209,210
  Alice L ........................................208
  Elsie L ..................................208,209,211
  J A ........................................98,100
  J H ..............................................211
  J Y ........................208,209,210,211
  Leola ....................208,209,210,211
MCCARTER
  Andrew L ...................................151
  Elberta G .....................................151

# Index

MCCARTNEY
  Elsie ............................................. 232
MCCLAIN
  Mary I ..................... 66,67,68,69,70
  Notre Dame ......... 65,66,67,68,69,70
  R L .................................................. 65
  Rufus L ..................... 66,67,68,69,70
MCCLARD
  C C ............................................... 318
MCCLEARY
  J E .................................................. 41
MCCLURE
  May Dell ...................................... 314
  Anna May ..................................... 315
  D C ............................................ 85,86
  Dora May .................. 14,15,16,17,18
  Harris Clay ..... 314,315,316,317,318
  Horace Clay ........................ 314,315
  Ida .............................. 14,15,16,17,18
  Lorena B ............................ 81,85,86
  Madell ........................................... 317
  Maydell ................. 315,316,317,318
  Napoleon B ..... 314,315,316,317,318
  P J ................................................... 15
  Poker J ...................... 14,15,16,17,18
  Rena ............................................... 84
MCCOY
  Wesley .................................. 325,326
MCCULLOUGH
  S S ................................................ 186
  S S, MD ........................................ 186
MCCURTAIN
  Mollie ........................................... 187
MCDANIEL
  R E ........................................... 20,22
MCGAHEE
  Arthur ........................................... 296
MCGAHEY
  Annie ............................ 292,293,294
  Arthur ................................... 293,295
  Arthur D ....................................... 292
  Author D ...................................... 294
  Authur D ...................................... 294
  Opal .............................. 292,293,294
MCGUIRE
  Carrie ..................... 159,160,161,162
  Emery O ................ 159,160,161,162

Joel B ................................... 160,161
Joel Burrel ................................... 158
Joel Burrell .................. 159,161,162
MCINTOSH
  Turner ....................................... 98,99
MACKEY
  David M .............................. 175,176
MCLAUGHLIN
  Claude .................... 246,247,248,249
  G W .................................... 247,248
  George W ..................... 246,247,248
  Lillie ............................. 246,247,248
MCLURE ........................................ 317
MCPHERREN
  Cas E ........................................... 139
MCREYNOLDS
  Thomas V ............................... 85,86
MADDOX
  B F ............................................... 312
MAHAR
  C H ............................................... 233
  Charles H ............................ 232,235
  Charles H, MD .............. 232,233,236
MANNING
  F ............................................... 28,29
MANSFIELD, MCMURRAY &
  CORNISH ................................... 102
MARCUM
  Cordelia .............................. 4,5,6,7,8
  Edward C ............................ 4,5,6,7,8
  Henry W ............................. 4,5,6,7,8
MARSHALL
  W H ...................................... 76,77,79
MARSTON
  Adda ......................................... 90,91
  Adde ............................................... 90
  Addie ..................................... 91,92,93
  Bulah .... 86,87,88,89,90,91,92,93,94
  Mary ......... 87,88,89,90,91,92,93,94
  Theodore M ............................. 87,88
  Theodore McKinley .. 86,88,89,94,95
MARTIN
  Wm .............................................. 260
MAXEY
  J T ................................................ 118
MAYO
  George ................... 225,226,227,228

337

## Index

J B .................................................. 226
John B ........................... 226,227,228
Tabitha ......................................... 226
Tabitha A ...................... 226,227,228
MAYTUBBY
  Peter, Jr .................................. 187,188
MELTON
  W J ..................................... 25,27,29
  W J, MD ...................................... 29
MENTZER
  J L ............................................... 180
MENTZER J L ............................... 181
MERRYMAN
  John S ........................................ 114
  Leonidas ................................... 324
  Leonidas E .......................... 320,321
MILKETT
  Mrs M J .............................. 320,323
  Nancy J ..................................... 320
MILLER
  H C ...................................... 204,206
MILLS
  Bellie .......................................... 276
MITCHELL
  S E ....................................... 261,262
MITTS
  Deali Estle ........................... 129,130
  Delie Estel ................................. 128
  Delie Estle ........................... 128,131
  James Isaac ................. 128,132,133
  Lucinda ........... 128,129,130,131,132
  W E ................. 128,129,130,131,132
MONDS
  Mollie ................................... 151,152
  Mollie L ................................ 153,154
  Oda ................. 150,151,152,153,154
  Richard ................................ 151,152
  Richard F ............................. 153,154
MOORE
  Christopher ................................. 45
  Christopher D ............................. 44
  D M ........................................... 222
  Jane ................. 194,195,197,199,200
  Jane A ....................................... 194
  Mary ................................ 98,99,100
MORGAN
  H Y ............................................ 238

Thena ............................................ 75
Thomas M .................................. 237
Thos M ................................. 238,239
Thos M, MD ........................ 238,239
MORTON
  Anna .......................................... 268
  Ike ....................................... 266,268
MOWDY
  Frank M ............................... 185,186
  Ruby ..................................... 185,186
  Viola ..................................... 185,186
NALSON
  R M ............................................ 251
NEEDLES
  T B
    1,5,81,112,120,121,138,159,183,190,
    196,203,209,231,236,240,251,257,
    266,273,293
NELSON
  Alice .................................... 40,41,42
  Allice ........................................... 42
  J R ............................................... 41
  Richard ........................... 40,41,42,43
  Simon .................................. 40,41,42
NEWTON
  Kate ........................................... 241
  Robert ....................................... 241
NORMAN
  Benjamin H ............................. 47,48
  Benjamin Hibbert ............... 47,49,50
  Reuben .................................... 47,50
  Reubin ........................................ 49
  Ruben ...................................... 47,48
  Sarah J .................... 47,48,49,50,108
O'DONBY
  W J ............................... 160,161,162
OLIVER
  H S ............................................ 184
  John H ...................................... 260
ONUBBY
  Emma .................... 190,191,193,194
  Robert L .......... 189,190,191,192,193
  Stella .................................... 192,193,194
  Stella Frances ............... 189,190,191
OWEN
  Stella ........................................... 26
OWENS

Estella .................................. 24,25
John ..................... 25,26,27,28,29
Katie ............... 24,25,26,27,28,29
Stella ........................ 26,27,28,29
OWNES
   John ............................................ 24
PAGE
   Wm C ......................................... 59
PARKE
   Frank E .............................. 280,281
PATCHELL
   O W .................................... 291,292
   Ora ............................................. 285
PATTERSON
   Carl ..................................... 188,189
PAXSON
   Calvin ................................... 17,18
PAYNE
   Lee ............................................... 27
PHILLIPS
   A Denton .................................. 158
   J W .................................. 218,219,220
   J W, MD ............................... 219,220
PISTOKACH
   Cornelius .................................. 158
POLK
   Taylor ................................. 308,310
PORTER
   Angeline .................................... 246
   Lily ............................................. 247
POWELL
   H A ............................................. 185
   W H ............................................ 184
   W H, MD ................................... 184
POWERS
   Maide ............. 281,282,283,284,285
   Vesta ........ 286,287,288,289,290,291
PRATLEY
   J R ............................................... 127
PUSLEY
   Frank William ......... 171,172,173,174
   Frank Williams ......................... 170
   John ..................................... 172,173
   Lizzie .................... 171,172,173,174
   Lyman ............. 170,171,172,173,174
   Osbon ................................ 172,173
RABON

J Mary E ................................... 225
James W ......... 221,222,223,224,225
Judith M E ...... 221,222,223,224,225
Otowa Thomas ................... 222,223
Otowa Tomas ........................... 221
Ruby Helen .................. 221,224,225
Ruby Hellen .................. 221,223,224
Rufus .................................. 222,225
RAPPOLEE
   J L ................................ 25,27,28,29
RATLEY
   J R .............................................. 247
RAYDON
   A W ............................................ 174
REAGAN
   Gertrude A ............. 110,112,113,114
   Robert L ..................................... 115
   Robert M ................................... 113
REEDER
   J G ................. 129,130,131,132,133
RENEGAR
   J F ....................................... 163,164
   J F, MD ...................................... 164
RHINE
   Birdie .......................................... 22
RICHARDS
   W L ............................................ 164
RIDDLE
   Cephus . 95,96,97,98,99,100,101,102
   Coleman ..................................... 96
   Joseph
      95,96,97,98,99,100,101,102,103,104
   Wash ......................................... 102
RIDDLES
   Cephus ........................................ 96
   Joseph ......................................... 96
RIDER
   Geo E ........................................ 212
RILEY
   Mose .......................................... 255
RISTEEN
   H C ................................................ 4
ROBERTS
   Sam T ........................................ 303
   Sam T, Jr ................................... 304
ROBINSON
   C A ..................................... 167,168

WELLS
  A J ............................ 159,161,162
  A J, MD ................................ 161
WEST
  C W ........................................ 20
WHITE
  J M .................................... 98,99
WILKINS
  L B ....................................... 167
  T B .................................. 169,170
WILLAM
  George .................................... 38
WILLIAM
  George .................................... 39
WILLIAMS
  Ada
    48,49,56,57,58,59,105,106,107,108,
    109,110
  B W ........................... 38,39,40,137
  Dessie ........................... 56,57,58,59
  George .................................. 137
  Joe B .................................. 71,72
  Lum ............................. 56,57,58,59
WILSON
  Cillen .................................... 175
  Edward H ............................. 13,14
  Emma ................................... 13,14
  G J, MD ............................ 309,310
  George J ............................ 309,310
  Josephine ........................... 298,299
  R F ..................................... 270,271
  Roberth R .............................. 13,14
  Samuel R .......... 57,106,107,108,109
  Tennessee .......................... 37,38,39
WILSON SAMUEL R ...................... 58
WISE
  John ...................... 288,289,291,292
  John E ........................... 286,287,290
  John E, Jr ........ 286,287,290,291,292
  John W, Jr ................................ 286
  Lela .................... 286,287,288,289
  Vesta. 286,287,288,289,290,291,292
WOLVERTON
  A A ....................................... 247
  M S ....................................... 247
WORLEY
  Annie ...................................... 30

Jesse A ..................................... 30
Mattie Fay ............................. 30,31
WRIGHT
  Ida .................................... 300,302
WYRICK
  Artie E ............................. 122,123
  John ..................................... 121
  Missie ................................... 121
  Mrs A E ............................ 119,125
  Susie .......................... 122,125,126
  Susie A .................................. 121
YANDELL
  J D ........................................ 115
YARBROUGH
  Annie 164,165,166,167,168,169,170
  James ....... 164,165,166,168,169,170
  Jas ................................... 166,167
  Nowita .... 164,165,166,167,168,169,
    170
YODER
  James .............. 281,282,283,284,285
  Maide .............. 281,282,283,284,285
  Maidie P ................................ 283
  Troy ............... 281,282,283,284,285
ZONALA
  John .................................. 152,153
ZONOLA
  Mildred ............................. 152,153

www.ingramcontent.com/pod-product-compliance
Lightning Source LLC
Chambersburg PA
CBHW020241030426
42336CB00010B/566